IN BAD FAITH

In Bad Faith

The Dynamics of Deception in Mark Twain's America

FORREST G. ROBINSON

Harvard University Press
Cambridge, Massachusetts
and London, England

First Harvard University Press paperback edition, 1992

Library of Congress Cataloging-in-Publication Data

Robinson, Forrest G. (Forrest Glen), 1940–
    In bad faith.

    Bibliography: p.
    Includes index.
    1. Twain, Mark, 1835–1910—Political and social
views.   2. Social problems in literature.   3. Deception in
literature.   4. Slavery and slaves in literature.   5. Racism in
literature.   I. Title.
PS1342.S58R63   1986   818'.409   86-4668
ISBN 0-674-44527-9 (alk. paper) (cloth)
ISBN 0-674-44528-7 (paper)

Designed by Gwen Frankfeldt

To Grace Gordon Robinson

Acknowledgments

It says something about me, and something about my peculiar, privileged vocation, that while I have often felt the pressure of solitude in the making of this book, I have at the same time enjoyed the generous help of many people. Myra Jehlen offered encouragement and numerous good suggestions at a luncheon some years ago. Michael Cowan has also read and responded in valuable ways from the beginning of the project. I am deeply grateful for all his support. I have had the benefit of weekly conversations over several months with Robert Coleman, whose remarkable penetration into Mark Twain has at many points helped me to sharpen my own perspective. John Jordan has gone over the entire manuscript with great critical acumen and more patient attention to detail and nuance and implication than I had the right to ask for or to expect. He has offered generous encouragement, dozens of valuable suggestions, and he has helped me to locate my project in the large, often baffling world of contemporary literary study. I am fortunate in his friendship.

A number of friends and colleagues have read parts of the work as it has developed, and they have offered suggestions and encouragement for which I am most grateful. I am thinking of John Dizikes and Will Vroman, David Hoy, Sharon Cameron, Michael Colacurcio, Susan Gillman, Page Stegner, Stephen Greenblatt, and Bill Bloodworth. Bill Wilson and his friends have provided vital support and illumination. Graduate students have also been invaluable sources of insight and suggestion. I want most especially to thank Michael Miller, Stewart Cooper, Tim Fitzmaurice, Mary Schultz, Jim Gurley, Pat Messer, Joanne Fordham, and Liam O'Mellin. Robert Hirst and Victor Fischer of the Mark Twain Papers very kindly permitted me to consult the new Mark Twain Library edition of *Huckleberry Finn* while it was still in proofs. Betsy Wootten and her assistants at the Kresge College Steno Pool, who have typed endlessly, most ably, and without complaint, have my lasting gratitude. Finally, I have an extraordinary debt to the members of my family. Grace, the eldest of my daughters, has been an especially bright source of light. Seeing Huck and Tom through her sharp young eyes showed me my way. Renate and Emma have arrived more recently, and have helped to make it all worthwhile. Most of all,

I thank my wife, Colleen, who has given me time, understanding, good humor, and a model of sanity. This book has grown as we have.

A version of the beginning of Part I appeared as "Social Play and Bad Faith in *The Adventures of Tom Sawyer*" in *Nineteenth-Century Fiction,* 39 (1984), 1–24; and a portion of Part II has been published in the same journal, 37 (1982), 50–74, as "The Silences in *Huckleberry Finn.*"

Contents

IN BAD FAITH

Introduction

THIS BOOK is an effort to retrieve, through the careful scrutiny of two of our favorite stories about ourselves, some of "the tragic aspects and the ironic implications" of American history that have been distorted, according to C. Vann Woodward, "by the national legend of success and victory and by the perpetuation of infant illusions of innocence and virtue."[1] At the same time I try to offer some insight into these distortions and the ways and means of their formation. I have been moved in this enterprise by the discovery that major strands of what Woodward has in mind are to be found—submerged, obscured, concealed, but not beyond recovery—in *Tom Sawyer* and *Huckleberry Finn*. I will argue, in fact, that we continue to return to these novels because they express, both by what they include and what they conceal or omit, some of our most enduring cultural self-conceptions. Obviously enough, "infant illusions of innocence and virtue" must figure prominently in any account of the cultural currency of these texts. Yet they contain an abundance of selfishness and malice, violence and injustice, and such prominent discordancies must also be reckoned with. This is especially the case in *Huckleberry Finn*, where the selfishness and malice and violence and injustice of white people find their center in poor Jim. The novel gives us such discord in forms and quantities that we can bear, and it rounds its tragic thrust with a comic resolution that is apparently compatible with our cultural prepossessions. I say "apparently" both to acknowledge that this assessment of *Huckleberry Finn* is a critical simplification, and to suggest that the novel's popularity is evidence of a much greater cultural appetite for darkness and ambiguity than is generally allowed. Americans are drawn almost reluctantly back to their favorite "classic," I will argue, because they are not fully, comfortably acquiescent in their comic reading of the novel's conclusion. Thus the virtual compulsion to review the fictional construction of "historical reality" in *Huckleberry Finn* is inseparable from the pressure of a submerged, generally unacknowledged resistance to the representation of that past as it unfolds, time after time, before us. The book and its popular reception are parallel variations on a theme formulated most pointedly by Louis Hartz—that "there can be an appalling complexity to innocence, especially if your point of departure is guilt."[2]

The key term in the literary and cultural analysis that follows is "bad faith." I define bad faith, as it appears and functions in *Tom Sawyer* and *Huckleberry Finn,* as the reciprocal deception of self and other in the denial of departures from public ideals of the true and the just. Bad faith functions to bridge the gap between codes and actual day-to-day behavior. It is, I assume, universally a feature of social arrangements, though the varieties and degrees of such deception, and tolerances for them, must vary quite considerably. As the "play" in a culture's bearings, bad faith has the potential to allay inevitable tensions, though it may also work to conceal problems of grave consequence. Thus *Tom Sawyer* provides numerous examples of the social unity and fellow-feeling to be derived from the deception of self and other. And we are emphatically of Huck's persuasion when he sidesteps cultural codes whose authority he concedes, but whose strict enforcement is incompatible with his comfort and satisfaction. Such hedging is most in evidence when we find the boy indoors in civilized circumstances; but it is also quite conspicuously at work, and as widely approved, when Huck assures himself that stealing watermelons and cantaloupes is morally acceptable so long as he abides faithfully by his decision to forego crabapples and persimmons. Similar but much more consequential varieties of bad-faith evasion are on display a few pages later when a murderer aboard the wreck of the *Walter Scott* declares that "it ain't good morals" to kill a man when you have the option of abandoning him to certain death by drowning. Huck's valiant attempt to remedy what he witnesses aboard the old boat is in turn a glimpse at the array of subtle bad-faith obstacles that may arise to obstruct the achievement of simple, utterly elusive, justice. In the upshot, Huck's pursuit of right ends necessitates the resort to devious means, results nonetheless in disaster, and leaves him outwardly resolute, but inwardly world-weary and ready to sleep like one of the "dead."

My notions about the reciprocal deception of self and other have emerged haltingly from the study of *Tom Sawyer* and *Huckleberry Finn;* but they surfaced long before I had a term for them. Thus I settled on "bad faith" belatedly, and with some misgivings. It is not a formulation that Mark Twain would have warmed to. The term is sometimes used as a translation of Sartre's *mauvaise foi,* and readers of *L'Etre et le néant* will recognize similarities between my notions and the French philosopher's more fully developed position. This imposing background to my own comparatively modest designs has been useful in its way; it has tended to confirm my impression that *Tom Sawyer* and *Huckleberry Finn* dramatize specific cultural variations on a universal human phenomenon; and it has obliged me to strive for clarity in my thinking. But, again, my concept arises directly from the study of Mark Twain, and should not be measured alongside *mauvaise foi*. Bad faith as I find it in Mark Twain's novels is social and cultural in its origins and operations, while *mauvaise foi* is manifestly an individual phenomenon. My own thinking in these matters is cognate with, and takes reinforcement from, the descriptions and discussion of collective world building in Peter L. Berger and Thomas Luckmann, *The Social Construction of Reality*. Their authority with me derives directly from their systematic elaboration of the Marxian insight "that man's consciousness is determined by his social being,"[3] and by what I take to be very liberal definitions of such notions as "ideology," "reification," and "false consciousness." That I have generally refrained from using these terms should not be construed as an implied criticism of *The Social Construction of Reality*. To the contrary, I am indebted to Berger and Luckmann not only because they have enriched my understanding of Mark Twain's "sociology," but also because they have opened a way to the avoidance of terminological refinements and disputes remote from my rather special purposes. On one side, my understanding of *Tom Sawyer* and *Huckleberry Finn* is reinforced by the emphatic assertion that "*All* social reality is precarious. *All* societies are constructions in the face of chaos." On the other, my impulse to ruminate at large with relative freedom finds endorsement in the declaration that the argument of *The Social Construction of Reality* posits "*neither* an ahistorical 'social system' *nor* an ahistorical 'human nature.'"[4] Finally, I place a high value on the implication in Berger and Luckmann that we are not the passive victims of our world building; rather, they clearly suggest, we have the capacity both to understand the processes and to alter the results of our reality construction.[5]

It is entirely consistent with the nature of influence, and with my vanity, that there should be more of Berger and Luckmann in this book than I recognize. I have been familiar with their ideas for some time, and wish properly to acknowledge their sway. I am able to identify a number of other significant parallels with specific aspects of my work, and I want to mention some of them here, but quite without claiming them as influences or authorities for what I do. First among these I would number Carolyn Porter's *Seeing and Being: The Plight of the Participant Observer in Emerson, James, Adams, and Faulkner*. Armed with a definition of reification derived from Georg Lukács, Porter addresses herself to a group of American writers whose work gives evidence of "a crisis in which the observer discovers his participation within the world he has thought to stand outside."[6] This preoccupation, as it is elaborated in Porter's learned, very skillful and penetrating study, overlaps in a number of important ways with my own more limited designs. Mark Twain, along with many of the observers in his works—Huck, obviously, but also Hank Morgan, David Wilson, and young Satan, among others—are deeply implicated in the worlds to which they seem marginal, or even complete strangers. And I find, as Porter does, though not precisely in her terms, that Mark Twain's "texts," like those of Emerson, James, Adams, and Faulkner, "constitute and record a series of 'social projects' in and of themselves, projects in whose rhetorical and narrative complexities lie sedimented the social contradictions generated by the reifying process."[7] I believe that it is accurate to say of Mark Twain in *Tom Sawyer* what Porter says of Henry Adams in *The Education*—that his "narrative strategy . . . is designed primarily to deny what the act of writing it demonstrates," that the novelist "was a participant in the social process he presumed merely to observe."[8] Her analysis of Faulkner, with its emphasis on the deep contradictions inherent in American slavery, runs along lines that parallel my own in a number of especially significant ways. What she observes of *Absalom, Absalom!*, for example—"by the time we find out what's going on, we are already implicated in it"[9]—applies with equal force, though with rather different emphasis, to *Huckleberry Finn*.

Having indicated a few of the ways in which Porter's questions and answers anticipate my own, let me add that her book is in some respects much more ambitious than mine. Most conspicuously in this regard, she situates her literary analysis in the context of a fully developed Marxist reading of American history. I do not quarrel with the impulse to historicize; to the contrary, I welcome both the strong thrust of Porter's challenge to "established" American literary history, and the wealth of critical insights that spring from her multidisciplinary approach. At the same time, however, I find her emphasis on capitalism rather too narrowly insistent to be completely persuasive as a way of reading American history or literature. There is, for example, much to commend the view that "Sutpen embodies that paternalism embraced by Andrew Jackson in the service of capitalist expansion," or that his refusal to recognize his son "exhibits the logical, if self-contradictory, consequence of a paternalism generated in the interest of

Capital."[10] But while this way of focusing the analysis is sharply illuminating, it also works to deny Faulkner's grand, elusive figure the
much broader range of literary and historical significance laid claim to
throughout the novel, most emphatically perhaps in its title.

Embedded as it is in a rather narrow construction of American history, Porter's analysis is often freighted with the implication, noted by
Gregory S. Jay in his long review of *Seeing and Being,* that there was a
"historical Fall from authenticity at the decisive juncture of capitalism's
appearance as a new mode of production." Thus Porter's opening definition of reification as "a process in the course of which man becomes
alienated from himself"[11] is clearly vulnerable to Jay's charge that it
"participates in a mythic historiography of truth's self-estrangement
and recovery in time. Is the 'plight of the participant observer' original
to capitalism," he goes on, pointedly, to ask, "or is there always already
'reification' when we employ matter and meaning to do our work?"[12]
For myself, I find Jay's overriding inclination to deconstruct history
much more limiting than Porter's generally successful attempt to make
sense of it. Nonetheless, I share some of his reservations on this vital
point of emphasis.

It is telling that Jay's differences with Porter on the score of reification have their theoretical foundation in Derrida, Lacan, and de Man,
while mine, though hardly as developed in their theoretical moorings
as his, lead me back to *The Social Construction of Reality.* Specifically, I
am persuaded by Berger and Luckmann that it is "a mistake to look at
reification as a perversion of an originally non-reified apprehension of
the social world, a sort of cognitive fall from grace."[13] Indeed, my reservations about Porter's historiography apply more generally to the majority of the Marxist literary criticism that I have read, but from which,
especially in probing the interactions of the literary and the social, I
have taken support and guidance. I am moved and enlightened by
Mikhail Bakhtin's *Problems of Dostoevsky's Poetics* (University of Minnesota Press, 1984), and quite struck by the similarities between what he
discovers in Dostoevsky and what I observe in Mark Twain. The more
general, but equally compelling theoretical formulations in *The Dialogic Imagination* (University of Texas Press, 1981)—most especially in
the final essay, "Discourse in the Novel"—have also been a source of
encouragement and confirmation. Such parallels notwithstanding,
however, I do not believe that the dialogic effects in the American novelist are as self-consciously designed as Bakhtin claims they are in the
works he studies. The multivocality in Mark Twain's major novels

arises from tensions within the dominant ideology, and not from a clear apprehension of alternatives to it. In taking this position, I find myself aligned in a variety of ways with Pierre Macherey's approach to Jules Verne. Macherey draws attention, as I do, to the omissions and unacknowledged disavowals in literature, and argues that such distortions can be traced back to ideological contradictions. "The interest of Verne's work," he says, "lies in the fact that, through the unity of its project—a unity borrowed from a certain ideological coherence, or incoherence—and by the means which inform this project (or fail in this enterprise) by specifically literary means, it reveals the *limits,* and to some extent the *conditions* of this ideological coherence, which is necessarily built upon a discord in the historical reality, and upon a discord between this reality and its *dominant* representation." [14] I have found much to reflect on in Louis Althusser's "Ideology and Ideological State Apparatuses"—not least his exposition of the interpellation of the subject and his provocative development of the notion "that ideology *has no outside.*" [15] And I have been edified and inspired to further study by my reading in, and by brief personal contacts with, Fredric Jameson. Finally, Terry Eagleton's *Criticism and Ideology* (New Left Books, 1976) is clearly and generally quite helpful; his more recent *Literary Theory: An Introduction* (University of Minnesota Press, 1983) is all of this, and also, at points, marvelously funny.

I have taken encouragement in my approach from other scholars whose work is less readily located within one or another critical camp. Stephen Greenblatt's writing combines learning and penetration and grace in an uncommon way, and I have taken something of value from all of it. "Invisible Bullets," his essay on "Renaissance Authority and Its Subversion," has been especially useful as a model for the analysis of what Greenblatt calls "the process whereby subversive insights are generated in the midst of apparently orthodox texts and simultaneously contained by those texts, contained so efficiently that the society's licensing and policing apparatus is not directly engaged." [16] His observation that the "ideal image" of the prince in *I Henry IV* "involves as its positive condition the constant production of its own radical subversion and the powerful containment of that subversion" [17] anticipates in a remarkable way my characterization of the creation and popular reception of Mark Twain's major works. D. A. Miller's "The Novel and the Police," in its development of the notion that "the genre of the novel belongs to the disciplinary field that it portrays" [18] also throws helpful light on my subject. Finally, readers interested in a description and analysis of some good uses of what I have termed "bad faith" may wish to consult Guido Calabresi and Philip Bobbitt, *Tragic Choices* (Norton, 1978).

These scholars have in various ways reinforced my inclination, strongly rooted in the study of Mark Twain, to regard the *badness* in bad faith as a relative quantity. As I have suggested, bad faith may serve to advance the health of a society. Some of our rules are unjust; others are out of date; and some, though perfectly reasonable in principle, fail in their rigid angularity to conform comfortably to the less precise, less stable contours of ordinary human impulse and desire. At its best, then, bad faith gives us room to breathe while our codes evolve. It may also provide occasional, salubrious relief from the daunting submission to a civilized regimen. Such violations of rules are in bad faith only if they are denied, and bad only in the sense that the strict letter of the law has been transgressed. This is not to suggest that bad-faith violations of a society's public standards of justice and right conduct are without potential for harm. To the contrary, and as Mark Twain's representation of American social arrangements strongly suggests, the bad-faith denial of injustice can achieve pathological proportions. But here we must remember that bad faith, at least as I define it, is relative in the additional sense that what passes for good in one cultural setting may be anathematized as evil in another. This familiar caveat is frequently overlooked because culture bearers, as the inevitable consequence of their acculturation, tend to assume that their standards of truth and justice are morally absolute. I can serve as my own best example in this regard. For while I recognize that slavery has in many cultural contexts been a morally acceptable practice, I am inclined nonetheless to regard the institution as self-evidently evil. Nor am I unaware of the ironies that attach to my righteous reflexes on this score. To take support for the condemnation of slavery from the culture that tolerated and even defended the institution, and to deplore the racism that persists in our midst, but without which the slavery had no justification, is to betray an epidemic of paradoxes. Readers will be patient with my lapses in this area, I trust.

Racism and slavery, or what I at times refer to as race–slavery, are the other key elements in the analysis that follows. Again, I have tried to take Mark Twain's lead in shaping my commentary, both in matters of definition and emphasis, and in centering the analysis of bad faith on the habits of deception requisite to the justification of slavery in a Christian democracy. "The rise of liberty and equality in this country was accompanied by the rise of slavery," observes Edmund S. Morgan. "That two such contradictory developments were taking place simultaneously over a long period of our history, from the seventeenth century to the nineteenth," he goes on, "is the central paradox of American history."[19] Mark Twain, whose perspective on America, like his humor, was rooted in the perception of contradiction, would have agreed entirely. How, Morgan asks, could men as morally scrupulous as Washington and Madison and Jefferson have arrived, in the matter of slavery, "at beliefs and actions so full of contradiction"?[20] Mark Twain confronted this vexing question in one form or another for several decades, and it was his enduring inclination to respond with versions of what I have defined as bad-faith denial. *Huckleberry Finn* is the consummate expression of his deep, complex involvement in this American dilemma.

Racism was the ideological cornerstone of American slavery, and its influence hardly abated, and seems at times to have increased, in the decades following the Civil War. Mark Twain was equally relentless in his attention to this bitter legacy, and he was strongly inclined, especially after his global lecture tour of 1895–96, to associate the bloody tide of domestic racial hatred and violence with post-bellum advances in military technology and expanding American imperialism. Promptings of this sort are clearly evident in *A Connecticut Yankee,* but they achieve their fullest elaboration in the social criticism of a decade later. My use of the compound "race–slavery" is intended to reflect and underscore Mark Twain's emphasis on this persistence in America of the cultural habits that formed the ideological foundation of slavery. My usage is also designed to suggest that this continuity in our history has served to nourish bad faith, and to vastly expand its sphere of influence. Thus in "To the Person Sitting in Darkness" Mark Twain observes that the chains cast off by Lincoln have been reforged in Cuba and the Philippines. The response to this development, he goes on, with grim, withering irony, is not outrage and reform, but denial and the retreat to righteous, self-serving delusion.

The pattern of bad-faith blindness to prominent cultural contradictions in matters of race–slavery is readily illustrated. Frederick Douglass is only the most eloquent of the ex-slaves who testified to the multiple strands of bad faith that stretched outward from the myth, fostered and strictly enforced by white masters and apologists, that slavery was a benign and morally correct institution. Douglass records that slaves were cruelly punished for revealing their true feelings about their owners, and consequently buried the truth under falsehoods designed to appease the master's conscience.[21] The same prudent compliance with white habits of bad-faith denial is everywhere to be found in John Langston Gwaltney's invaluable oral history of contemporary black America, *Drylongso*. Gwaltney's respondents offer endless testimony to the readiness among white people to be deceived.

> White men say they love justice, which they fear worse than hell. If I were a good white man, I don't know what I would do. I would not want to see my children braggarts and cheats, but I would know that justice would be fatal for them.

> Don't never tell whitefolks that they are wrong. I know that they are wrong most of the time, but you will save yourself a kick in the ass if you just go on like you thought they knew what they was talking about. Like I told you, they are how folks. They want to know how you can make everything be like they would want it to be. Don't tell them *what* anything is. They do not want to hear it and they will give you a hard time.

> Now, the biggest difference between us and white people is that we *know* when we are playing . . . Play is pretending what's out here is not really out here. If you are black you just cannot make it like that because we can't buy our way out of things or make somebody say that square is round. Whitefolks lie so much that they can' tell the difference now between a lie and the truth. Now, that is because they are livin' a lie. Everything they do they must lie about![22]

We may glimpse cognate varieties of cautious simulation and equivocation in the behavior of Jim. I will pause at some length over his seeming attempt to measure and to influence Huck's disposition toward the king and the duke, and I make note in passing of what may be the self-interested motive for his refusal to share with Huck what he knows about the corpse that floats into Chapter 9. But there is more to be done along these lines. To what extent, for example, is his powerfully moving farewell in Chapter 16 a calculated appeal to Huck's wavering loyalty? In this instance, and in others, there is evidence that Jim is maneuvering, deftly, almost imperceptibly, perhaps by a kind of reflex, within the twisted bad-faith fabric of slave culture.[23]

Let me emphasize that it is not my intention to ground the analysis of Mark Twain's works in the larger patterns of American history. To the contrary, I intend to draw inferences about American history and culture, with rather special attention to race–slavery, from the close and sustained critical analysis of two literary texts. I am persuaded that our enduringly popular works compress *multum in parvo,* and offer us as full and clear a window on ourselves as we are likely to find. Among other things, this book may be said to test that sanguine point of view. At the same time, however, I cannot doubt that my perspective on the past as it emerges from *Tom Sawyer* and *Huckleberry Finn* is itself influenced by assumptions and attitudes that I bring with me to the study of those books. Such assumptions and attitudes, most especially as they bear on the issue of race–slavery, have their foundation in my reading of some standard works on the subject. There is general agreement among historians that American slavery had its roots in a brand of racial prejudice so comparatively extreme that its influence would continue to be felt long after legal emancipation. Nor have I come across dissent from the conviction that racism and slavery have been the grossest of the contradictions in a culture of many and deep paradoxes. David Brion Davis speaks for most observers when he locates "the inherent contradiction of slavery . . . in the underlying conception of man as a conveyable possession with no more autonomy of will and consciousness than a domestic animal."[24] In fact, of course, there was no doubt that slaves were human beings who submitted to their harsh fates only because they were forced to, utterly against their wills and by both threat and example of terrible violence. The attempt to submerge this bald contradiction of American ideals in equally bald, equally contradictory rationalizations, may be viewed as illustrative of the extreme bad faith at the core of the national experience of race–slavery. It is also clear that here, as elsewhere, the perfectly predictable cultural response to the harsh truth of race–slavery was recoil, rationalization, outright denial. In the outcome, the grand-daddy of contradictions in the land of the free was half-submerged in a spawn of lesser delusions. "Everywhere," according to Davis, "the more thoughtful masters" indulged hopes that

> the obvious evils of slavery would wither away and the grateful Negro would willingly give his service without coercion. But all such dreams and hopes ran aground on the simple and solid fact . . . that a slave was not a piece of property, nor a half-human instrument, but a man held down by force.[25]

Lacking the will to resolve the dilemma, the culture withdrew into the strangely voluntary and yet unacknowledged blindness of bad faith. "Thus the stars wink upon the bloody stripes," wrote the grimly satirical Dickens; "and Liberty pulls down her cap upon her eyes, and owns Oppression in its vilest aspect, for her sister." [26]

Once again, it is not my intention to yoke literature to history in some literal way. Accordingly, I will restrain an impulse to elaborate on the case that the historians have made, both for the essential and quite monumental bad faith of American race–slavery, and for the spread of bad faith from that dark cultural center. Nonetheless, a few more names and comments are in order. C. Vann Woodward is absolutely indispensable, both for his testimony to the endurance of racial hatred after the Civil War—in *The Strange Career of Jim Crow* (Oxford, 1957)—and his treatment of the ironic reversal that overtook the South in the 1830s, from a strong swell of emancipationist sentiment to a dogged resistance to the mention of abolition. In the space of a few years, the same people who had risen in condemnation of slavery were concentrating their "energies upon the repression of heresy . . . The institution that had so recently been blamed for a multitude of the region's ills was now pictured as the secret of its superiority and the reason for its fancied perfection." [27] Here were the seeds of an especially troubled, especially intractable brand of bad faith.

Though Winthrop D. Jordan's *White Over Black* formally terminates its survey of "American Attitudes Toward the Negro" in 1812, it has manifest implications for the understanding of race–slavery in the nearly two centuries since. Jordan is everywhere clear and emphatic that guilt and fear, and their denial—the nagging sense that something was profoundly wrong, and the impulse to seek relief from that anxiety—were cultural staples in the deepening bad faith of race–slavery after 1776. He illustrates this point in reflections on our marked failure to find words adequate to the offspring of miscegenation; on the desire, which exceeded "a reasoned fear of domestic insurrection," to "banish" from consciousness "the reality of St. Domingo"; and on "the successful movement against the slave trade" in the first years of the nineteenth century, a cause which "engrossed much reformist energy and, more important, salved the nation's conscience that *something* was being done about slavery." In fact, he goes on, the abolition of the slave trade in 1808 "said nothing definite about Negroes already in America and afforded a comfortable alternative to thinking about that problem." Further examples of bad faith abound in Jordan's magisterial study, prompting him at one point to allude, almost wearily, to "the old shell game." The most powerfully sustained and most telling of such examples is his discussion of Thomas Jefferson, founder and cultural progenitor, whose passionate advocacy of freedom and equality appears in painful juxtaposition to his equally fixed opinions on the racial inferiority of black people and the "tragic necessity" of slavery. As Jordan deftly demonstrates, our great forbear's response to this deep division within himself was evasion, a persistent impulse, clearly manifest in *Notes on the State of Virginia*, "to dodge the implications arising from his deep-seated sentiments." In the dilemma and in his bad-faith response to it, Jefferson appears to Jordan as "an effective sounding board for his culture." [28]

Eugene Genovese's *Roll, Jordan, Roll: The World the Slaves Made*, though addressed in different methodological terms to a different period of time, is as impressive in its way as *White Over Black*, and as illustrative of the pervasive bad faith of American race–slavery. Genovese argues that the peculiar institution had its foundation in a system of class rule which, in combination with racism, led to the formation of a highly paternalistic relationship between the masters and their human possessions. It was the preeminent bad faith of this culture to submerge the fact of violent coercion in cozy familial images of grateful black children submitting humbly to the firm but loving guidance of beneficent white parents. Genovese goes on to observe that this fanciful conception, which was

> accepted by both masters and slaves—but with radically different interpretations—afforded a fragile bridge across the intolerable contradictions inherent in a society based on racism, slavery, and class exploitation that had to depend on the willing reproduction and productivity of its victims. For the slaveholders paternalism represented an attempt to overcome the fundamental contradiction in slavery: the impossibility of the slaves' ever becoming the things they were supposed to be. Paternalism defined the involuntary labor of the slaves as the legitimate return to their masters for protection and direction. But, the masters' need to see their slaves as acquiescent human beings constituted a moral victory for the slaves themselves. Paternalism's insistence upon mutual obligations—duties, responsibilities, and ultimately even rights—implicitly recognized the slaves' humanity. [29]

It was at root a system of evasion potent with maddening ambiguity at every level. The fact of miscegenation was as visible as its suppression was desperate. Mary Boykin Chesnut noted in her diary for March 14, 1861, that "Any lady is ready to tell you who is the father of all the mulatto children in everybody's household but her own. Those, she seems to think, drop from the clouds." [30] More broadly, the carefully cultivated illusion of domestic calm could never fully dispel the tremors of hatred and fear that arose from the brutal injustice at the heart of the slave system. Thus, Genovese observes, "the panic of the slaveholders at the slightest hint of slave insurrection revealed what lay beneath their endless self-congratulations over the supposed docility, contentment, and loyalty of their slaves. Almost every slaveholder claimed to trust his own slaves but to fear his neighbor's." This enslavement of the masters to their own illusions is nowhere more graphically evident than in the traumatic "moment of truth" they endured in 1865. So deep was the slaveholder's investment in the image of his slaves as docile black children that he was utterly unprepared for the revelations of bitter resentment and hostility that surfaced at the end of the war. The masters

> had expected more than obedience from their slaves; they had expected faithfulness—obedience internalized as duty, respect, and love. They had had little choice, for anything less would have meant a self-image as exploitative brutes. This insistence on the slaves' constituting part of the family and these expressions of belief in their loyalty lay at the heart of the masters' world-view and, abolitionist criticism notwithstanding, embraced little insincerity. Thus the leading southern ideologues, who wrote the proslavery polemics of the late antebellum period, were deceiving none so much as themselves.[31]

Such clear historical parallels notwithstanding, I am principally concerned in what follows with bad faith as it manifests itself in two novels by Mark Twain—how it works, how it connects with race–slavery, how it figures in the telling of the stories, and how it has worked to shape the popular reception of those most familiar American "classics." In the last of these considerations my argument may be viewed as a detailed elaboration of a position set forth some twenty years ago in the best critical book in the field, James M. Cox's *Mark Twain: The Fate of Humor.* "The judgment which the last ten chapters" of *Huckleberry Finn* "render on Tom," Cox contends,

> is surely the judgment rendered upon the moral sentiment on which the book has ridden. If the reader sees in Tom's performance a rather shabby and safe bit of play, he is seeing no more than the exposure of the approval with which he watched Huck operate. For if Tom is rather contemptibly setting a free slave free, what after all is the reader doing, who begins the book after the *fact* of the Civil War? This is the "joke" of the book—the moment when, in outrageous burlesque, it attacks the sentiment which its style has at once evoked and exploited. To see

that Tom is doing at the ending what we have been doing throughout the book is essential to understanding what the book has meant to us. For when Tom proclaims to the assembled throng who have witnessed his performance that Jim "is as free as any cretur that walks this earth," he is an exposed embodiment of the complacent moral sentiment on which the reader has relied throughout the book. And to the extent the reader has indulged the complacency he will be disturbed by the ending.[32]

Here, as elsewhere, I am indebted to the extraordinary insight, clarity, and critical rigor of Cox's analysis. His scholarship on Mark Twain represents a standard of excellence toward which I have aspired, however haltingly, in my own. Even when we disagree, I find that my own critical preoccupations have a bearing on, and often spring from, what he has had to say. I am not persuaded, as he is, that "conscience . . . is the real tyrant" in *Huckleberry Finn*.[33] Racism and slavery, I argue, and the pathological bad faith that they entail, are at the center of the trouble. This is, it must be obvious, a disagreement of no little consequence. But I acknowledge a debt even in major differences, and trust that the critical tension will help to energize new perspectives in the midst of continued, spirited debate.

PART ONE

"The Truth Is Always Respectable"

Tom Sawyer

THOUGH it is generally granted a place among Mark Twain's "major" works, *Tom Sawyer* has not attracted critical attention commensurate with its high canonical station. Indeed, it is not unusual to find professional students of American history and literature who admit that they have not gone back to *Tom Sawyer* since they first read it—or since it was first read to them—as children. Such benign neglect is not altogether surprising. Though they should know better, many readers have been influenced by Mark Twain's caveat that his "book is intended mainly for the entertainment of boys and girls."[1] Undoubtedly, many others have acquiesced in the view, advanced for decades in survey courses around the country, that despite its interest as a formal departure, and its chronological significance as Mark Twain's first sustained meditation on "the matter of Hannibal," *Tom Sawyer* is nonetheless a mere foretaste of greater things to come. Some read the book as an adjunct to *Huckleberry Finn;* and such readers are perhaps understandably predisposed to regard Tom as a conventional, rather mindless proto-entrepreneur. For the most part, however, *Tom Sawyer* has been widely accepted as a minor juvenile classic—"the supreme American idyll," in Bernard DeVoto's familiar characterization.[2]

DeVoto's brief but very suggestive qualifying remarks on the novel are probably less well known. Though he viewed *Tom Sawyer* as "a book eternally true about children," he was careful to add that its pastoral setting "is a part not of cloudland but of America. It is capable of violence and terror." Hinting perhaps that the culture which it portrays, idyll and violence and all, has been rather childlike, if not childish, DeVoto concludes:

> The St. Petersburg of Tom Sawyer is a final embodiment of an American experience many layers deep, from the surface to whatever depths one may care to examine, each layer true. What finds expression here is an America which every one knows to be thus finally transmuted into literature . . . In the presence of such a finality, technical defects, here freely acknowledged, are trivialities. It does not matter much that some of the artist's inventions are weak, that some of the situations and dialogue fail rather dismally, or that, by some canon of abstract form, the

book lacks a perfect adjustment of part to part. It does matter that here something formed from America lives as it lives nowhere else.[3]

Subsequent critics have been slow to explore the layers of meaning and truth that DeVoto first hinted at a half-century ago. Walter Blair has written exhaustively on the history of the novel's composition, on the real-life models for its main characters, and on Mark Twain's literary sources. Critically speaking, however, he finds *Tom Sawyer* "a light book suitable for children and for adults satisfied with a funny story."[4] Henry Nash Smith, having reviewed a similar array of background materials, argues that grave weaknesses in the structure and style of *Tom Sawyer* were obstacles to an effective treatment of "the problem of values to which Mark Twain had devoted so much attention in his early work."[5] In effect, Blair and Smith make much more of the alleged flaws in *Tom Sawyer* than DeVoto does, and they have helped to promote the view that the novel is either inconsequential, or confused, or both, and to be valued primarily for the way it anticipates *Huckleberry Finn.*

Rather more recently, James M. Cox has implicitly accepted the critical challenge laid down by DeVoto two generations ago. Taking the novel seriously in its own terms, Cox dismisses the charge of flimsy plot construction on the grounds that "the reality of the adventures lies not so much in their order as in their relations to Tom." Centered on its juvenile protagonist, the action of the story is defined by Tom's unwavering commitment to a dream of himself as hero in a world of play. With the discovery that coherence resides in a dominant character rather than plot, Cox insists that "every episode of *Tom Sawyer* enacts . . . the conversion of all 'serious' community activity—all duty, pain, grief, and work—into pleasure and play. Tom Sawyer himself is the agent of this conversion."[6]

The appeal of Cox's argument has several dimensions. Most crucial, his analysis and implicitly positive assessment of *Tom Sawyer* arise from principles and standards generated from close critical attention to the text. Cox is aware of history and biography and chronology, but he is not blinded by them. And though he equivocates on the question of plot construction, Cox nonetheless provides the reader with a plausible, comprehensive understanding of the novel's organization. His application of the pleasure principle and the notion of play strikes us as apt, for it describes Tom's behavior quite accurately and at the same time serves admirably to illuminate his motivation and his relationship to the community. Finally, in asserting that "play is the reality principle in the book," Cox points briefly but very usefully to one of the "layers" of meaning, "formed from [Mark Twain's] America," that DeVoto discovered in the novel. Tom's penchant for play, Cox explains, is a direct manifestation of his creator's "inability to 'believe' in conventional fiction . . . Mark Twain had no real use for conventional fiction because his entire genius—the 'Mark Twain' in Samuel Clemens—had his being in the tall tale, a form which presented the truth as a lie, whereas the fiction he condemned presented the lie as the truth."[7]

My debt to Cox's penetrating chapter on *Tom Sawyer* will be evident enough in what follows. I want to develop his insight into Mark Twain's rejection of conventional fiction by pursuing the axiom that artistic forms replicate at one remove the prior social conventions which they figure forth. The commitment to what Cox calls "play" reflects Tom's—and, in a rather different way, Mark Twain's—deeply ambivalent attitude toward the lies masquerading as truth in the adult world of *Tom Sawyer*. In pursuing this line of thought, I will find it necessary to refashion Cox's concept of play, and I will attempt to adumbrate and defend a plot structure for the novel.

II

From that moment at the very beginning of *Tom Sawyer* when aunt Polly looks over, rather than through, her spectacles, because "they were her state pair, the pride of her heart, and were built for 'style,' not service" (39), we are alerted to the importance of social appearances in St. Petersburg. All of the important phases of village life are governed by ordinarily unspoken but evidently rigid rules and conventions. Domestic affairs, school, church, the political and legal establishments, the status hierarchy—in all of these areas a strict code works to enforce order and maintain "degree." For the most part, the members of the community have learned to accept, and even to take pleasure in, shaping themselves to the severely angular construction of their reality. The adults know their places in church, just as the children know theirs in school. All take parts, and play them, accepting apparent inconvenience and discomfort in the dutiful adherence to proper form. The young men of the community, for example, are willing to endure "sit-

ting with their toes pressed against a wall for hours together" in order
to achieve "the fashion of the day," boot toes turned sharply up "like
sleigh-runners" (61). Though the social regimen of the little society
may strike us as comically extreme, our reaction is certainly in some
degree the result of our failure—one we share with the residents of St.
Petersburg—to recognize the constraints, objectively numerous and
rather bizarre, that we bend to in our own daily lives. In larger part,
we respond as we do because the novel directs our attention with un-
remitting persistence to the potent rigor of convention in the village
society. Quite evidently, amidst his fretting about whether he was writing for adults or children, in *Tom Sawyer* Mark Twain yielded to a deep,
though incompletely acknowledged, impulse to write a novel of social
analysis.

Though the status hierarchy in St. Petersburg is rather rigidly fixed,
the social ladder stretches generously from "the aged and needy post-
master, who had seen better days," through a broad range of middling
families like the Sawyers and Harpers, to "the widow Douglas, fair,
smart and forty" (66), with her amiably aristocratic ways, and to such
eminences as the "fine, portly, middle-aged gentleman with iron-gray
hair . . . the great Judge Thatcher, brother of their own lawyer" (62).
The outcasts are surprisingly few. Huck Finn and Muff Potter are tolerated, and even granted condescending sympathy, so long as they keep
their places on the margin. Only Injun Joe, half-breed and suspected
felon, is forced completely outside the capacious orbit of local society.
The great majority of the villagers accept their assigned ranks unre-
flectingly, without any apparent desire to resist the codes that order
and limit their lives. Rather, they assert themselves through public
display of conspicuous mastery of their roles. The necessity for spelling
and spectacles and hymns is never questioned; thus the clear objective
is to be the best speller, to wear the most fashionable spectacles, and,
with the Rev. Mr. Sprague, to recite hymns "with a relish, in a peculiar
style which was much admired in that part of the country" (67). To be
sure, the desire for approval occasionally reaches lunatic proportions.
Consider the lamentable example of the young biblical enthusiast who
once vaingloriously "spread himself" before the congregation by recit-
ing from memory "three thousand verses without stopping." Unfortu-
nately, "the strain upon his mental faculties was too great, and he was
little better than an idiot from that day forth" (60). In spite of such
hazards, however, all St. Petersburg joins in the scramble for public
acclaim. This is especially the case at church, where rituals of devotion

and edification readily give way to an orgy of showing off. The superintendent, the librarian, the young men, the teachers, the boys and
girls—members of every age and rank vie for attention. "And above it
all" Judge Thatcher "sat and beamed a majestic judicial smile upon all
the house, and warmed himself in the sun of his own grandeur—for he
was 'showing off' too" (63).

Despite appearances, such wholesale self-indulgence reinforces
rather than threatens the social order, for the ostentation is an expression of pride of place, not the ambition to subvert or climb. The showing off merely confirms the status quo. Following the urbanely superior
narrator, the reader will undoubtedly be amused by the inflated posturings of the villagers; but he will be wrong if he supposes, as Cox
does, that "the adult rituals" of St. Petersburg "are nothing but dull
play."[8] We may find them dull, but only after we have enjoyed the
show. More to the point, the villagers themselves take manifest pleasure in their relatively artless affectations. Hopelessly encumbered as
they may appear, the members of the little community adhere to rigidly structured roles and routines with evident gusto. Our assessment
of his style notwithstanding, the Rev. Mr. Sprague

> was regarded as a wonderful reader. At church "sociables" he was always
> called upon to read poetry; and when he was through, the ladies would
> lift up their hands and let them fall helplessly in their laps, and "wall"
> their eyes, and shake their heads, as much as to say, "Words cannot
> express it; it is too beautiful, *too* beautiful for this mortal earth."   (67)

These people have an enviable latitude and ingenuity when it comes to
pleasure. Is it dull in the schoolmaster that he responds to news of a
murder by declaring a "holiday for that afternoon"? Not in the view of
his neighbors. Indeed, "the town would have thought strangely of him
if he had not" (105).

Cox's characterization of St. Petersburg features an extreme contrast
between the real play of Tom Sawyer and the somehow inauthentic play
of the adults. He equates Tom with the "world of boyhood . . . where
play, make-believe, and adventure are the living realities defining the
false pieties and platitudes which constitute the dull pleasure of the
adult world."[9] In addition to his misapprehension of adult amusements, Cox errs in both the breadth and the extremity of his definition
of the "world of boyhood." The definition is too broad in that it ignores
the vast majority of children in St. Petersburg who conform without
protest to the values and behavior patterns prescribed by grownups.

When we observe them at play, we find the children of St. Petersburg imitating their elders, holding "a juvenile court that was trying a cat for murder, in the presence of her victim, a bird" (166). And if we remind ourselves of Sid and Mary Sawyer, of the Thatcher children and Amy Lawrence, of the impeccably dressed newcomer whom Tom scuffles with in Chapter 1, of "the Model Boy, Willie Mufferson, taking as heedful care of his mother as if she were cut glass" (66), of the scriptural prodigy who damages his brain, and of the nameless, obedient juvenile assemblage at school and church, then the "world of boyhood" shrinks dramatically.

Cox's contrast is also too extreme in its clear suggestion that Tom inhabits a world of imagination and action that is radically different in degree, and possibly in kind, from the world of the grownups. The error here derives in good part, I believe, from limitations inherent in Cox's notion of play. He construes the term in the theatrical sense, with Tom cast as the central actor who performs before a receding audience composed of townspeople, the narrator (who handles props and draws the curtain), and a multitude of adoring readers. The advantages of this approach are very considerable, especially in opening up the pervasive theatricality of the novel's action and mode of presentation. But the method is misleading when it draws attention away from the fundamental realism of Mark Twain's social analysis, and when it leads to audience-response measurements of the alleged dullness of adult performances. In fact, Tom shows off like everyone else in town, and he does so for the same reasons, according to the same rules, and with the usual amount of zest and pleasure. Tom is willing, for example, to strive for excellence in spelling; but he extends himself at school principally because success earns him a "pewter medal which he had worn with ostentation for months" (80). Moreover, there is abundant evidence that Tom advocates the strict observance of orderly, established procedures. "After the hymn had been sung," we learn, it was the convention for the minister to turn "himself into a bulletin board and read off 'notices' of meetings and societies and things till it seemed that the list would stretch out to the crack of doom." The narrator's amusement betrays a rather sharper edge when he observes, "Often, the less there is to justify a traditional custom, the harder it is to get rid of it." As if to add insult to injury, the minister goes on to his regular, and regularly interminable, prayer for "the church, and the little children of the church; . . . for the oppressed millions groaning under the heel of European monarchies and Oriental despotisms" and "the heathen in the far islands of the sea." We are hardly surprised to find that Tom "did not enjoy the prayer, he only endured it—if he even did that much." But despite the fact that he "was restive, all through it," Tom

> kept tally of the details of the prayer, unconsciously—for he was not listening, but he knew the ground of old, and the clergyman's regular route over it—and when a little trifle of new matter was interlarded, his ear detected it and his whole nature resented it; he considered additions unfair, and scoundrelly.   (67–68)

The reader may be inclined to share the narrator's view that the prayer is mechanically prolix and therefore, like the recital of "notices," somehow unjustified. For Tom, however, the prayer is justified simply because it is "a traditional custom," and he objects to the slightest departure from its familiar, outward dullness. In this light, Tom's scrupulous adherence to literary "authorities" in his adventures, and his urging Huck to submit to the widow's civilizing influence—"we can't let you into the gang if you ain't respectable, you know" (235)—point to the unmistakably adult models which inform his values and conduct.[10]

We can move toward an even clearer sense of Tom's behavior if we shift briefly from the theatrical frame of reference to a notion of play as spontaneous activity taking rise from the relatively unencumbered promptings of the imagination.[11] The nearest approach to such "free" play occurs at the beginning of the famous whitewashing episode, when Ben Rogers appears on the scene.

> He was eating an apple, and giving a long, melodious whoop, at intervals, followed by a deep-toned ding-dong-dong, for he was personating a steamboat. As he drew near, he slackened speed, took the middle of the street, leaned far over to starboard and rounded to ponderously and with laborious pomp and circumstance—for he was personating the "Big Missouri," and considered himself to be drawing nine feet of water. He was boat and captain and engine-bells combined, so he had to imagine himself standing on his own hurricane deck giving the orders and executing them:
>
> "Stop her, sir! Ting-a-ling-ling!" His headway ran almost out and he drew up slowly toward the side-walk.
>
> "Ship up to back! Ting-a-ling-ling!" His arms straightened and stiffened down his sides.
>
> "Set her back on the stabboard! Ting-a-ling-ling! Chow! ch-chow-wow! Chow!" His right hand, meantime, describing stately circles,—for it was representing a forty-foot wheel.   (47–48)

Meanwhile, apparently absorbed in his own activity, Tom goes on with the whitewashing, and "paid no attention to the steamboat" (48). In fact, however, and in contrast to Ben's total oblivion to his actual surroundings, Tom is alive to the possibilities of the objective circumstances. While Ben plays at being a steamboat, Tom plays—in a very different way—at seeming not to notice. On one side, we have virtually unselfconscious make-believe; on the other, alert, self-conscious and purposive dissimulation. While Ben plays, Tom schemes. In the upshot, of course, artless play succumbs to artful plotting.

In following the inevitable logic of the child- versus adult-play argument, Cox is inclined to minimize what he calls the "embryo businessman" in Tom, and focuses instead on "the essential criticism the episode . . . makes of the original chore." Viewed from this angle, the whitewashing incident exposes the poverty of adult initiative—aunt Polly's demands are a "dull-witted stratagem for getting work done at low pay in the name of duty"—and the concomitant superiority of a juvenile rejoinder in which "Tom shows off his handiwork" while completing the task "in the name of pleasure."[12] In thus preserving his critical line of thought, however, Cox ignores the force of the contrast between Tom and Ben, and seriously overstates the contrast between the behavior of aunt Polly and Tom. If we acknowledge—as I think we must—that the episode demonstrates Tom's prodigious mastery of deception and the strategies of self-interest, then we must go on to observe that his conduct, unlike Ben's, is hardly spontaneous and free. In fact, if it is true that aunt Polly contrives to get "work done at low pay," then the same can be said of Tom, except that he gets it done at a considerable profit to himself, and that the name of pleasure serves his purposes better than "duty."

I will return to a much fuller analysis of Tom's highly self-conscious maneuverings in a moment. First, however, it remains to point out a final liability in the interpretation of the whitewashing episode as an example of play-as-performance in which "Tom shows off." While it is undeniable that Tom adopts a role in his dealings with his friends, it is wrong to assume that his role is abandoned and the action completed when the curtain closes on his aunt's freshly painted fence. Tom's fellows fall into this error, and they do so at the cost of becoming victims once again. For the very next day Tom capitalizes on an extremely depressed market when he trades the proceeds of his artistic enterprise for enough tickets to win a Bible. No one in the congregation is so foolish as to believe that Tom has actually memorized enough verses to earn the tickets, but there is no denying that he possesses the requisite number. Thus all doubts are carefully suppressed, and Tom is

> elevated to a place with the Judge and the other elect, and the great news was announced from head-quarters. It was the most stunning surprise of the decade; and so profound was the sensation that it lifted the new hero up to the judicial one's altitude, and the school had two marvels to gaze upon in place of one. The boys were all eaten up with envy—but those that suffered the bitterest pangs were those who perceived too late that they themselves had contributed to this hated splendor by trading tickets to Tom for the wealth he had amassed in selling white-washing privileges. These despised themselves, as being the dupes of a wily fraud, and guileful snake in the grass. (63)

To a much greater extent than in the whitewashing incident, there is a conspicuous element of spectacle here; Tom is indeed the happy hero in a kind of performance. But there is a good deal more to be observed in his triumph. As I have already suggested, Tom's elevation is hardly an isolated episode; rather, it is the final step in a carefully orchestrated sequence of events that first took life when Tom spotted Ben ("Big Missouri") Rogers and decided to feign indifference. This opening move led, in turn, to the successful duping of Joe and a host of friends, the effortless completion of an onerous chore and the masterful evasion of punishment, the gathering of unearned treasure, the subsequent doubling of profit from the very advantageous conversion of capital (at the expense of the original, and still unsuspecting, victims), and the final, admittedly dramatic, cashing in. At one level, the elegance and boldness of the scheme strongly suggest that Tom takes as much pleasure from the conception and execution of his elaborate plot as he does from its spectacular denouement. Much of the fun, it appears, is in the doing. At another level, the complex attenuation of Tom's scheme is evidence of greater development and continuity between episodes than the isolated performance model recognizes. Events are related not merely because Tom is *in* them, but also to a large extent because he *orders* them. Thus in this cluster of incidents, as in others I will turn to, Tom Sawyer's plotting serves to emplot *Tom Sawyer.*

In winning his way to the top, Tom outwits and exploits members from every age group and class in the community. The other children are twice taken in, and provide ready sources of free labor and capital. The adults are equally easy prey; for, as Tom shrewdly divines, their incredulity is not as deep as their craving for amusement. Along the way, Tom makes a mockery of honesty and good faith; but he does so in a manner that is, paradoxically, easily detected and yet impervious to public disapproval. We can begin to unravel this paradox by observing that in moving toward his objectives, Tom has enjoyed the cooperation, both willing and unwilling, of the community. His victims either get what they asked for, or have themselves to blame for their undoing, or both. In effect, Tom has collaborated with his neighbors in "bad faith," the reciprocal deception of self and other, generally in the denial of departures from public codes of correct behavior. A telling feature of such acts is their incorporation of silent prohibitions against the admission that they have occurred. For their part, Tom's neighbors can never fully acknowledge to themselves or others the full extent to which they have been deceived. To do so would risk a humiliating revelation of their willingness to be misled. On Tom's part, full acknowledgment of bad faith would entail the potential for an unbearable assault of guilt, or the loss, through their public disclosure, of the social intuitions which form the basis of his power. This delicate equipoise of threats to the collective peace of mind would collapse were it not for the fact that bad faith is the ruling characteristic in the social dynamics of the village.

St. Petersburg society is a complex fabric of lies: of half-truths, of simulation, dissimulation, broken promises, exaggeration, and outright falsehoods. Tom is exceptional only in the sheer quantity of his showing off; Huck's faith is more than once betrayed; the local ladies are easy marks for vendors of quack cure-alls and exotic religions; the entire community turns a blind eye to Injun Joe's grave robbing and the presence of liquor in the Temperance Tavern; and the Judge himself is moved to deliver an encomium on lies of the generous, magnanimous stripe. One imagines, in fact, that St. Petersburg is hardly unusual in all this, and that varieties of bad faith are universally a feature of complex societies. They are the covert mechanisms of flexibility and resilience that work imperceptibly to mitigate rigid customs and laws, and thus provide a measure of latitude adequate to the accommodation of apparently incompatible demands for conformity and individual self-expression. As I am using the term, then, "bad faith" describes the spectrum of unacknowledged and sublimated deceits that a society tolerates as the price of stability and equanimity. It is the "give" in the outwardly stiff St. Petersburg system.

It must be obvious by now that if Tom is playing at all, he is playing a sustained, purposeful, relatively complex social game. His success is the index of his masterful mimicry of adult strategies, and of his possession, to an uncommon degree, of social intuition, audacity, and an arsenal of artifice. Their skillful use enables him to gain glittering notoriety and the pinnacle of the social ladder, and at the same time to avoid censure. But if Tom is like Icarus in his mastery of artifice and in the swiftness and dizzying pitch of his ascent, he is Icarian as well in his precipitous vulnerabilities. Tom's genius for manipulation makes it possible for him to play at the perilous margins of social tolerance for bad faith. As we have seen, the potential for exploitation is great; but susceptible as he is to the pride of mastery, Tom is prone to the kind of false move that threatens a fall as abrupt as his climb. The radical extremes of Tom's potential are precisely, if somewhat obliquely, evident to those villagers "that believed he would be President, yet, if he escaped hanging" (173).

Tom's outward vulnerability to his neighbors has its inward counterpart in his vulnerability to himself. The indispensable key to Tom's power is his unique, even transcendent, intuitive grasp of the mechanisms of bad faith that govern behavior in St. Petersburg. The other villagers are all but blind to their immersion in the quotidian round of deceit, and thus complacently unaware of what we might be inclined, in a righteous mood, to call their hypocrisy. Indeed, it is the essential first article of bad faith that its agents live in the illusion that they are virtually free of the impulse to deceive or be deceived. Thus the local residents, fully and unconsciously acculturated as they are, deceive themselves and each other without frequent or significant misgivings. For Tom, however, the correlative to enhanced social acuity is heightened vulnerability to a crippling double consciousness. On one side, Tom recognizes and subscribes to the overt code of his community. On the other, he is the possessor of a profound subliminal insight into the dynamics of the social game. But this insight is an asset only so long as it works below the threshold of consciousness; for full self-awareness would be accompanied by the onset of guilt and the collapse of manipulative social power. At some submerged level, Tom knows that he cannot afford to know what he knows. Thus he is obliged to expend large sums of psychic energy in the abridgment of self-knowledge. As we shall see, though he is generally successful in this enterprise, he is never completely out of danger of an upsurge of painful emotion from beneath the surface of consciousness.

It will also become clear that the novel's failure to fully resolve Tom's dilemma is the price Mark Twain paid for the preservation of his fictional point of view. For if Tom's intuitive manipulation of pervasive bad faith produces both plotting and plot, the same perception in the reader, issuing from our privileged view of Tom's intrigues, produces humor. It follows, of course, that the key to the novel's humorous consistency of tone is the narrator's ability to preserve his good-natured condescension to the villagers' double standards. On those occasions when his superior detachment from village eccentricity gives way to anger at perceived hypocrisy, we are reminded of Tom's dilemma and made aware of the fine line that separates humor from the angriest variety of social satire.

III

Tom's glittering climb from truculent whitewasher to triumphant church hero is marred by a final, nearly catastrophic, reversal. Having mounted the platform to join the local bon ton, Tom is encouraged to honor the audience with a brief demonstration of his pious learning. "Now I know you'll tell *me*," urges the Judge's perfectly ingenuous wife: "The names of the first two disciples were—" When Tom responds, "DAVID AND GOLIAH!" the upper case type is alone adequate to suggest the enormity of his lapse. Sudden and steep though it is, however, the hero's fall does not end in disgraceful defeat. With the reader, the members of the community appear to be much more amused than offended by Tom's antics. The bubble of their pretensions has been pricked, but much of the potential for resentment has been dissipated in the embarrassment of the quondam celebrity. Moreover, there is an ample measure of triumph in Tom's apparent humiliation. For the adults, he has been the source of entertainment and the occasion for a gratifyingly spontaneous expression of communal high spirits. For his juvenile peers, Tom's egregious lapse serves to ameliorate feelings of envy and betrayal. Most important of all, even in defeat Tom is precisely where he wants to be—at the center of the stage—when the narrator good-humoredly draws "the curtain of charity over the rest of the scene" (65).

Once again, there is good reason to press beyond the play-as-performance analysis of the text. To be sure, this approach draws ample justification from the setting and language of the episode. But Tom's moment on the stage is also an important phase in his education as the leading gamesman in St. Petersburg. Superficially, the lesson of Tom's exposure is that schemes of deception are morally wrong and therefore doomed to failure. In fact, Tom learns that strategies of self-aggrandizement on his ambitious scale must be complete to the last detail if they are to succeed. In plotting his course of action, he fails to anticipate developments—in this case, questions about apostles—that exceed his admittedly formidable resourcefulness and dexterity. Thus in entering and playing the game Tom's error is strategic rather than ethical.

In confirmation of this general lesson, and as a potential guide for the future, Tom is well placed to make observations on some of the finer points of the social game. First, it must be evident to him that his neighbors are perpetually ready to be deceived. In this case, the congregation's craving for amusement, along with the superintendent's understandable ambition to show off a prize pupil, combine to envelop an obvious falsehood in a mantle of bland credibility. Thus the episode illustrates the axiom that community tolerance for lies is directly proportional to the service the deceit renders to the desires and vanities, almost always unacknowledged, of those who endure the deception. Given the right return on their gullibility, the villagers will swallow almost anything. As a corollary to this rule, there is an evident premium on falsehoods that are offered up in the name of some noble or educational cause. This feature lends a sort of pious plausibility to the decision to be deceived and, should the deception be exposed, it provides the grounds for a gratifying outburst of righteous indignation.

Second, Tom learns that failure—outright exposure of the act of deception—can sometimes be converted to personal advantage. This is so because the community investment in varieties of duplicity is so fundamental and far-reaching that the detection of group acquiescence in a single lie points by implication to the complex fabric of deceptions and half-truths that they have all silently agreed to accept, and to ignore. The admission that one has been deceived threatens to trigger the awareness that one is perpetually deceived. Since this awareness is humiliating to the individual and threatening to the stability of the group, the most seasoned and successful deceivers will always be ready with new lies to veil old ones, or with smooth palliatives to ease the sting of the victim's anger and embarrassment. Tom's apparent failure at church works substantially to his advantage because it alleviates the anger of his juvenile victims, draws attention away from the foolish gullibility of the adults, and averts discord with the happy illusion that the episode is a harmless prank. Meanwhile, his success tarnished slightly but still intact, Tom remains the central attraction.

The exposition and oblique analysis of the dynamics of village social behavior is the primary business of the early chapters of *Tom Sawyer,* and a major theme and principle of organization in the novel as a whole. The narrator directly addresses this preoccupation when he pauses, in Chapter 2, to observe that Tom "had discovered a great law of human action, without knowing it—namely, that in order to make a man or a boy covet a thing, it is only necessary to make the thing difficult to attain" (50). Mark Twain's survey of the community is remarkably comprehensive and systematic, moving from the domestic scene to the peer group, through a host of institutional arrangements, and including along the way a glimpse of the relations between the sexes. As we shall see, this preliminary anatomy of village "sociology" forms the quite essential background to our understanding of later, more complicated variations on basic social themes. Notable throughout is the consistency with which the novel's actors adhere to patterns of behavior set forth in the opening chapters. The principal agent and structural focus of this unfolding analysis is, of course, Tom Sawyer. Tom's consistency derives in part from his sure intuitive grasp of the subtle ways and means of St. Petersburg society. As the narrator says, Tom masters these principles "of human action, without knowing it." It derives, too, from his prolonged exposure to, and astute mimicry of, the artful manipulative strategies of his aunt Polly. In the finer points of the social game, Tom's education begins right at home.

Though aunt Polly views herself as a fool in her relationship to Tom, and though she insists that "old fools is the biggest fools there is" (40), she is in fact a worthy opponent and an able mentor in the fine art of St. Petersburg gamesmanship. A substantial strand of *Tom Sawyer* is given to the description of the running, apparently interminable, battle between the good-hearted old woman and her nephew. Superficially, the contest pits aunt Polly's insistence on honesty, probity, obedience, propriety—in a word, respectability—against Tom's pursuit of freedom and the pleasure principle. To all appearances, it is the familiar conflict between youth and age, nature and civilization. In fact, however, the apparent terms of the struggle are merely a conventional pretext for what is, at root, a battle of wills. When aunt Polly rewards Tom for his good work with the fence, she forces him to endure "an improving lecture upon the added value and flavor a treat took to itself when it came without sin through virtuous effort. And while she closed with a happy Scriptural flourish, he 'hooked' a doughnut" (51–52). While the humor in this brief encounter springs in part from a perception of sprightly pleasure subverting leaden piety, there is a deeper human comedy in the spectacle of naked willfulness masquerading in the liveries of virtue and desire. Aunt Polly is much more in love with her own voice, and with her power to hold her nephew captive, than she is with virtue. And her nephew will relish his doughnut principally because it bears palpably sweet testimony to the triumphant autonomy of his own will. It is the comedy, then, of the devious ingenuity we humans bring to having things, even the most trivial things, our own way.

Tom is blessed by nature and training with ample resources for the domestic struggle. He is physically quick enough to scale a fence in the wink of an eye. And he is mentally quick as well. Aunt Polly complains that you "can't learn an old dog new tricks," but in the same breath she acknowledges that Tom "never plays them alike, two days, and how is a body to know what's coming?" (40). Moreover, in laying his plans, Tom displays increasingly close attention to matters of detail. Improvement in this area is vital, for when his foresight falters—as it does when he neglects the apostles, or when he sews his collar closed with black instead of the original white thread—Tom becomes vulnerable to the consequences of discovery. But even in tight places Tom can rely on his sharp intuitive judgment of his aunt's limits. "He 'pears to know just how long he can torment me before I get my dander up," aunt Polly observes, "and he knows if he can make out to put me off for a minute or make me laugh, it's all down again and I can't hit him a lick" (40). Finally, and most crucially, Tom is absolute in his control of his face. He views it as a weakness in Becky that her expression often betrays her feelings: "Girls' faces always tell on them. They ain't got any backbone" (154). Muff Potter and Huck Finn are equally prone to give themselves away. But Tom has the ability to feign or dissimulate moods as his perceived self-interest would seem to require. He is a pillar of apparent indifference as he lays schemes for Joe Harper, and though he knows he is late for school, "he strode in briskly, with the manner of one who had come with all honest speed" (77). This consummate mastery of face is the clearest outward manifestation of the gamesman's inward self-control, and it aptly expresses his ruling ambition to give nothing away.[13]

The contest between Tom and his aunt appears to involve him in the effort to avoid the punishments meted out for the violation of her rules.

To an extent this impression is accurate, though it should be emphasized that Tom errs not when he breaks rules, but only when he gets *caught* breaking rules. That aunt Polly is surprised to find the fence whitewashed betrays her assumption that Tom will defy her will whenever it conflicts with his own. Indeed, we may go even further in this direction and argue that the old woman's expectation that her nephew will break her rules is the indirect manifestation of the fact that she places great value on Tom's rebelliousness. To be sure, she is totally unaware of this contradictory wrinkle in her makeup. It is equally evident, however, that the rules are relatively unimportant except as occasions for the game, and that the game cannot begin until a rule has been broken. Paradoxically, then, Tom serves his aunt best when he seeks to escape detection in the violation of her orders. Tom shares his aunt's blindness to this dimension of their relationship; yet he values the game as much as she does, and is perfectly happy to play along. In effect, the woman and the child unconsciously collaborate in the creation of a pleasurable contest of wills. As the following passage clearly illustrates, when the contest is finally joined the issue of compliance with rules appears in its true colors, as the merest pretext for an exhilarating round of artful deception and cat-like pursuit.

> While Tom was eating his supper, and stealing sugar as opportunity offered, aunt Polly asked him questions that were full of guile, and very deep—for she wanted to trap him into damaging revealments. Like many other simple-hearted souls, it was her pet vanity to believe she was endowed with a talent for dark and mysterious diplomacy and she loved to contemplate her most transparent devices as marvels of low cunning. Said she:
> "Tom, it was middling warm in school, warn't it?"
> "Yes'm."
> "Powerful warm, warn't it?"
> "Yes'm."
> "Didn't you want to go in a-swimming, Tom?"
> A bit of a scare shot through Tom—a touch of uncomfortable suspicion. He searched aunt Polly's face, but it told him nothing. So he said:
> "No'm—well, not very much."
> The old lady reached out her hand and felt Tom's shirt, and said:
> "But you ain't too warm now, though." And it flattered her to reflect that she had discovered that the shirt was dry without anybody knowing that that was what she had in her mind. But in spite of her, Tom knew where the wind lay, now. So he forestalled what might be the next move:
> "Some of us pumped on our heads—mine's damp yet. See?"

Aunt Polly was vexed to think she had overlooked that bit of circum-stantial evidence, and missed a trick. Then she had a new inspiration:

"Tom, you didn't have to undo your shirt collar where I sewed it to pump on your head, did you? Unbutton your jacket!"

The trouble vanished out of Tom's face. He opened his jacket. His shirt collar was securely sewed.

"Bother! Well, go 'long with you. I'd made sure you'd played hookey and been a-swimming. But I forgive ye, Tom. I reckon you're a kind of a singed cat, as the saying is—better'n you look. *This* time." (41–42)

Quite appropriately, when it begins to appear that Tom has in fact complied with her instructions, aunt Polly responds with a marked division of feeling. On one side, she is "half glad that Tom had stumbled into obedient conduct for once." "Stumbled" betrays her as-sumption that Tom's apparent obedience has been an unintentional ac-cident, and points to her submerged preference for disobedience and the preservation of the game. That she is "half sorry her sagacity had miscarried" (42) complements this sentiment, for it is an expression of regret that her suspicions turned out to be groundless. Thus the sum of aunt Polly's response is rather grudging approval of Tom's seeming compliance, and much more emphatic disappointment that his inad-vertent obedience has spoiled the fun. In reality, of course, Tom has bested her in the game of cat-and-mouse, for her reluctant acknowledg-ment of his good behavior is ironically premature. But the match of wits is hardly revitalized when young Sid reminds his aunt that "you sewed his collar with white thread, but it's black" (42). This intrusion of solid, irrefutable fact resolves the question of objective right and wrong, but it also levels the uncertainty which first gave the contest life. There can be no doubt that Tom would have preferred to avoid detection; the rewards of disobedience would have been immeasurably sweetened by the success of his subterfuge. As it is, victory is wrenched from his grasp, aunt Polly is spared the mild embarrassment of miscar-ried sagacity, and Tom rushes from the room vowing vengeance on Sid. But Tom's abrupt defeat is augmented by the loss, which he shares with aunt Polly, of the game which they have both so obviously and thor-oughly enjoyed. It is richly paradoxical that in a debate ostensibly com-mitted to the discovery of truth, the actual ingress of truth should spell the end of pleasure. Yet this is precisely what happens. And it is a paradox which will bring us back, in due course, for a longer look at Sid. After all, though Tom loses the battle, Sid is the true villain of the piece. His betrayal of Tom is self-righteous and small. But his much deeper offense is to take up truth as a weapon against pleasure. Sid would be less contemptible if we believed that his crushing revelations were prompted by innocent literal-mindedness. In fact, however, Sid is a pharisaical kill-joy. His intuitive understanding of the terms and pleasures of the game is as complete as his inability to join the fun. As compensation, he vents his arid malice in outwardly pious disclosures of revealing facts that he has hoarded as hostages against the pleasure of others. Thus Sid's bad faith is worse than bad, for he values truth only as it advances his perverse compulsion to expose the small lies that vitalize and sustain the socially beneficial game.

It is one measure of Sid's alienation from the game that he is invulnerable to punishment of misdeeds that would earn Tom the swiftest retribution. This is partly the result of the fact that Sid is very seldom out of line. His behavior is so narrowly and scrupulously—one is tempted to say, unnaturally—correct that he offers no challenge to his aunt's superiority, or to her poised craving for combat. Sid may spoil the game, but he is no contest. Thus when aunt Polly hears the sugar bowl fall and break, she is quick to lay the blame on Tom. The subsequent revelation that Sid is at fault betrays yet another miscarriage of her sagacity, but prompts nothing in the way of punishment. Viewed in this light, Sid's immunity is as much the reflex of his aunt's indifference as of her approval, while Tom's vulnerability is the reward of his gratifying readiness to play along. And just as surely as Sid's resentment is fueled by the faint praise that greets his rectitude, Tom's pleasure in the game is enhanced and sustained by aunt Polly's attention to his every move.

At the same time, however, it would be wrong-headed to suppose that the penalties for detection lack sting. Error in this regard might arise from a too ready acquiescence in aunt Polly's persuasion that Tom "hates work more than he hates anything" (41). The truth of her position aside, the imposition of chores as punishment fails because Tom demonstrates an effortless facility for converting work to play and personal profit. In fact, aunt Polly knows better than she says; she knows that the real penalty for being found out is enforced and humiliating acknowledgment that one has been outwitted. The heaviest immediate consequence of losing is *not* winning. Moreover, aunt Polly's own actions and responses betray her awareness that the most dread adjunct to the simple sting of defeat is the infliction of guilt.

Though Tom is relatively unmoved by threats of work or the rod, he is overcome with crippling remorse when aunt Polly "wept over him and asked him how he could go and break her old heart so . . . This was worse than a thousand whippings, and Tom's heart was sorer now than his body" (103). The boy's susceptibility to assaults of guilt mirrors a tendency more broadly characteristic of the community as a whole. Widespread sensitivity on this front is quite evidently the price paid by all for their subliminal collusion in bad faith; the collective moral economy exacts apparently gratuitous or excessive attacks of conscience as the return on numberless unacknowledged duplicities. This phenomenon is perhaps clearest in the plangent appeal by the St. Petersburg women for a posthumous pardon of Injun Joe. The apparent irrationality of their plea begins to make sense if we view it as the manifestation of an unconscious admission that the half-breed terror of the village is in fact the victim of a cruel racial lie, and is hounded to his misdeeds, and ultimately to his death, by heartless prejudice. Similar dynamics are at work when aunt Polly admits that she shares Tom's sense of complicity in Dr. Robinson's death. "Sho! It's that dreadful murder. I dream about it most every night myself. Sometimes I dream it's me that done it" (107). Mary confesses to the identical reaction, and only Sid—as removed from the penalties as he is from the benefits of bad faith—retains his composure.

The intense guilt that afflicts Tom when his aunt appears to suffer on his account is a unique element in his general attitude toward questions of right and wrong. As we have seen, he is coolly detached in his departures from accepted norms of behavior; he is indifferent to rules, relatively indifferent to punishment except as it testifies to his failure in the game, and seriously constrained only by the grief he brings to others. Thus he assures the family slave, Jim, that aunt Polly "never licks anybody—whacks 'em over the head with her thimble—and who cares for that, I'd like to know. She talks awful, but talk don't hurt—anyways it don't if she don't cry" (47). Most obviously, we are reminded that Tom is inclined to view his own transgressions as strategic rather than as moral phenomena. Aunt Polly indirectly reinforces this attitude, and gives it an added dimension, when she complains, "Tom, don't lie to me—I can't bear it" (51). Her injunction is not premised on the conventional Christian abhorrence of deceit as inherently sinful; rather, she condemns Tom's lies because they give her pain. By implication, and in a manner wholly consonant with a climate of bad faith, the old woman is taking arms against detection, but not against deceit. Moreover, her cry of pain is as much a threat as it is an appeal. If Tom lies to her, as she expects and even hopes he will; and if she is able to detect the lie and plausibly demonstrate that it has caused her suffering; then, paradoxically, she has him where she wants him. The guilt that Tom suffers will handsomely compensate the old woman for the pain she claims to have endured, for to her triumphant riposte in the duel with her nephew she can add the gratifying illusion that victory has been the reward of moral superiority. Thus while aunt Polly is hardly insensitive to pain, it is nonetheless evident that she views it primarily as an element in the game. Or, to put it another way, aunt Polly's suffering is most important to her when she is able to persuade Tom that he is its cause, and thus turn its consequences, with redoubled energy, upon him. Likewise, I am not suggesting that Tom has a charitable or empathic aversion to giving hurt. To the contrary, on numerous occasions the suffering of others is perfectly compatible with his self-esteem. What he fears, though, is the guilt that follows as the consequence of being caught.

To highlight the major part played by guilt in the struggle between Tom and his aunt is to recognize that both players are vulnerable to attacks of conscience. This shared susceptibility serves to diminish the advantage that aunt Polly appears to enjoy in her role as pursuer and enforcer. After all, Tom is no more prone to error than she, and he is quite as skilled in the strategies of the game. It follows that aunt Polly must proceed with great caution, for her errors in planning and timing can result in sudden reversals. Such a turnabout occurs, for example, when the old woman learns that she has mistakenly punished Tom for breaking the sugar bowl.

> Then her conscience reproached her, and she yearned to say something kind and loving; but she judged that this would be construed into a confession that she had been in the wrong, and discipline forbade that. So she kept silence, and went about her affairs with a troubled heart. Tom sulked in a corner and exalted his woes. He knew that in her heart his aunt was on her knees to him, and he was morosely gratified by the consciousness of it. . . . He pictured himself lying sick unto death and his aunt bending over him beseeching one little forgiving word, but he would turn his face to the wall, and die with that word unsaid. Ah, how would she feel then?   (54)

Though aunt Polly rationalizes her failure to apologize as a disciplinary necessity, it is quite transparently the case that she is unwilling to amplify Tom's triumph with an outright admission of her own error. But Tom does quite well without apologies. Past experience in the game gives him a clear window on his aunt's feelings, and he answers her silence with a much more punishing silence of his own. Since Tom's inner delight is directly proportional to his aunt's inner discomfort, he exploits her inadvertent tactical blunder by the artfully contrived failure to disguise simulated pain. So levitating is his feeling of triumph—the rapturous "Ah" betrays his pleasure in tightening the screws of his aunt's remorse—that he indulges himself in one of his many fantasies of death. Here, as elsewhere, such fantasies may point to a measure of self-pity, but they serve more primarily to express Tom's imagined conception of total victory based on the infliction of maximum, irremediable guilt. While the drawback to the actual employment of such a strategy is perfectly obvious, it is an index to Tom's exultation that he regales himself with this imagined spectacle of consummate mastery.

The perilous pleasures of the game with aunt Polly—issuing from impulses toward self-assertion and dominance in a context of bad faith, and contingent on the acquisition of the various "moves" necessary to the infliction of guilt and the ascent to victory—are virtually duplicated in Mark Twain's presentation of the battle between the sexes. Once Tom has settled on Becky Thatcher as his amorous objective, a whole array of familiar strategies come into play. At first, he makes a bid for Becky's attention while disguising his own interest behind a bland exterior. "He worshiped this new angel with furtive eye, till he saw that she had discovered him; then he pretended he did not know she was present, and began to 'show off' in all sorts of absurd boyish ways in order to win her admiration" (53). Such preliminary maneuvers—frequently involving the controlled presentation of "face"—lead to an "engagement" which is almost immediately broken off when Tom makes the tactical blunder of mentioning his earlier interest in Amy Lawrence. His ensuing frustration prompts a temporary flight to fantasy, where he enjoys an imagined return to favor and supremacy resulting from the infliction of guilt. "Now as to this girl. What had he done? Nothing. He had meant the best in the world, and been treated like a dog—like a very dog. She would be sorry some day—maybe when it was too late. Ah, if he could only die *temporarily!*" (87).

The volatile relationship moves through various shifts in the balance of power, during which Becky displays a remarkable aptitude for the game. At one juncture, for example, Tom is "maddened . . . to see, as he thought he saw, that Becky Thatcher never once suspected that he was even in the land of the living." But Tom is deceived by Becky's mastery of her own face, for "she did see . . . and she knew she was winning her fight, too, and was glad to see him suffer as she had suffered" (147). But Tom finally reasserts himself in a series of brilliant moves. First, he earns Becky's grudging gratitude by concealing the fact that she has accidentally torn the teacher's prized anatomy book. Appearances notwithstanding, however, Tom's generosity is a calculated concession, and does nothing to modify his determination to regain the upper hand. "Well, of course *I* ain't going to tell old Dobbins on this little fool," he reflects, "because there's other ways of getting even on her, that ain't so mean" (154). In reality, Tom's seeming generosity is shrewdly veiled self-interest. Since he assumes, with considerable justice, that Becky's face will betray her culpability to the teacher, his concealment of her secret does nothing to protect her from the punishment that she fears, and that he anticipates with vindictive relish. Thus even in holding back he will get "even on her," all the while preserving the strategic advantage he derives from seeming to act in her interest. As a final bonus, Tom's apparently charitable silence will save him from the guilt that he would suffer if he spoke out against the culprit.

Though the scheme is admirable in its elegant intricacy, it has at least two important shortcomings. First, it subordinates the primary goal of victory in amorous conflict to the secondary satisfactions of revenge. Second, the suave passivity of the strategy, while undeniably gratifying in its way, is fundamentally incompatible with the melodramatic elan of Tom's manipulative impulse. As if in response to these imperatives, Tom is at the last moment inspired by a final stroke of tactical genius. In an act that at first seems to nullify all the advantages of silence, and to positively invite disaster, he rushes to Becky's defense by boldly announcing that he is guilty of the heinous offense.

> The school stared in perplexity at this incredible folly. Tom stood a moment, to gather his dismembered faculties; and when he stepped forward to go to his punishment the surprise, the gratitude, the adoration that shone upon him out of poor Becky's eyes seemed pay enough for a hundred floggings. Inspired by the splendor of his own act, he took without an outcry the most merciless flaying that even Mr. Dobbins had ever administered; and also received with indifference the added cruelty of a command to remain two hours after school should be dismissed—for he knew who would wait for him outside till his captivity was done, and not count the tedious time as loss, either. (156–57)

To the eyes of his peers, Tom has stepped forward in a spirit of magnanimity and willing—even foolhardy—self-sacrifice. In fact, his satisfaction is rooted in the secret, gratifying knowledge that his ready submission to brief discomfort has placed him at center stage in a heroic melodrama, and has earned him the melting gratitude of the elusive Becky Thatcher. Thus there is a fine irony in Becky's adoring outburst, "Tom, how *could* you be so noble!" (157) The emphasis on *"could"* arises from her perception that Tom has requited "her own treachery" toward him—which she admits to "with shame and repentance" (157)—with an act so apparently selfless and forgiving that it would strain her credulity were it not so nourishing to her self-esteem. At one level of consciousness, Tom obviously shares Becky's view, and basks in the warm "splendor of his own act." At another, he recognizes that whether or not he *"could . . .* be so noble" is utterly beside the point. Virtue may have its rewards, and Tom Sawyer may be virtuous; as a route to victory in the game of deception, however, the successful simulation of nobility is more richly satisfying than the achievement of the merely real thing.

IV

Tom's education as a gamesman reaches its climactic fruition in the planning, execution, and aftermath of the mock-resurrection that appears in Chapter 17. For sheer virtuosity in boldness, exploitation of bad faith, anticipation of details, mastery of face, and the strategic scope of its engagement with St. Petersburg society, the episode is the finest flowering of Tom's genius. The first seed of the elaborate plot is planted when Tom, recently rejected by Becky and feeling himself "a forsaken, friendless boy," decides to abandon the village for a life of crime. Characteristically, the plan is rooted in self-pity, and has the kindling of guilt in faithless hearts as its principal objective. "Nobody loved him; when they found out what they had driven him to, perhaps they would be sorry" (114). Tom finds similarly long-suffering allies in Joe Harper and Huck Finn, who join him in an escape to Jackson's Island.

A much more elaborate scheme begins to germinate when a steamboat loaded with townspeople circles the island in search of the victims of a drowning accident. In a flash of insight Tom grasps the implication of the situation: "Boys, I know who's drownded—it's us!" Just as quickly, he recognizes that his fondest fantasy has come true, and revels with his companions in the happy consequences of being imagined dead.

> They felt like heroes in an instant. Here was a gorgeous triumph; they were missed; they were mourned; hearts were breaking on their account; tears were being shed; accusing memories of unkindness to these poor lost lads were rising up, and unavailing regrets and remorse were being indulged; and best of all, the departed were the talk of the whole town, and the envy of all the boys, as far as this dazzling notoriety was concerned. This was fine.   (124–25)

At the same time, however, Tom is initially uneasy that aunt Polly will suffer unnecessarily on his account, and so steals away from camp with a note, inscribed on a sycamore scroll, that he plans to deliver when she is asleep. He returns to the village, finds a secure hiding place in his aunt's sitting room, and listens in as Mrs. Harper and the members of his own family give way to their feelings. The women overflow with expressions of love for their good-hearted boys, and bewail in unison the remorse that afflicts them for their cruel mistreatment of the dearly departed. Tom's vanity is thoroughly gratified by what he overhears— indeed, he is "more in pity of himself than anybody else"—and he can barely resist "the theatrical gorgeousness" (129) of stepping forward to relieve his aunt's misery. With instinctive anticipation of emergent opportunities, however, Tom holds back long enough to learn that the funeral will be held if the boys do not return by Sunday, four days hence. With this sad announcement, the bereaved party breaks up for the night and aunt Polly falls into a restless sleep. Moved by pity for her evident suffering, Tom approaches her bed, the saving message in hand. "But something occurred to him, and he lingered, considering. His face lighted with a happy solution of his thought; he put the bark hastily in his pocket. Then he bent over and kissed the faded lips, and straightway made his stealthy exit, latching the door behind him" (130). So much for good intentions.

As we soon learn, Tom abandons his aunt to her guilty suffering because he fears that the disclosure of his actual circumstances will threaten the success of his grandest scheme yet. It is a matter, simply, of priorities; and Tom's first priority, the "happy solution of his thought," is to attend his own funeral. The scheme is admittedly irresistible in its audacity, and the timing of its execution is perfect. Tom restrains his companions until the assembled community has worked itself into a fever of grief. "At last the whole company broke down and joined the weeping mourners in a chorus of anguished sobs, the preacher himself giving way to his feelings, and crying in the pulpit." Then, while "the minister raised his streaming eyes above his handkerchief, and stood transfixed," Tom leads the small band into the church. "First one and then another pair of eyes followed the minister's, and then almost with one impulse the congregation rose and stared while the three dead boys came marching up the aisle." The community's initially breathless response has the quality, one imagines, of the stunned dazzlement that would accompany the glimpse of an avatar. The minister's text, "I am the resurrection and the life," is still fresh in the minds of his listeners as the boys enter the room, and the unfolding of the familiar religious mystery in palpable form must seem to verge on the miraculous. At the least, the young trickster is transcendent to the extent that his seeming return from the grave confers spiritual renewal and an affirmation of unity on the gathered congregation.

> Suddenly the minister shouted at the top of his voice:
> "Praise God from whom all blessings flow—SING!—and put your hearts in it!"
> And they did. Old Hundred swelled up with a triumphant burst, and while it shook the rafters Tom Sawyer the Pirate looked around upon the envying juveniles about him and confessed in his heart that this was the proudest moment of his life.
> As the "sold" congregation trooped out they said they would almost be willing to be made ridiculous again to hear Old Hundred sung like that once more.   (141)

It is remarkable that the sudden descent from credulous wonderment does not leave the St. Petersburg citizenry in a mood of vengeful embarrassment. They have been "sold," and they know it. Yet they are amiably—and for the moment even consciously—disposed to be pleased with what amounts to an admission of their immersion in bad faith. This happy brand of hypocrisy is in fact a secular *credo quia absurdum est* in which the suspension of disbelief is proportional to the perceived social dividends of knowing gullibility. The most realistic measure of resurrections, it appears, is not their demonstrable proximity to truth, but their power to affirm and enhance the common life. No one is finally deceived by Tom, but no one fails to be moved by his timely reenactment of an ancient, equally unbelievable, fable of rebirth and regeneration. The community's resentful embarrassment at the exposure of its credulity is thus readily dissipated in the deeper revelation of its capacity for hope, unity, fellow feeling, and the tolerance of harmless folly. As the bearer of such gratifying news, Tom serves briefly as a kind of high priest in a ritual affirmation of the paradoxes that facilitate daily social life. The master and fullest embodiment of that complex social game, he is temporarily immune from ordinary justice because the exposure of his scheme serves to highlight the social benefits to be derived from bad faith. He "sells" his neighbors with impunity because he leads them to apprehend that his strategy of deceit is in fact a replica, in high relief, of the cultural status quo. The gamesman's final victory is thus to give the game away—to show his victims, in a manner compatible with their equanimity, what they are.

This is not to suggest that the community reaction to Tom's exploit is unmingled approbation. Bad faith will permit in one mood what it will condemn in another, and Tom has transported his neighbors to the outermost limits of their tolerance for self-knowledge. It is a telling symptom of this ambivalence that "Tom got more cuffs and kisses that day—according to aunt Polly's varying moods—than he had earned before in a year" (141). Once her sense of relief and exhilaration make room for more settled reflection, the old woman is able to bring the source of her punitive impulse into clearer focus; and, appropriately enough, the game resumes.

> "Well, I don't say it wasn't a fine joke, Tom, to keep everybody suffering 'most a week so you boys had a good time, but it is a pity you could be so hard-hearted as to let *me* suffer so. If you could come over on a log to go to your funeral, you could have come over and give me a hint some way that you warn't *dead,* but only run off."
> "Yes, you could have done that, Tom," said Mary; "and I believe you would if you had thought of it."
> "Would you Tom?" said Aunt Polly, her face lighting wistfully. "Say, now, would you, if you'd thought of it?"
> "I—well I don't know. 'Twould a spoiled everything."
> "Tom, I hoped you loved me that much," said Aunt Polly, with a grieved tone that discomforted the boy. "It would been something if you'd cared enough to *think* of it, even if you didn't *do* it."   (142)

Aunt Polly's initial emphasis on her own suffering comes as little surprise. But her next move betrays the fact that Tom's recent tour de force has shaken her confidence. For rather than press the complaint that Tom should have notified her of his well-being, she shifts to Mary's much softer plea for a concession that he would have done it if he had thought of it. The shift makes all the difference in what follows. Had aunt Polly pursued her opening line, Tom would have been forced to produce the sycamore scroll as proof of his original good intentions. This would have met his aunt's demands at least half-way, and thus relieved him from the conscience-wrenching spectacle of her anguish. But the sudden adoption of Mary's much softer position is a sure sign that the balance of power has undergone a marked shift in the boy's favor. Tom is quite evidently quick and shrewd in measuring his strategic advantage. He sees that the sycamore scroll would more than meet his aunt's modified demand—it would give palpable testimony to his thoughtfulness, where she has asked for no more than verbal assurances. At the same time, however, he astutely senses that his aunt's conciliatory tone is an appeal for sympathy and a comforting evasion rather than a demand for a remorseful apology. It follows that he is virtually invulnerable to the threat of guilt, and thus free to pursue the game on terms of his own choosing.

Tom's first choice is to reject the slender gratifications to be derived from making charitable, but strategically unnecessary, concessions to his aunt's weakened position. Instead, he holds the scroll in reserve for later deployment, and rather cruelly implies that the thought of letting aunt Polly in on the scheme never crossed his mind: "I—well I don't know. 'Twould a spoiled everything." Tom is now so proof against guilt that he is totally unmoved by Mary's indirect accusation that "he never thinks of anything," or by his aunt's final, desperate thrust: "Tom, you'll look back, some day, when it's too late, and wish you'd cared a little more for me when it would have cost you so little" (142). It is perfectly ironic, of course, that the small price Tom would have to pay to appease his aunt is the simple admission that he did in fact consider her feelings. But resolute and supremely confident gamesman that he is, Tom refuses to give an inch because to do so would compromise his advantage and end the game. Instead, he indulges himself in a display of his leverage, and in the promise of extending the feline play, by compounding the deception. "'I wish now I'd thought,' said Tom, with a repentant tone; 'but I dreamed about you, anyway. That's something, ain't it?'" The sheer audacity of the claim bears witness both to Tom's confidence in his strategic edge, and to his relish for playing it to the hilt. The headiness of his mood is amply reinforced by aunt Polly's evident willingness to grasp at straws. "It ain't much—a cat does that much—but it's better than nothing. What did you dream?" (143) Assured that he has the hapless mouse where he wants her, Tom now proceeds to give a meticulously detailed account—on the pretext that it was all a dream—of his nocturnal visit to the house. Sid injects a note of doubt, but aunt Polly is determined to accept the utterly implausible, but even more comforting, fraud. Indeed, she is so delighted to be deceived that she is in a rush "to call on Mrs. Harper and vanquish her realism with Tom's marvelous dream" (145).

Given Tom's flawless control of the game to this point, we are perhaps initially surprised to find him without a convincing response when aunt Polly returns from Mrs. Harper's with a new perspective on his remarkable "dream."

> "Tom, I've a notion to skin you alive!"
> "Auntie, what have I done?"
> "Well, you've done enough. Here I go over to Sereny Harper, like an old softy, expecting I'm going to make her believe all that rubbage about that dream, when lo and behold you she'd found out from Joe that you was over here and heard all the talk we had that night. Tom I don't know what is to become of a boy that will act like that. It makes me feel so bad to think you could let me go to Sereny Harper and make such a fool of myself and never say a word." (150)

Tom stumbles rather recklessly for a moment or two, but then perceives that his aunt's anger is little more than a bluff. The truthful declaration that "I wanted to keep you from grieving—that was all that made me come," restores her to a mood of pliant acquiescence in reassuring lies: "I'd give the whole world to believe that—it would cover up a power of sins Tom" (151). His tactical advantage thus effortlessly recovered, Tom pauses to weigh the options available to him in the handling of his remaining strategic asset, the sycamore scroll. At no time, we imagine, does he seriously consider handing the message over to his aunt. Such simplicity goes against the gamesman's grain in a number of ways. To present aunt Polly with the scroll would be uncomplicated and truthful; but the gamesman values complexity and all varieties of indirection—especially outright lies. The direct approach would bring the game to an early end, and this drawback would be compounded by the failure to fully exploit the opportunities for heightened drama and protracted deception. Perhaps most important, the simple handing over of the scroll would violate a leading principle of the game—that you never give more than you are absolutely obliged to. Since Tom knows that aunt Polly will settle for a barely plausible lie, he is constitutionally disinclined to reveal the whole truth until he can take the fullest advantage of its disclosure.

Most of these considerations come into play as Tom concludes the account of his secret visit home from Jackson's Island. "Why, you see, auntie, when you got to talking about the funeral, I just got all full of the idea of our coming and hiding in the church, and I couldn't some-how bear to spoil it." Then, as if in passing, he adds a detail that is as unnecessary to the persuading of aunt Polly as it is essential to the success of Tom's emergent scheme. "So I just put the bark back in my pocket and kept mum." Her response—"What bark?"—amply re-wards his foresight, for it is an unmistakable sign that her interest has been excited. Having planted the thought, Tom brushes it aside with the blandest indifference, and turns to seemingly more important mat-ters. "The bark I had wrote on to tell you we'd gone pirating. I wish, now, you'd waked up when I kissed you—I do, honest." Tom is un-doubtedly gratified to see that his aunt's interest is only briefly engaged by this endearing distraction. For he knows, as she hustles him out of the house—"be off with you to school, now, and don't bother me any more"—that alleged kisses cannot be as sweet to the old woman as the discovery of palpable testimony to his good intentions. Thus Tom does not have to be in the room to know, and to relish, what happens in his absence.

> The moment he was gone, she ran to a closet and got out the ruin of a jacket which Tom had gone pirating in. Then she stopped, with it in her hand, and said to herself:
> "No, I don't dare. Poor boy, I reckon he's lied about it—but it's a blessed, blessed lie, there's such comfort from it. I hope the Lord—I *know* the Lord will forgive him, because it was such good-heartedness in him to tell it. But I don't want to find out it's a lie. I won't look."
> She put the jacket away, and stood by musing a minute. Twice she put out her hand to take the garment again, and twice she refrained. Once more she ventured, and this time she fortified herself with the thought: "It's a good lie—it's a good lie—I won't let it grieve me." So she sought the jacket pocket. A moment later she was reading Tom's piece of bark through flowing tears and saying: "I could forgive the boy, now, if he'd committed a million sins!" (151–52)

This brief episode compresses a complex *multum in parvo,* for with extraordinary economy it dramatizes the leading paradoxes of St. Petersburg social life. There is the shameless, virtually unconscious, resort to devious means; the enlistment of an ostensibly scrupulous God in the endorsement of bald deception; and, at the root of it all, there is bad faith, the deep, if deeply uneasy, acquiescence in a culture of lies. It is perhaps the most brilliantly telling irony of all that aunt Polly should stake her comfort and self-esteem, but hardly her sense of morality, on the fond hope that Tom's lie is not a lie. Her nephew's well-laid bait is finally impossible to resist, but in taking it aunt Polly risks a painful confrontation with her own, and her society's, capacity for self-deception. At the same time, the episode demonstrates Tom's absolute intuitive mastery of the game of bad faith. His control is so sure and so artfully disguised that, almost without her knowing it, aunt Polly is stripped of the power, and even the desire, to enforce her own will. Instead, she is reduced to the furtive scramble for such crumbs of comfort as her nephew casts in her way. Meanwhile, Tom enjoys rewards reserved for a small elite among gamesmen—the confidence, never articulated or even fully conscious, that his lies are virtually interchangeable with the truth, and that his best laid schemes succeed, as if by magic, even when he is not there to oversee their unfolding.

V

Tom's masterful manipulation *in absentia* of aunt Polly's thoughts and actions is strikingly reminiscent of Stephen Dedalus' artistic ambition to be "like the God of the creation, [who] remains within or behind or beyond or above his handiwork, invisible, refined out of existence, indifferent, paring his fingernails." [14] What the boys share is a desire for control that is at once irresistible in force, without apparent source in its energy and design, and invisible in its operation on those who endure or witness its sway. They want to be as potent and as impalpable as Fate. The analogy between Tom's gamesmanship and Stephen's art intersects, in turn, with Mark Twain's acknowledged methods and objectives as America's premier literary entertainer. He argues that the indigenous humorous story, as distinct from the foreign comic and witty story, depends for its success on the narrator's ability "to conceal the fact that there is anything funny about it." As a key element in his simulated innocence, the teller must provide his auditors with "a nub, point, snapper, or whatever you like to call it," that he pretends not to recognize for what it is, and that they recognize only too late, when the insight betrays the fact that they have been taken in. Thus the "trick" in the humorous story is *on* the audience rather than within the tale itself. [15] The joke is even richer, though much more exclusively the teller's pleasure, if the audience fails to recognize, or refuses to acknowledge, that it has been gulled into credulity. This is the case, of course, in "The Jumping Frog," where the inside narrator's iron-clad hauteur is hilariously impenetrable to mirth. It is the case, too, when aunt Polly fidgets over Tom's coat. She has responded swiftly and predictably to her nephew's carefully planted "nub," and she submits to his unseen control in all that follows. Indeed, it is the final measure of her absolute submission, and the capstone to Tom's triumph, that aunt Polly's now fragile self-esteem will never permit her to recognize that she has been fooled.

The important difference between the telling of "The Jumping Frog" and *Tom Sawyer* is that in the latter narrative the principal speaker appears to be "in" on the joke, where in the former he is its butt. As witnesses to the undoing of poor aunt Polly, we join the narrator in his mood of superior and good-humored condescension; but generations of readers have found out too late that identifying with the narrator of "The Jumping Frog" is perilous business. Having said this much, it remains to add that the narrator of *Tom Sawyer* may not be as fully "in" on the novel's nubs and snappers as we would like to think. I am not suggesting that readers of *Tom Sawyer,* following an apparently knowing teller, have been tricked in quite the same way as Simon Wheeler's auditors. But it can be argued that our inclination to smile knowingly at the novel, and then to dismiss it as "a light book suitable for children and for adults satisfied with a funny story," is the leading symptom of our immersion in the culture of bad faith that the story portrays. There is no evidence that the narrator is aware of Tom's controlling hand in aunt Polly's "discovery" of the sycamore scroll, or, for that matter, of any of the manifold subtleties of Tom's gamesmanship. Concomitantly, there is no evidence that the critics have been at all closely in touch with the complex dynamics of St. Petersburg's elaborate social game. To be sure, we have been alerted to examples of rather harmless hypocrisy and comical pretensions to "style"; but we have not been invited to pause for long over what is, once it has been recognized and pursued, a remarkably clear pattern of social interaction. I am suggesting, of course, that our close cultural kinship with the citizens of St. Petersburg, and with the teller of their story, manifests itself in our inability to objectify and scrutinize the world we share with them. Paradoxically, intimate cultural familiarity has fostered its special kind of blindness. As deep insiders to the St. Petersburg brand of social deception, we are apparently unable to recognize bad faith for what it is.

This paradox is most profound and intriguing when we apply it to Mark Twain. He is without doubt our most experienced, perceptive, and articulate observer of small town culture on the American frontier of his day. To iterate Bernard DeVoto, in *Tom Sawyer* "something formed from America lives as it lives nowhere else." And yet in recording that life—with admittedly remarkable accuracy of detail and fidelity to its essential quality—its author could not quite see what he meant. His rather baffled and inconclusive effort to locate his proper audience is an expression of this failure to grasp his own point. Mark Twain was too deep inside his world to see it from without. Thus in following his confident lead in *Tom Sawyer* we are at once as omniscient, and as fundamentally blind, as he. But we hardly resist or complain. For Mark Twain is indeed our cultural leader; he unfolds our world before us, and all unknowingly abets the willing blindness that makes us feel, in a good-naturedly superior way, at home. Culturally speaking, this is precisely as it should be.

But if our culture erects obstacles to our critical penetration, it also—as I have suggested—imposes limitations on our power of critical vision. Our inability to see is reinforced by our unwillingness to see. Once again, Mark Twain is our guide. For in following him through *Tom Sawyer* we have been consistently acquiescent in his refusal to acknowledge fully the manifestations of bad faith, even when they are baldly present to sight. With aunt Polly, we have displayed a marked preference for comfortable, "blessed" lies. The most compelling evidence of this shortsightedness is the nearly total failure of scholars and critics to focus their analysis on those frequent, if brief, intervals in the novel when the narrator pauses over, and then recoils from, the perception of fractures beneath the placid surface of St. Petersburg society. When such insights occur, Mark Twain is suddenly angry and satirical; for a moment he loses his detachment. Yet in every case his impulse is to regain composure as quickly as possible, at the price of suppressing the truth that he has glimpsed. Rather than confront his unsettling insights, he turns immediately away; and, once again, his readers have been willing to follow.

This tendency is first in evidence at the end of Chapter 5, when the narrator decides to "draw the curtain of charity" over Tom's disastrous failure to name the first two disciples. The mood of the moment, as we have seen, is one of amused tolerance. Nonetheless, Mark Twain's abrupt truncation of the scene occurs at the precise moment that the essential bad faith of the situation comes fully—and as abruptly—to light. Tom has lied to gain notoriety, and for the sheer pleasure of the game. With characteristic shrewdness, he has contrived a deceit which invites the congregation to rationalize its self-indulgence in amusement as the dutiful recognition of proven (the tickets!) merit. In short, the community succumbs to willing self-deception in seeming to honor Tom's incredible claim. Thus the subsequent exposure of Tom's dishonesty reveals far more than a boyish prank; it lays open the subtle fabric of bad faith that the village society surreptitiously fosters and submits to, and that Tom so effortlessly exploits.

If this reconstruction of the situation is correct, then it is fair to suppose that Tom's neighbors' amusement is mixed with bafflement and shock and upswellings of anger. The source of these feelings can hardly be Tom; the revelation of his duplicity, after all, is in no sense a surprise. The villagers are upset, rather, by a glancing recognition that their amusement has been purchased at the price of subliminal collusion in a lie. For a painful moment they are face to face with the vexing contradiction between their conscious, public values and the deeper sources of their pleasure and social stability. And it is precisely the nature of their bad faith that it can never appear to them as necessary and even socially beneficial. Thus they recoil from their insight in a flash of confused anger, and then collectively close their eyes. Having glimpsed their.duplicity, they promptly laugh it off. This rather complex social reflex is mirrored, at one remove, in the narrator's sudden decision to terminate the scene. It is a perfectly unconscious irony, of course, that the principal beneficiary of the "charity" that moves him to "draw the curtain" is not Tom Sawyer, but the narrator himself, the community, and the generations of readers who have been culturally predisposed to overlook the bad faith behind the humor.

This is merely the first, and certainly the most oblique, example of Mark Twain's reluctance to confront and explore the emergent implications of his social portrait. On several subsequent occasions his equanimity is more visibly shattered by a momentary perception of bad faith; and on each occasion the abrupt suppression of a surge of anger betrays his personal entanglement in the object of his scorn. This is clearly the case, for example, when his attention alights on the townspeople's uncharitable haste in convicting Muff Potter of murder.

> A gory knife had been found close to the murdered man, and it had been recognized by somebody as belonging to Muff Potter—so the story ran. And it was said that a belated citizen had come upon Potter washing himself in the "branch" about one or two o'clock in the morning, and that Potter had at once sneaked off—suspicious circumstances, especially the washing, which was not a habit with Potter. It was also said that the town had been ransacked for this "murderer" (the public are not slow in the matter of sifting evidence and arriving at a verdict,) but that he could not be found. Horsemen had departed down all the roads in every direction, and the Sheriff "was confident" that he would be captured before night.   (105)

The anger—almost, but not quite, buried in the parenthesis—is aimed at the villagers' indulgence in the comfortable illusion that their craving for excitement is in fact the honorable pursuit of justice. A trace of temper also spills out on the Sheriff, who seems more attentive to the crowd than to due process. But Mark Twain's ironic indignation is more the product of his own self-indulgence than of superior self-knowledge or integrity. After all, his ridicule of the villagers is premised on the privileged knowledge that Muff Potter did not kill Dr. Robinson. Were his information as limited as the villagers', he would almost certainly rush to their conclusion. Our confidence on this score is reinforced when we reflect that as narrator of the tale Mark Twain has demonstrated a more urgent itch for melodrama than the one he condemns in the crowd. Perhaps it began to dawn on him that his scorn, if fully unleashed, would inevitably find its way back to its source. If we grant him the intimation that the angry exposure of others threatened to reveal the same fault in himself, we can begin to make sense of his hasty retreat to safer ground. For then Mark Twain's apparent return to superior detachment from village hypocrisy appears in its true colors as an uneasy truce with his own bad faith.

Prudent composure gives way to anger again when Mark Twain addresses the townspeople's craven concessions to their arch villain.

> The villagers had a strong desire to tar-and-feather Injun Joe and ride him on a rail, for body-snatching, but so formidable was his character that nobody could be found who was willing to take the lead in the matter, so it was dropped. He had been careful to begin both of his inquest-statements with the fight, without confessing the grave-robbery that preceded it; therefore it was deemed wisest not to try the case in the courts at present.   (108)

Once again, the barbed ironies spring from the perception of a collective lie—in this case, fear masquerading as deference to "character" and the "wisest" timing. And, once again, the invective subsides almost immediately into a mood of detached calm. The counter-irony in this instance is further to seek, but it is surely present in Mark Twain's subsequent treatment of Tom Sawyer's day in court. As a witness to the murder of Dr. Robinson, Tom knows that Muff is not guilty. But his fear of Injun Joe causes him to hesitate until the last minute in coming forth with the saving evidence. The villagers respond by treating Tom as a hero, and there is no mention made, even by Muff Potter, of the strange delay. This enigmatic silence is not the result of a failure of perception, or of a charitable desire to let Tom off the hook; rather, it is a residual manifestation of the villagers' own fear of Injun Joe. They know that drawing attention to Tom's weakness would serve as a reminder, by clear and direct implication, of their own. And since Tom has overcome his fear of Injun Joe, they know that they would suffer badly in the inevitable comparison. Thus their initial bad faith compounds itself, for they are now compelled to ignore in Tom what they have previously refused to recognize in themselves.

Mark Twain's reaction to Tom's delay is not so readily explained. Consistency would seem to demand that he fault Tom in the same manner that he has already faulted the community; but he moves on without comment. Perhaps his identification with the boy, and a characteristic preference for heroism of the untarnished variety, enforced this lapse in consistency. In any case, such anger as he expresses, though it may well be unconsciously deflected from Tom, finds its way back to "the fickle, unreasoning world [which] took Muff Potter to its bosom and fondled him as lavishly as it had abused him before. But that sort of conduct is to the world's credit; therefore it is not well to find fault with it" (173). The willingness to "credit" the "unreasoning world" is almost certainly ironic; for Mark Twain's tone is freighted with the clear implication that he is less impressed with the people's impulse to amend their error than he is angered by their "fickle" inconsistency. At a second glance, we may find cause to resist the narrator's irony; indeed, we may want to turn it back on him. After all, Mark Twain's prejudicial treatment of Tom betrays an inconsistency as great as the townspeople's, while his readiness to admit to and amend his errors is much less evident than theirs. Since bad faith is quite evidently the name of the St. Petersburg game, and since cultural rules are notoriously resistant to change, it is emphatically "not well to find fault with" the occasional stirrings of goodness that emerge from the social round. Given this much, Mark Twain's irony is unconsciously at his own expense; for in refusing to properly "credit" the potential for good in the villagers' bad faith, he would seem to betray the lack of a comparable component in his own.

Mark Twain's final surrender to anger is the most unguarded and sustained in the novel, and bears the clear suggestion that his composure grew more fragile as his material grew familiar to his hand. The occasion for this last outburst is "the petition to the Governor for Injun Joe's pardon"; and his target, as usual, is village hypocrisy.

> The petition had been largely signed; many tearful and eloquent meetings had been held, and a committee of sappy women been appointed to go in deep mourning and wail around the governor and implore him to be a merciful ass and trample his duty under foot. Injun Joe was believed to have killed five citizens of the village, but what of that? If he had been Satan himself there would have been plenty of weaklings ready to scribble their names to a pardon-petition and drip a tear on it from their permanently impaired and leaky water-works.   (221)

There is undoubtedly a diffuse sexual component to the women's grief; they mourn the final passing of an energy too wild for their civilization, but alluring nonetheless as a dark, concentrated, haunting vitality on the margins of their lives. More manifestly perhaps, the plangent appeal of the village women is an oblique admission that the half-breed was the victim of white society before he was its villain. Ironically enough, Mark Twain seems to have shared in this strange mingling of fascination and guilt-inspired pity. It was singularly uncharacteristic of him, for example, to soil his narratives with details as explicitly sexual and perverted as those in Injun Joe's bloody designs on the widow Douglas: "When you want to get revenge on a woman you don't kill her—bosh! you go for her looks. You slit her nostrils—you notch her ears, like a sow's!" (198) And his own sentiments on the outcast are hardly as severe as his sarcastic outburst might lead us to suppose.

> When the cave door was unlocked, a sorrowful sight presented itself in the dim twilight of the place. Injun Joe lay stretched upon the ground, dead, with his face close to the crack of the door, as if his longing eyes had been fixed, to the latest moment, upon the light and the cheer of the free world outside.   (220)

Subsequent references to Joe as "prisoner," "captive," "the poor unfortunate," and "the hapless half-breed" (220–21) contrast dramatically with the diatribe against "sappy women" that immediately follows. Quite obviously, in fact, Mark Twain was guilty of the same brand of inconsistency that he so vigorously condemns in the village women. That he was so directly, if inadvertently, the object of his own wrath undoubtedly accounts for both the sharpness and the brevity of his attack. The outward edge of his frustration took on added sharpness as it veered to its true target, then flattened out as suddenly in the retreat to prudent detachment.

In every instance, then, the abrupt upsurge of Mark Twain's anger is almost immediately curbed by the chilling intimation that his contempt for the villagers' hypocritical inconsistency threatens to return on his own head. It is for this reason, I believe, that he restrained the potent impulse toward satire in his otherwise searching analysis of St. Petersburg society. Had his own hands been less evidently dirtied in the culture of bad faith, *Tom Sawyer* would have been a much different—which is to say, a much more overtly angry—book. As it is, and at times against nearly irresistible promptings, Mark Twain settled into the safe, rather nervously studied, and thoroughly untoward persona of an urbane, slightly condescending outsider. Had it been narrated from the point of view of an illiterate, humorless, in almost all ways innocent insider, however, the world of *Tom Sawyer* would have appeared to be what in fact it is: the world of *Huckleberry Finn*.

We can press a bit further along this line of thought if we pause over Mark Twain's apparent blindness to all but the rather benignly superficial features of Tom's gamesmanship. We have seen one example of his neglecting to probe in Tom's behavior what he probes and condemns in the villagers'; in fact, there are several omissions of this kind. Drawing "the curtain of charity" is a complex gesture, but its most conspicuous result is to veil the villagers' shocked resentment behind the narrator's superior readiness to be amused. And while we are brought face to face with the community's willingness to convict Muff Potter of murder, we are not invited to reflect that Tom acquiesces in that verdict though he knows it is wrong. The villagers know that Injun Joe is a grave-robber, and they are chided for their hypocritical failure to act on that knowledge. Tom has the same information, but his failure to act is ignored. The "unreasoning world" is criticized for the "fickle" haste with which it forgives and fondles Muff Potter; but the really glaring hypocrisy of

Tom's visiting the prisoner, and accepting his gratitude for small favors, all the while holding the keys to the old man's freedom, is allowed to pass unnoticed. Having observed this pattern, we may be tempted to speculate, as I have already, that in granting Tom Sawyer such exemptions Mark Twain was slipping into an identification with his youthful hero. The plausibility of this position is enhanced when we place the narrator's sympathy for Injun Joe alongside Tom's: "Tom was touched, for he knew by his own experience how this wretch had suffered. His pity was moved" (220). But whatever its depth, the forgiving force of Mark Twain's identification with his hero was substantially reinforced by the threat of self-exposure that reared up each time he took a tilt at the villagers. To confront Tom's masterful manipulation consciously was inevitably to come face to face with his own. Ironically, however, the unconscious resistance to a perception of his close kinship with Tom does nothing to obscure that connection from the reader. For it must be clear by now that Mark Twain's refusal to acknowledge his hero's hypocrisy is the exact replica, at the level of narration, of Tom's blindly intuitive mastery of bad faith, at the level of narrative incident.

It is a signal insight into the deeper imperatives of Mark Twain's creativity that in *Tom Sawyer* he unconsciously placed himself in the direct line of his own fire. As I have already pointed out, bad faith is inherently blind to itself; it follows as a corollary that bad faith has little in the way of alternatives to rather fixed patterns of behavior. This is clearly borne out in Mark Twain's relationship to Tom Sawyer. To show his good faith as narrator, he would have had to expose his hero; but in unveiling Tom's bad faith he would have glimpsed his own. In effect, he left himself no protection against the barbs of his own contempt. Thus entangled as teller in the web of his tale, he unconsciously elected—in perfect bad faith—to avoid the trap he had set for himself by retreating from a harsh to a humorous view of his hero. In the upshot, the attempted evasion backfired, for it merely confirmed the pattern of willing blindness and extended it to the outermost margins of the narrative structure.

We can make the same point in reverse by arguing that Mark Twain's selection of a point of view settled in advance the array of meanings that would emerge in *Tom Sawyer*. To have written a different book, Mark Twain would have had to adopt a narrative persona whose attitude toward bad faith was less ambivalent, and therefore less prone to paradoxical ensnarement, than his own. Huck Finn comes immediately to mind. Huck lies constantly and comfortably and well. He expects the same from others, and he is quite amiably astute in recognizing both the inevitability and the social utility of conscious deception. He is hardly taken in, for example, by the flea-bitten intruders on the raft; but he plays along with their preposterous claims, and even aligns himself with the would-be deceivers, on the grounds that

> it would a been a miserable business to have any unfriendliness on the raft; for what you want, above all things, on a raft, is for everybody to be satisfied, and feel right and kind towards the others.
>
> It didn't take me long to make up my mind that these liars warn't no kings nor dukes, at all, but just low-down humbugs and frauds. But I never said nothing, never let on; kept it to myself; it's the best way; then you don't have no quarrels, and don't get into no trouble. If they wanted us to call them kings and dukes, I hadn't no objections, long as it would keep peace in the family; and it warn't no use to tell Jim, so I didn't tell him. If I never learnt nothing else out of pap, I learnt that the best way to get along with his kind of people is to let them have their own way.[16]

If Tom employs his understanding and mastery of bad faith to gain dominance and notoriety, Huck does it simply to survive. If Tom plays the game with blind intuition, and is subject to the guilty recoil of his deeply acculturated ambivalence, then Huck plays with his eyes wide open, and with an acceptance of the rules that renders him proof against the snares of remorse. Huck is characteristically practical when he reflects that "a body that ups and tells the truth when he is in a tight place, is taking considerable many resks"; and he goes further, in resolving to deceive a friend, and concludes that lies are "the little things that smoothes people's roads the most, down here below" (239, 242–43). Paradoxically, in his phlegmatic indifference to the accepted mores of St. Petersburg society, Huck arrives, all unwittingly, at a set of values not unlike those that the respectable conventions disguise.

The important difference between the juvenile pariah and his neighbors, then, is that while they are all immersed in bad faith, Huck is unique in giving conscious assent to the unacknowledged terms of the dominant culture. As narrator of *Tom Sawyer,* on the other hand, Mark Twain is less tolerant of social deception than the villagers. Indeed, his imperfectly restrained fury with what he viewed as hypocrisy, in combination with his urbanely superior tone, foster the impression that he could conceive of alternatives to the culture of bad faith. In fact, of course, Mark Twain's conception of human nature worked consistently to undermine what little there was of the ameliorative and utopian in his social vision. His final installment on the theme of bad faith was to despair utterly of human social progress, and to take a shred of bitter consolation in finding God to be the grandest hypocrite of all. Meanwhile, bereft of hope or plausible alternatives to the social condition he at once shared in and deplored, Mark Twain took refuge in humorous denial. What he could not abide in St. Petersburg and himself, he laughed off.

The habit of resistance to the obvious may be a characteristic, in some form or other, of all cultures. But at the very least—as *Tom Sawyer* clearly shows—it is endemic to our culture's brand of self-deception. Given this much, it is perfectly appropriate that the circle of denial should enclose the readers, as well as the narrator and the actors. Indeed, it is the surest sign of our cultural kinship with Mark Twain and Tom and aunt Polly and the others that we have shared their unwillingness, or inability, to acknowledge the bad faith that runs so conspicuously through both the telling and the tale. For generations now, we have recognized *Tom Sawyer* as especially and even intimately our own, and at the same time failed almost completely to see what it means. Rather furtively suspecting, perhaps, that the joke is somehow at our own expense, we have surrendered nonetheless to the strange, nervous laughter.

In principle we join our cultural leader in a fundamental abhorrence for the myriad varieties of deception and manipulation that constitute what I have called bad faith. Such devious maneuverings, we have been inclined to believe, are somehow foreign to our way of life, and belong in the old world, where we left them. In drawing back from what we perceive to be corrupt and hypocritical, we have committed ourselves to a national myth of innocence so pure and uncomplicated that it has proven itself incompatible with all save the most naive, virginal, and finally incomplete human embodiments. It is an innocence as blindingly white and, in its way, as appalling, as the one we have wished (I believe wrongly) on Huckleberry Finn.[17] The paradox in all of this is perfectly overwhelming. The contrast between the Huck Finn of our fond imaginings, and the haunted fugitive who cons his way south on the big river, is a fair measure of our uneasy cultural equilibrium. In fact, Huck's innocence consists not in his being above the game of deception, but in the relative freedom from guilt that he enjoys as the result of his often conscious submission to its rules. If Huck is innocent at all, he is so because he is much less deceived about himself than most of his admirers have been.

There is quite a direct line to be drawn between Huck's really profound moral authority and his clear-eyed acceptance of the necessity for dirty hands. Knowing and accepting that he must deceive, he is free to do so fairly. Huck lies and steals constantly, but he does so in the service of the happiness and satisfaction and survival of himself and others. The implicit social teaching, that we must acknowledge and accept our true condition before we can transcend it, is obvious and familiar enough. But Mark Twain also provides us with (again implicit) warnings against a too simple or sanguine understanding of this tempting inference. On one side, we will find that Huck is not nearly so free of bad faith as we suppose, or as we might like him to be. On the other, it requires little more than a glance at those characters who share Huck's perspicuity to recognize that the possession of such heightened awareness is rarely very appealing. Susan Wilks, for example, is astutely distrustful of the fraudulent claims of the king and the duke, and skillfully probes the inconsistencies in Huck's pathetic account of their lives in England. Ironically, however, Mark Twain contrives to align Susan's clairvoyance with what is generally unattractive about her. She is cast as an unimaginative, ungenerous, doggedly suspicious hare-lip, and we are easily seduced into approving when Mary Jane, her pretty, totally gullible older sister, chastises her into silence. We have a similar reaction to characters like Dr. Robinson ("a big iron-jawed man") and Levi Bell ("a sharp looking gentleman" [216, 250]), who are made to appear overbearing and intrusive in their perfectly reasonable resistance to the imposters. If we join Mark Twain in finding these sharp-eyed, forthright truth-tellers unattractive, and even unnatural, it is because they threaten to expose the game for what it is, and to bring it to an abrupt end.

Mark Twain interposes yet another obstacle to our sympathy for those eagle-eyed realists who recognize and acknowledge bad faith when they see it. We are inclined to join him in discountenancing such characters because their perception of the impulse to deceive and manipulate in others does not seem to free them from equivalent impulses in themselves. Few characters are consciously aware of the game they play; but fewer still rise above it. Huck is the unique exception in this regard, for his knowledge of bad faith in others often liberates the impulse toward good faith in himself. Much more generally, as Tom's example clearly suggests, insight into the intricate mechanisms of gamesmanship leads to even more subtle variations on the basic social pattern. Or, when the perception of bad faith is more fully conscious than Tom's, it can foster the sniping, self-righteous, thoroughly disagreeable variety of passive aggression that we recognize almost immediately in Sid Sawyer.

VI

Critical comment on Sid Sawyer has been limited to observations in passing that he serves as a foil to Tom. Henry Nash Smith presses a bit further, but inclines strongly toward the conclusion that Sid contributes little to the main business of the novel.[18] Sid is at once much less enigmatic and much more interesting when he is viewed as a representative player in Mark Twain's analysis of the villagers' social game. As we have already seen, Sid's example tends to deflate the optimistic equation of social acuity with social virtue. A more detailed review of his peculiar operating style yields even richer critical perspectives on Tom, on the narrator, and on our curious collaboration in the novel's idiosyncratic humor.

Sid Sawyer suffers all the penalties, and enjoys none of the advantages, of participation in the culture of bad faith. On one side, he is perfectly literal and scrupulously exacting in his conformity to the dominant St. Petersburg code of respectability. He is clean, prompt, obedient, studious, deferential to adults, and fond of Sunday school; or, in the words of the narrator, "he was a quiet boy and had no adventurous, troublesome ways" (41). We imagine that Sid's absolute submission to the "good boy" mold is the outward manifestation of an inward diffidence and timidity; his craving for attention and sway is apparently slender, and quite evidently in total subordination to his desire to avoid punishment and garner such approval as falls to the well-behaved. In short, he is aunt Polly's boy—and he is no doubt the child she always thought, quite mistakenly, she wanted.

Sid would be content enough—as content, say, as his sister, Mary—were it not for the side of his consciousness which knowingly surveys the undercurrent of bad faith beneath the respectable surface of village society. Sid understands the game perfectly. Yet unlike Huck, he cannot accept the terms of bad faith; and unlike Tom, he is too fully conscious of them to be able to forget. He suffers perpetually what the narrator suffers during his occasional moments of angry insight—the sputtering, indignant frustration of an insider to the culture whose impulse to get out renders him an outsider powerless to get fully in. Much more than Huck, Sid is marginal; he is cursed with a consciousness so sharply divided between the poles of bad faith that it can never rest comfortably at either. As the result, he is nervous and furtive, ever suspiciously vigilant against deceit, almost always vindicated in his doubts, and therefore confirmed in the habit of narrow-eyed suspicion. He is the only member of the household free enough from the hidden seductions of self-deception to recognize the patent fraudulence of Tom's "dream." But "Sid had better judgment than to utter the thought that was in his mind as he left the house. It was this: 'Pretty thin—as long a dream as that, without any mistakes in it!'" (145)

Sid's "better judgment" is perfectly characteristic, and consists of bending to the paired pressure of fear and calculation—fear that the immediate exposure of the truth will earn him disbelief and ridicule, and the calculation that a more timely revelation of the same truth will result in greater humiliation for Tom. Quite typically, Sid's impulse is to hoard his secrets until that moment when their discovery will do most to expose bad faith and subvert the game. His principal target in this enterprise is the premier gamesman in St. Petersburg, his half-brother, Tom; and his favored strategy is to be sharply vigilant from within a guise of indifference. Thus on three occasions we find Sid feigning sleep—ears poised and eyes imperceptibly at attention—as Tom steals in from one of his adventures. In the first instance, after carefully avoiding any reference to his roommate's compromised condition, Sid makes a "mental note" of the fact that "Tom turned in without the added vexation of prayers" (56). Some time later, "when Tom crept in at his bedroom window" after witnessing Dr. Robinson's murder, "the night was almost spent. He undressed with excessive caution, and fell asleep congratulating himself that nobody knew of his escapade. He was not aware that the gently-snoring Sid was awake, and had been so for an hour" (103). And, finally, when Tom's evident anxiety over the murder prompts comment from the family, Sid glimpses an opportunity to capitalize on his secret. "Tom, you pitch around and talk in your sleep so much that you keep me awake about half the time." Aunt Polly obligingly pursues the issue, thus opening the way for Sid's more direct insinuations. "And you do talk such stuff," Sid said. "Last night you said 'it's blood, it's blood, that's what it is.' You said that over and over. And you said 'Don't torment me so—I'll tell.' Tell *what?* What is it you'll tell?" (107) As we have already noted, Tom is spared the embarrassment that Sid has planned for him when aunt Polly and Mary admit that they have also dreamt about the horrible murder. Sid's vengeful drift is nonetheless perfectly clear, and his intended victim takes appropriate precautions. "After that he complained of toothache for a week and tied up his jaws every night." But Sid's serpentine malice is more than a match for his step-brother's defenses. Tom "never knew that Sid lay nightly watching, and frequently slipped the bandage free and then leaned on his elbow listening a good while at a time, and afterward slipped the bandage back to its place again" (108).

In his respectability, as in his suspicious probings, it is Sid's paradoxical fate to be as repellent as he is correct. Lurking at Tom's bedside, he must inevitably appear to us as a diminutive Satan—alienated, slightly mad, predatory, ruthlessly vindictive, and finally hopeless and pathetic and darkly comical. We may understand and even sympathize with his dilemma, yet the sum of our response—shared and even cultivated by Mark Twain—is a repulsion so complete, and so out of proportion to its object, that it demands further scrutiny. Why is our reaction to Sid so extreme?

In the broad literary and mythic sense, we despise Sid because Mark Twain's portrayal of him puts us in mind of the archetypal betrayer. But the unfortunate child is a special kind of devil whose offenses seem most grievous in a very specific cultural context. Sid is quintessentially the kill-joy and the spoiler; and the world he threatens to corrupt is the all-American boyhood paradise embodied and preserved in the characters and setting and action of *Tom Sawyer.* In the extremity of our reaction to him, we betray the fact that we know in advance, refuse to accept, and therefore reject out of hand the oblique but unmistakable truths that he levels at our fondest cultural prepossessions. We condemn Sid not because he is wrong, but precisely because, deep down, we sense that he is right. He is right, and in perfect conformity with overt, respectable values, to expose Tom's gamesmanship for what it is. We may declare him a self-righteous prig, but in doing so we blind ourselves to the objective propriety of his position, and declare indirectly that our deepest cultural commitment is not to respectability at all, but to the game. Our deeply ingrained hostility to gamesmanship, along with the pleasure that we derive from its pervasive but unacknowledged operation, combine to foster our strange resistance to Sid Sawyer. The extremity of our reaction to Sid, in other words, is the leading symptom of our own bad faith.

Henry Nash Smith is certainly correct to point out that the majority of Sid's carefully hoarded secrets are never revealed, and therefore come to nothing.[19] Mark Twain reveals his own awareness of this apparent anomaly when he speculates, at the conclusion of the bedside vigil: "If Sid really managed to make anything out of Tom's disjointed mutterings, he kept it to himself" (108). Our *prima facie* inclination must be to join Smith in condemning these blind leads as flaws in the novel's design. At the same time, we must be struck by the fact that Mark Twain was aware of at least one such will-o'-the-wisp, and yet left it in. We can begin to unfold this enigma by pointing out that Sid gathers his secrets with the long-range objective of unveiling them at the time when they will most nakedly reveal bad faith. His larger mission is to expose what he views as hypocrisy. To some extent, as we have seen, Mark Twain shared this angry impulse; and his general conception and portrayal of the young spoiler is surely one manifestation of his desire to pillory village hypocrisy. An important strand of his imaginative energy allied itself with Sid, and expressed itself in the creation of vengeful designs on the community's mechanisms of deceit. Sid's secrets are thus the displaced shafts of his creator's wrath. But we have also seen that Mark Twain's reaction to his periodic glimpses of bad faith in the villagers is to retreat from anger as a check against the discovery of bad faith in himself. In parallel fashion, his failure to permit the disclosure of Sid's secrets falls into place as the unconscious resistance to the exposure of his entanglement in the hypocrisy he so deplores. From this point of view, Sid's covert knowledge—especially since it is primarily knowledge about Tom—can be understood to be Mark Twain's suppressed indictments against himself. The meaning of Sid's secrets thus inheres squarely in the fact that they come to nothing.

The final step in this line of analysis brings us to one occasion when Sid actually reveals his secret knowledge—an occasion, significantly, when the revelation does *not* directly involve his step-brother. In the closing movements of the novel, Tom and Huck are invited to a surprise party in honor of Mr. Jones, the Welchman who came to Huck's assistance in saving the widow Douglas. When Tom inquires, "What's all this blow-out about, anyway?" Sid replies:

"Why old Mr. Jones is going to spring something on the people here to-night, but I overheard him tell auntie to-day about it, as a secret, but I reckon it's not much of a secret *now.* Everybody knows—the widow, too, for all she tries to let on she don't. Oh, Mr. Jones was bound Huck should be here—couldn't get along with his grand secret without Huck, you know!"

"Secret about what, Sid?"

"About Huck tracking the robbers to the widow's. I reckon Mr. Jones was going to make a grand time over his surprise, but I bet you it will drop pretty flat."

Sid chuckled in a very contented and satisfied way.

"Sid, was it you that told?"

"O, never mind who it was. *Somebody* told—that's enough."

"Sid, there's only one person in this town mean enough to do that, and that's you. If you had been in Huck's place you'd 'a' sneaked down the hill and never told anybody on the robbers. You can't do any but mean things, and you can't bear to see anybody praised for doing good ones. There—no thanks, as the widow says"—and Tom cuffed Sid's ears and helped him to the door with several kicks. "Now go and tell auntie if you dare—and to-morrow you'll catch it!"   (229–30)

This is our last view of Sid, and it comes amply freighted with details guaranteed to seal our general disapproval of him. As he scurries out of Tom's line of fire, we readily concede that he is a coward, and note that he is a kill-joy of all pleasures, and not merely those involving bad faith.

We are not as attentive, perhaps, to an equally important, but much less evident spur to Tom's—and, conceivably, to our own—wrath. The ostensible source of Tom's righteous indignation is his step-brother's skulking sabotage of Huck's well-deserved acclaim. Tom overlooks the fact that Huck, who shirks in abject terror from the public eye, probably nods in mute gratitude for Sid's inadvertent favor. The oversight is innocent enough, but it at least hints that Huck's welfare is not as central to Tom's motivation as it might appear to be. After all, the novel contains abundant evidence that Tom's interest in his friends rises and falls with their perceived potential for exploitation. He warms to people when he sees opportunities to use them. The question follows, what ulterior objective is implied in his heated advocacy of his friend's cause? The answer is *spectacle.* Sid's deepest offense is not his subversion of Huck, but his subversion of Mr. Jones's "surprise." The real pleasure that the party promises is the exhilarating shock that will result from the sudden disclosure of a carefully guarded secret. Huck is as incidental to the community's gratification with such a stimulating diversion as he is to the satisfaction that Sid takes in spoiling it. What we witness in Tom's anger, then, is not the outrage of a loyal friend, but the frustration of a master showman who bristles at the notion that "a grand time" should be made to "drop pretty flat."

Tom's general commitment to spectacle is of course fueled by his personal ambition to be the central attraction whenever such spectacles occur. This genuinely compulsive need for attention is at least threatened by Sid's successful machinations, for as events unfold it becomes clear that Tom valued Mr. Jones's "surprise" primarily as a minor prelude to his own much more dramatic disclosure. Expert showman that he is, he knows that the force of contrast lends added grandeur even to the most astonishing revelations. But he is little daunted by minor setbacks. Predictably enough, Mr. Jones's "little speech" falls flat.

> He sprung his secret about Huck's share in the adventure in the finest dramatic manner he was master of, but the surprise it occasioned was largely counterfeit and not as clamorous and effusive as it might have been under happier circumstances. However, the widow made a pretty fair show of astonishment, and heaped so many compliments and so much gratitude upon Huck that he almost forgot the nearly intolerable discomfort of his new clothes in the entirely intolerable discomfort of being set up as a target for everybody's gaze and everybody's laudations. (230)

Tom patiently endures the forced gaiety until it completes its descent to utter boredom. Then, seizing a potential for contrast much greater than the one he had foreseen, he drags the heavy treasure into the room and pours "the mass of yellow coin upon the table."

> The spectacle took the general breath away. All gazed, nobody spoke for a moment. Then there was a unanimous call for an explanation. Tom said he could furnish it, and he did. The tale was long, but brim full of interest. There was scarcely an interruption from any one to break the charm of its flow. When he had finished, Mr. Jones said—
>
> "I thought I had fixed up a little surprise for this occasion, but it don't amount to anything now. This one makes it sing mighty small, I'm willing to allow." (231)

It is only when we begin to appreciate the levitating exultation of Tom's final triumph that the precise nature of his deep resentment against Sid becomes clear. For in assaulting the game Sid also threatens the show, and this adds intolerable insult to grievous injury. And the offense, if we reflect upon it, is as surely one against the sensibilities of Mark Twain, our premier literary showman, as it is against his fictional alter ego. For there can be little resistance to the conclusion that our narrator's description of Tom's triumph is the imaginative projection of what he would most fondly wish for himself: to be the acknowledged master of "spectacle," and to take "the general breath away"; to inspire stunned silence, followed by a cry in unison for more. To be able to meet that demand with a "tale [that] was long, but [so] brim full of interest" that there is "scarcely an interruption from any one to break the charm of its flow." And to cap it all, to have the competition admit publicly that by comparison their own efforts "sing mighty small." Can there be any doubt that Mark Twain indulged himself freely in Tom's magnificent exploit?

But if the final spectacle in *Tom Sawyer* is grand, it is also the product of rigorous self-restraint and several close calls with disaster. For the potent counter-impulse to subvert Tom's masterful manipulation of bad faith was as surely Mark Twain's as it is Sid's. How else can we explain our narrator's conspicuous blindness to Tom's often selfish and sometimes cruel gamesmanship? how else account for the barely suppressed outbursts of anger at perceived hypocrisy, and the enigmatic impulse to arm Sid with arrows against bad faith that never find their target? And how else, except by recourse to the hypothesis that his audience joined him in his deeply acculturated habit of deceit and self-deception, can we account for more than a century of critical neglect of the broad strand of outrage in the novel's mingled texture? In this larger perspective, Sid's mute secrets appear as threats not merely to Tom's games, but to the comic tale, "long" and "brim full of interest," that Mark Twain felt compelled to tell. Tom Sawyer is the record of Mark Twain's uneasy truce with disruptive imaginative energies that strained upward against the seemingly placid surface of his fragile idyll. If Tom's complex nature is fully explored; or if the social dynamics of village life are squarely faced; or, finally, if Sid finds occasion to disclose his subversive secrets, then the narrator's superior detachment will collapse into an angry and embarrassed confrontation with the bad faith of both the tale and the telling. This is not allowed to happen. Tom is conveniently blind to the deeper reaches of his own subtlety; Mark Twain prudently restrains his ricocheting anger; and Sid's secrets come to nothing. Finally, for more than a century now the novel's enormous audience has unconsciously collaborated in the refusal to acknowledge the bad faith that is everywhere at work in *Tom Sawyer*. Paradoxically, our mute acquiescence in the larger round of deceit and self-deception is the surest tribute to the tale's profound cultural authority. *Tom Sawyer* may be a humorous book, but only because we have joined Mark Twain in the determined struggle to have it that way. Read the novel to children, to young people not yet fully adult in their cultural prepossessions; and watch their eyes as you go.

VII

Sid's literal compliance and attempted enforcement of the overt code of St. Petersburg respectability earn him the contempt of his neighbors, the narrator, and the audience of *Tom Sawyer*. To put the matter another way, the fragile humor of Mark Twain's all-American idyll of boyhood freedom and innocence rests precariously on the acquiescence of the novel's actors, teller, and admirers in the rejection of the kinds of truths that Sid has to tell. It does not follow from this that Mark Twain erred in giving Sid a place in the narrative. To the contrary, Sid's threat to spectacle, and to the complex fabric of subliminal deceptions that enables such amusements, is an essential ingredient in the overall dynamics of bad faith. We join Tom and the narrator in rejecting Sid because, as one virtually inevitable consequence of our immersion in bad faith, we do not want to be made conscious of its terms. But while we can turn away from him and rather self-righteously condemn him, we can never completely do away with Sid; for the truths that he represents and spitefully advances are inextricably woven into the shaded levels of consciousness that constitute our own bad faith. With his righteousness, his spoiling motives and all, Sid is not merely one of us, he is part of all of us.

Given this much, it can be argued that Sid's function in the deeper psychological organization of the novel is to complicate and disrupt the flow of consciousness—Tom's, the narrator's, the reader's—as it passes through experience. At all levels, he serves as a guilt-threatening reminder of the varieties of deception they indulge in. It seems clear enough that Tom, were he left to himself, would be content to exercise his masterful gamesmanship in the prolonged indulgence of his imperious will. The only serious obstacle to his success in the fabrication of heroic personal roles in numberless public dramas is the guilt that would inevitably arise from the full awakening to his entanglement in bad faith. As we have seen, Mark Twain and his audience have their own stake in the game, and are unconsciously complicit in Tom's myopia. Aunt Polly threatens briefly with allegations of heartless and self-serving duplicity, but Tom rather effortlessly sidesteps her assault, and lays the dread charges to rest. Sid is not so easily dealt with; indeed, Sid is not really dealt with at all. Instead, by some subtle and silent collaboration between actors and teller and audience, he is ridiculed, ignored, and then roughly shuffled off the stage. Nonetheless, at the end of the novel Sid is as fully knowing about bad faith in general, and about Tom in particular, as he has ever been. He knows that Tom neglects his prayers; he justly doubts Tom's lies; and he lurks by the bedside in the perfectly acute anticipation of Tom's damaging revelations. To some extent, Sid functions as the embodiment of Tom's super-ego— his conscious, respectable, sternly judgmental side. Unlike his half-brother's conscience, however, Sid will not be pacified or deceived into silence.

In the doggedness of his meddling, Sid submits simultaneously to the imperatives of his own nature, to the strategic design of the novel's rhetoric, and to his vocation within the integrated structure of St. Petersburg society. It is his lonely task to remind his neighbors and his audience that such social stability as they achieve is won at the price of manifold deceptions. It is essential that Sid perform this duty, yet inevitable that his message should fall on virtually deaf ears. After all, if he succeeded, the social order would surrender to confusion. But if he cannot keep people honest, he can at least make them uncomfortable. Relentlessly intruding with hints and suggestions and outright accusations of deceit and hypocrisy, Sid interposes obstacles to Tom's schemes, disrupts the placidity and symmetry of the tale, and sends intermittent tremors through the reader's complacency. Little wonder that Tom fears and hates Sid, and that the narrator and generations of readers have condemned him as a sanctimonious snitch and then dismissed him from consciousness. Nor, upon reflection, is it surprising to discover that Mark Twain felt murderous impulses toward Sid's real-life model, Henry Clemens. To be sure, the differences between the real and the fictional brothers are significant and undeniable. But Henry was an infuriatingly good, quiet, rather unadventurous boy, too; and like Sid, as readers of *Life on the Mississippi* will recall, he was given to laying awake at night, a witness with righteous malice to the dark and guilty revelations that emerged from his sleeping brother's tormented dreams.[20]

If we resist the strong impulse in *Tom Sawyer* to press Sid out of mind, our sense of the relationship between Tom's plotting and the novel's plot becomes somewhat more complex. On one side, as we have seen, the novel's organization directly reflects its youthful hero's elaborate maneuverings toward high social status and acclaim. This most evident layer of the action was first discussed by Walter Blair, and has since been elaborated by Hamlin Hill and others. Blair advances the position (here ably summarized by Hill) that *Tom Sawyer* is "organized as the story of a boy's maturation, presented to the reader through four lines of action—the Tom and Becky story, the Muff Potter story, the Jackson's Island adventure, and the Injun Joe story—each of which begins with an immature act and ends with a relatively mature act by Tom."[21] It is true, as Judith Fetterley has insisted, that the text of the novel does not support the distinction—clearly implied by Blair and Hill—between "mature" adults and "immature" children. "The adults in *Tom Sawyer*," she argues, "are in all essentials like the children."[22] But Fetterley does not deny that Tom's social climbing leads him through the "four lines of action" originally outlined by Blair. To this extent at least, Blair's position is sound.

But it is also incomplete. In general terms, this is so because it is premised on an incomplete conception of Tom's relationship to his community. Specifically, it fails to consider bad faith. As we have seen, Tom can rise socially only if he is successful at ignoring or repressing the knowledge that Sid, or the Sid in himself, threatens to reveal. If he is to complete his education in gamesmanship and thereby assume his place as the most visible exemplar of St. Petersburg culture, Tom must learn to reckon with the guilt that menaces all actors in bad faith, but that is especially threatening to one as bold and ambitious as he. It follows that any comprehensive account of the novel's organization should recognize his developing intuitive grasp, and ultimate mastery, of the St. Petersburg variety of self-deception. Indeed, we may go further and insist that a fully satisfying structural analysis should also recognize the ways in which Tom's flight from self-knowledge is mirrored at different levels in the evasive maneuverings of his neighbors, his narrator, and generations of admiring readers. Only then will our notion of plot be commensurate with our understanding of the novel's full social and cultural implications.

In offering this more comprehensive analysis, I have no wish to deny the significance of such episodes as those involving Becky Thatcher, Muff Potter, Injun Joe, and Jackson's Island. But it is essential to recognize that these intermittent actions derive their meaning from their relationship to the plotting of Tom's education in bad faith. Viewed as an account of the molding of a gamesman, the novel falls most readily and naturally into another four-part structure, but one that is linear rather than alternating and episodic in form. Each section or movement in this linear progression has Tom as its prime mover, and each describes and implicitly analyzes a stage in Tom's mastery of bad faith. Sections two and three are by far the most substantial in size, and take rise from major challenges to the hero's psychic resources and equilibrium. Section one serves essentially as a descriptive introduction, and section four is a brief but illuminating coda.

Chapters 1–8 form the novel's first structural division, and amount to a compendious "sociology" of life in St. Petersburg. We are introduced in these chapters to village domestic arrangements, to the church, the school, and to aspects of work, play, the social hierarchy, and the style and exigencies of courtship. At the same time, we become familiarly acquainted with the prime candidate for local heroism and future leadership, Tom Sawyer. Through Tom, in his interactions with the village community, and more specifically with his mentor, aunt Polly, his adversary, Sid, the object of his romantic energy, Becky, and a number of his friends, we are initiated into the terms and dynamics of gamesmanship. In effect, we as readers are presented with a broad and detailed perspective on bad faith as we oversee the final stages in the education of its most adept practitioner. It is clear as well, as I have already shown in my analysis of Tom's shrewd management of the whitewashing, that the novel's episodes—thanks to the hero's constant plotting—are much more tightly seamed together than has generally been realized. In the course of these early chapters we have the impression that the consequences of pervasive bad faith are mild, and even socially beneficial.

This impression changes abruptly and quite dramatically in Chapter 9, the opening of the novel's long (Chapters 9–23) second movement, when Huck and Tom witness a bloody murder. For the first time, we as readers are the observers of Tom Sawyer in circumstances where deeds have serious personal consequences. Tom and Huck are appropriately horrified by what they have seen. Their horror is materially increased by the dawning awareness that they alone know that Injun Joe, and not Muff Potter, killed Dr. Robinson. In unison, and without apparent reflection, they decide to "keep mum." As Huck puts it, "That Injun devil wouldn't make any more of drownding us than a couple of cats, if we was to squeak 'bout this and they didn't hang him" (99). Thus they seek security in a sanguinary oath of absolute silence.

For both boys, the decision to "keep mum" issues out of the simple and perfectly reasonable fear of making themselves the targets of Injun Joe's formidable vengefulness. Obviously, neither of them has the slightest confidence in the town's ability to protect them from the dread half-breed. In Huck's case, the fear is an all-consuming motive, and he never registers any concern over the fact that his silence may be fatal for Muff. For Tom, on the other hand, the fear that prompts the oath is from the beginning accompanied by guilt over the omission to tell the life-saving truth. Characteristically, Tom's instinctive reflex to the threat of guilt is to press its cause out of consciousness. This impulse is first evident when he bows to Huck's initiative in the elaboration of the oath. Ordinarily, Tom is utterly contemptuous of Huck's notions about adventure and intrigue. In this case, however, he bends to his friend's judgment because the vexing intimation of his own bad faith is temporarily muted in the illusion that the design and energy behind the deception are Huck's. But the reprieve is as brief as the secret knowledge is potent with guilt. Tom falls asleep that night "congratulating himself that nobody knew of his escapade." What he does not realize is that "the gently-snoring Sid was awake, and had been so for an hour." Worse yet, he is not yet fully aware of the extent to which he is "on" to himself. As usual, Sid is justified in his suspicions; and for once Tom is fated to become fully conscious of what his half-brother merely suspects.

The next morning, Tom awakens to a mood of vague but oppressive dread. Eyes are averted at the breakfast table, and there is little relief in the confession that he was out after hours, or in the standard plea for forgiveness from aunt Polly. Tom knows something about his "escapade" that his aunt doesn't, and so he leaves the table "feeling that he had won but an imperfect forgiveness and established but a feeble confidence." Answering to and appeasing his guardian won't do in this case; so Tom retreats, "too miserable to even feel vengeful toward Sid" (103), because he knows, however vaguely, that he is up against the most relentless informer and judge of all, himself.

Tom's valiant but finally futile resistance to the emergence of guilt defines the second structural division of the novel. This substantial movement within the larger action begins at the graveside in Chapter 9 and ends with Tom's courtroom disclosure of Injun Joe's guilt and Muff Potter's innocence in Chapter 23. All of the action in the intervening chapters arises from Tom's progressively more desperate attempts to ignore or forget or repress what he knows to be true about the murder. It is a chronicle, in other words, of the failure of bad faith.

Initially, Tom must devote all of his ingenuity to diverting the thoughts of others from speculation about the murder. He ducks aunt Polly's questions about his somber mood and attempts, unsuccessfully, to foil his half-brother's nocturnal snooping. At the same time, he must struggle to keep troublesome thoughts from surfacing in his own consciousness. This is especially difficult, for "it seemed to Tom that his schoolmates," obviously inspired by the recent sensation, "never would get done holding inquests on dead cats, and thus keeping his trouble present to his mind." Sid is on hand to note that Tom declines to act as coroner or witness in the hearings, "though it had been his habit to take the lead in all new enterprises." Fortunately, however, "even inquests went out of vogue at last, and ceased to torture Tom's conscience." As the final step in this preliminary stage of denial and repression, Tom makes furtive visits to "the little grated jail-window and smuggled such small comforts through to the 'murderer' as he could get hold of." We are assured that such "offerings greatly helped to ease Tom's conscience" (108). Meanwhile, as if to confirm the boy's darkest fears, the craven townspeople turn a blind eye to Injun Joe's part in the body-snatching.

Once the town has settled back into its daily routines, and once he has reduced his own conscience to relative quiescence, Tom embarks on what amounts to a program of self-induced distraction from the guilty knowledge that prowls along the borders of his consciousness. Impelled by the imperatives of bad faith, he takes shelter from self-reckoning in a series of intense, and therefore diverting, preoccupations. At first, his "mind . . . drifted away from its secret troubles [because] it had found a new and weighty matter to interest itself about. Becky Thatcher had stopped coming to school." Since diversions work best when they lure consciousness to extremes, Tom is inclined to an exaggerated intensity of response. Thus when he learns that Becky is ill, he rushes to a vision of total calamity: "What if she should die!" There is undoubtedly a measure of concern in Tom's surmise, but there is, quite ironically, a much more generous measure of relief. The narrator inadvertently confirms this irony for us when he remarks that "there was distraction in the thought" (109) of Becky's death.

Tom's inflated concern for Becky quickly gives way to an equally exaggerated depression; and this, happily enough, moves aunt Polly to action. Imagining herself a solicitous nurse—"she never suspected that she was not an angel of healing and the balm of Gilead in disguise" (109)—she subjects her patient to a series of experimental treatments and quack medicines. In turn, Tom performs experiments of his own on Peter the cat, and then abandons the role of patient for that of disappointed lover. These initial diversions are characteristically of brief duration, and are punctuated by momentary descents into depression. One such mood swing occurs when Tom learns that Becky is ill, and another—"He was gloomy and desperate. He was a forsaken, friendless boy" (114)—follows his unhappy encounter with Becky at school. These moments of melancholy are disproportionately intense, and will seem puzzling until they are recognized as the manifestations of Tom's submerged agitation over Muff Potter. His gloom increases when his consciousness is emptied of immediate diversions and thus open to the surfacing of barely repressed anxieties. Appropriately enough, the intervals of depression end not with the resolution of the problem at hand, but with the discovery of yet another distraction.

Tom breaks out of his amorous melancholy by resorting to a much more extreme, and therefore more durable, deviation from the true source of his discontent. In a carefully nourished fit of self-pity, he decides "to escape from hard usage and lack of sympathy at home by roaming abroad into the great world never to return" (114). This resolve leads to the exhilarating flight to Jackson's Island, the discovery of the advantages of being thought dead, and the triumphant mock-resurrection (Chapters 13–17). This is followed by a brief interval of glory, the masterful exploitation of the sycamore scroll, various developments in the courtship of Becky, and magnificent revenge on the sadistic schoolmaster during "Examination" day exercises (Chapters 19–21). But the end of the school year brings a slackening of routines that is hardly welcome to a boy with trouble deeply in mind. Tom is briefly diverted by membership in the Cadets of Temperance, but this amusement pales into the revelation "that his coveted vacation was beginning to hang a little heavily on his hands" (164). In rapid and desperately random order he seeks amusement in a diary ("but nothing happened"), a minstrel show, the Fourth of July ("it rained hard"), the circus, and a phrenologist and mesmerizer, whose departure "left the village duller and drearier than ever." Children's parties are exciting, "but they were so few and so delightful that they only made the aching voids between ache the harder." Besides, Becky is away for the summer, "so there was no bright side to life anywhere." In fact, the paucity of summertime activities leaves Tom's consciousness vulnerable to the gathering pressure of his stricken conscience. Finally, when all distractions seem exhausted, and all energy for self-deception is spent, Tom's resistance collapses in an acknowledgment that "the dreadful secret of the murder was a chronic misery. It was a very cancer for permanency and pain" (164–65). Consciously face to face at last with what has been surreptitiously haunting him all along, Tom takes such relief as he can from confession to the local attorney and saving testimony in Muff Potter's trial.

The order and type of incident in the second movement of the novel are thus directly tied to the hero's first really significant encounter with the burden of guilt that threatens all serious gamesmen. The events that Tom witnesses in the cemetery set the plot in motion by confronting him with a dilemma that seriously challenges his moral resourcefulness. For the first time in his life, Tom's consciousness is exposed to some of the darker facts of adult reality. He must be jarred by the knowledge that apparently upright men such as Dr. Robinson are capable of grave moral departures; he must be shocked, too, at the terrible price paid by the victims, and by the deluded perpetrators, of racial injustice; and he is undoubtedly struck by the harshness of consequence that circumstance may cast in the path of such feckless innocence as Muff Potter's. It could be argued, of course, that Tom has been an accidental witness of realities that the townspeople have pushed to the margins of society in order to protect the delicate sensibilities of children. In fact, subsequent developments make it clear that the protection of adult sensibilities figures quite prominently in the motivation for suppressing such knowledge. As we have seen, Injun Joe's part in the grave-robbing is quietly ignored because the local authorities fear the consequences of prosecuting the vengeful half-breed. Dr. Robinson's obvious involvement in the crime prompts nothing in the way of comment; the less said about gross improprieties among the respectable classes, we suspect, the better. Meanwhile, it is poor Muff Potter's unhappy fate to serve as scapegoat in this tacit but socially broad-based subterfuge. His implication in the murder is plausible enough, and his hapless degeneracy is thorough enough, that the townspeople feel no compunctions about rushing prematurely to a verdict. Ostensibly, of course, the citizens are simply serving Muff his just deserts; in fact, their hasty judgment creates the illusion that the demands of justice have been met, and thus relieves them of the need to dwell further on the embarrassing cases of Injun Joe and Dr. Robinson. Thus this surge of apparent righteousness is quite evidently a cover for the community's refusal to deal with its own fear. Outwardly, Muff is jailed in the service of justice; in fact, he is jailed in the service of bad faith.

Against this larger social background, it is little wonder that Tom should respond to equally dire revelations by deciding, almost immediately, that they never happened. In the wake of the graveyard calamity, he is confronted with the same dilemma that later confronts his neighbors; and his surrender to fear, followed by the decision to suppress what he knows in order to sidestep conscience, anticipates in precise detail the later maneuvers of the village as a whole. Tom is no more self-conscious about the terms of his dilemma, or the fact that he has made a choice, than his neighbors are. Such parallels between the behavior of the child and the adult community are the surest index to the vitality and consistency of the local culture of bad faith, and of its continuity between generations. Just as surely, once Tom's unconscious decision to deceive himself and others has been made, the course and design of subsequent actions are determined. Thus the episodes involving Becky and Jackson's Island, and even the visit to Muff at the jail, are primarily in the service of Tom's unconscious determination to distract himself from what is in the back of his mind.

In effect, Tom's bad faith functions quite directly in the formation of plot. Mark Twain's works to the same result, only at a further remove. His outrage at the behavior of his characters erupts from time to time, but it is quickly suppressed, and never permitted seriously to disturb the apparently placid surface of the tale. Readers have contributed to this illusion of calm by preferring not to pursue vigorously or systematically the clues that the novel provides to its troubled undercurrents. Rather than acknowledge what is unmistakably there, the book's admirers have chosen to ignore the narrator's occasional lapses, to dismiss Sid as an incomplete or superfluous character, and to memorialize Tom's frantic distractions as the endearing antics of an all-American boy. At all levels, then, there is a failure to see what has actually happened; and this evasive behavior, in turn, has been the key determinant in the shaping of the novel's action.

The subtle force of bad faith as it interpenetrates the novel is especially clear in Tom's last-ditch effort to elude the guilt that has hounded him since the murder of Dr. Robinson. All ingenuity for self-deception having failed, Tom is helpless to resist the emergence into consciousness of his secret knowledge about Muff Potter. Once it has become conscious, that knowledge is unbearably painful to his conscience, and Tom seems poised for a confession. Instead, however, without apparent premeditation, Tom is rescued from his mind by the timely intervention of his body—which is to say, he comes down with a sudden and quite virulent case of the measles. The principal benefit of this happy affliction is distraction at once seemingly "natural" in its origins and consuming to the point of oblivion in its effects. "During two long weeks Tom lay a prisoner, dead to the world and its happenings. He was very ill, he was interested in nothing" (165).

Tom's surrender to this unconsciously self-induced illness is a telling index of both the intensity of his guilty suffering and the determination of his resistance. It is also testimony to Mark Twain's intuitive grasp of the role of psychosomatic illness in the covert dynamics of bad faith. This deft sure-handedness in Tom's characterization stems directly, if perhaps inadvertently, from the author-gamesman's personal experience. In "The Turning-point of My Life," and again in *The Autobiography,* Mark Twain reports that as a boy of about Tom's age, during an epidemic of measles in Hannibal, he purposely exposed himself to, and thereby contracted, the disease. In the first account, he explains that his fear of contagion became an intolerable burden.

> My soul was steeped in this awful dreariness—and in fear. At some time or other every day and every night a sudden shiver shook me to the marrow, and I said to myself, "There, I've got it! and I shall die." Life on these miserable terms was not worth living, and at last I made up my mind to get the disease and have it over, one way or the other. I escaped from the house and went to the house of a neighbor where a playmate of mine was very ill with the malady. When the chance offered I crept into his room and got into bed with him.[23]

The Autobiography similarly records suffering "continually under the threat of death" and the subsequent decision "to end this suspense and settle this matter one way or the other and be done with it." Both accounts agree, then, in representing the resort to physical suffering as a distraction from unbearable psychological pain. Both agree, too, in judging the maneuver a success. The more detailed version in *The Autobiography* is positively jubilant about the disease, and registers regret only when it comes to recording the final return to good health.

> It was a good case of measles that resulted. It brought me within a shade of death's door. It brought me to where I no longer felt any interest in anything, but, on the contrary, felt a total absence of interest— which was most placid and tranquil and sweet and delightful and enchanting. I have never enjoyed anything in my life any more than I enjoyed dying that time. I was, in effect, dying. The word had been passed and the family notified to assemble around the bed and see me off. I knew them all. There was no doubtfulness in my vision. They were all crying, but that did not affect me. I took but the vaguest interest in it and that merely because I was the center of all this emotional attention and was gratified by it and vain of it.
>
> When Doctor Cunningham had made up his mind that nothing more could be done for me he put bags of hot ashes all over me. He put them on my breast, on my wrists, on my ankles; and so, very much to his astonishment—and doubtless to my regret—he dragged me back into this world and set me going again.[24]

If we keep this extraordinary autobiographical background in mind, we can hardly minimize the extremity of Tom's suffering, nor can we question for long his reluctance to relinquish the psychological relief that he derives from physical illness. On one side, the measles provide an occasion for the indulgence of self-pity and a concomitant drift into blissful forgetfulness of life's cares; on the other, they gratify his voracious appetite for public acclaim and copious expressions of grief. In succumbing to both sides in an extreme way, Mark Twain and Tom Sawyer flirt perilously along the borders of physical and mental health. For both, the desperate capitulation to the measles serves as a reminder of the mental fatigue and world-weariness that gamesmanship imposes on its most ardent practitioners, and may even provide us with a glimpse of the form bad faith might assume in a pathological phase. At the very least, however, the autobiographical materials are the surest evidence that the intricate web of Tom's maneuverings was first woven in the childhood experience, conscious and unconscious, of his maker. This is no truer of Tom's sudden contraction of the disease than it is of his equally sudden descent into depression when his physical health is restored. As if to mirror the deeper sources of his mood, a dreadful storm, complete with thunder and lightning and driving rain, appears to threaten imminent retribution. There is no getting round it now; the terrible truth must at last be told.

VIII

While Tom's efforts to circumvent guilt end in frustration, it would be wrong to conclude that he experiences anything approaching total defeat. To the contrary, in giving way to the imperatives of conscience, Tom never loses sight of the imperatives of the game. The best evidence here is his masterful orchestration of the public disclosure of Muff Potter's innocence, where by the shrewdest measuring of his circumstances and audience, Tom converts potential humiliation into a self-aggrandizing spectacle. First, he assures himself that Huck has not leaked the secret. Next, he times his private conference with Muff's lawyer so that it accords perfectly with the young jurist's craving for courtroom melodrama. Armed with this stunning new evidence, the attorney "plays" to the gathered townspeople, first goading their impatience with the bland failure to defend his hapless client, and then electrifying them with the sudden introduction of Tom Sawyer. In thus seizing on the occasion to "show off," the lawyer unknowingly sets the stage for the indulgence of a vanity at once greater and more resourceful than his own. For even at the moment of surrender to conscience, Tom manipulates the counselor's bad faith to the service of his own, and thus maneuvers himself into the center of attention before a large, breathlessly attentive audience.

> Tom began—hesitatingly at first, but as he warmed to his subject his words flowed more and more easily; in a little while every sound ceased but his own voice; every eye fixed itself upon him; with parted lips and bated breath the audience hung upon his words, taking no note of time, rapt in the ghastly fascinations of the tale.   (172)

Once again, we are reminded of the parallels between Tom's showmanship and Mark Twain's—of the ways, for example, that their storytelling simultaneously serves, exploits, and profoundly interprets the culture from which it springs.

In submitting to the pressure of guilt, Tom gives ground in the game of deception he has set for himself. At the same time, however, he converts apparent defeat to victory by making his confession under circumstances that at once mitigate immediate losses and provide a generous supply of compensating personal gains. He accomplishes this by shrewdly anticipating the bad faith of the community, and by bringing it into alignment with his own objectives. This process commences, as we have seen, with the subtle manipulation of the lawyer, who obligingly prompts his young witness: "Speak out my boy—don't be diffident. The truth is always respectable" (171). The irony that attaches itself to this equation of "truth" with virtue is telling in several ways. Most obviously, perhaps, there is the broadly comical discrepancy between the forthright veracity that the lawyer preaches and the vain theatrics that he practices. A similar contradiction emerges when we apply the lawyer's definition of "truth" to the testimony it describes; for while Tom's confession is ostensibly "respectable" because it serves justice, its actual respectability resides in its masterful manipulation of pervasive bad faith. Tom's "truth" is "respectable," in other words, because it arises out of and reinforces—it "plays" to—a cultural fabric of lies.

The lawyer's unconscious irony points to the manifold revelations of bad faith set in motion by the young gamesman's surrender to conscience. This rather climactic unfolding occurs in Chapter 24, which immediately follows the trial scene, and which functions as a kind of watershed between the second and third movements of the novel. In drawing together and summarizing what has preceded, this chapter demonstrates that respectability has as its leading condition the silent acquiescence of its beneficiaries in the many inconsistencies—we may be tempted to call them "hypocrisies"—committed in its name. In Tom's case, for example, the benefit of subtle bad faith is sudden preeminence: he "was a glittering hero once more—the pet of the old, the envy of the young." It is the absolute condition of such gratifying notoriety that Tom and his neighbors permit the spectacle to distract them from what could only be an awkward and ignominious public reckoning. Tom's appetite for attention cannot be satisfied unless the townspeople silently agree not to pry into his motives for delaying so long with his life-saving revelations. Thus the evasion of guilt and the ascent to the summit of respectability go hand in hand. In much the same way—and as Tom acutely intuits—the villagers' willingness to overlook their young hero's negligence repays them with a pleasurable confirmation of the upright efficiency of their civic institutions, and, quite paradoxically, with the tacit permission to overlook their own delinquencies in matters of justice. We must imagine that the community experiences a brief tremor of puzzlement and surprise as it takes "Muff Potter to its bosom and fondle[s] him as lavishly as it had abused him before" (173). Meanwhile, though he must be troubled by Tom's tardiness in stepping forward, and utterly baffled by the town's readiness to overlook his (and, not at all coincidentally, Dr. Robinson's) part in the grave-robbing, Potter joins in the happy round of respectability by keeping his awkward questions to himself.

As if to complete its compendious summary of bad faith in action, Chapter 24 turns an ironic eye to the narrator's—and, more glancingly, to the reader's—entanglement in the same cultural web that enfolds the citizens of St. Petersburg. In the course of telling his story, as we have seen, Mark Twain cannot restrain intermittent outbursts of ironic indignation at village behavior. Such barbed observations are relatively abundant in this section, and are always swift and sure in finding their targets. This is the case, for example, when the bad faith of the town's "respectable"—which is to say, totally inconsistent—treatment of Muff Potter is ironically approved: "That sort of conduct is to the world's credit; therefore it is not well to find fault with it." It is the key to the acuity of this remark that while it obliquely acknowledges the apparent folly of the town's behavior, it also directs attention—by mimicking the passively self-interested refusal to "find fault"—to the motive and mechanism of its inevitable persistence. Mark Twain's observation that some villagers believed that Tom "would be President, yet, if he escaped hanging" is equally crisp in its implicit analysis of the contradictory impulses at work in the culture. Characteristically, however, the narrator's powers of insight soften considerably when he turns to the activities of Tom Sawyer. Thus it is an irony of a different sort that emerges from Mark Twain's failure to note that Tom's keeping "faith" with the community necessitates that he break his "faith" with Huck, whose "confidence in the human race was well nigh obliterated" (173). A similar irony arises when he ignores the intricacy of his own characterization, and resorts instead to the narrowly prejudicial announcement that it was "Tom's harassed conscience" that led him to the lawyer's house. In blinding himself to the manifest inconsistencies of his hero, Mark Twain places himself squarely in the line of fire that he has directed against the myopia of the townspeople. Just so, if we as readers have smiled knowingly at the folly of the townspeople, but failed to grasp the ironies that attach to Tom and the narrator, then we become entangled in similar ironies ourselves.

At the same time that it summarizes the novel's concentric circles of unwitting complicity in bad faith, Chapter 24 also serves as a point of departure for the third division of *Tom Sawyer*. Moreover, it supplements this transition with a strongly implied and quite plausible hint as to the continuity between the book's "parts." On one side, we are witness to the levels and varieties of self-deception prompted by the desire to avoid guilt. On the other, our understanding of bad faith is substantially advanced when we learn that the successful removal of the source of guilt can result in a confrontation with fear. This is quite clearly the case with Tom, who enjoys the rewards of a clear conscience at the cost of renewed fear for his life. After the trial, we learn, his days "were days of splendor and exultation to him, but his nights were seasons of horror. Injun Joe infested all his dreams, and always with doom in his eye. Hardly any temptation could persuade the boy to stir abroad after nightfall" (173). By contrast with Tom, Huck's response to the courtroom disclosures is a dramatic intensification of his already paralyzing fear. To live on the margins of St. Petersburg culture, it appears, is to experience a minimum of guilt but a steady and pretty full diet of terror. From graveyard to courtroom to the final discovery of Injun Joe's death, Huck is seldom free from fear. To live as fully within bad faith as Tom does, on the other hand, is to encounter guilt and fear in a kind of alternating cycle. More concretely, Tom's initial fear of Injun Joe prompts the evasive decision to "keep mum," which in turn stirs guilt over Muff Potter; the guilt, intensifying over time, necessitates the confession, which leads to Injun Joe's escape and restores Tom to his original, terror-stricken condition. It is the main business of the novel's third movement to complete the exposition and implied analysis of Tom's initiation into this cultural cycle.

This process commences gradually, and in rather clear stages. At the beginning of Chapter 24 we find Tom at peace with his conscience and—not at all coincidentally—the cynosure of an adoring public. But this mood of unmingled pleasure gives way almost immediately to a state of alternating extremes. "Daily Muff Potter's gratitude made Tom glad he had spoken; but nightly he wished he had sealed up his tongue." Finally, the serenity that the confession seemed to promise is totally eclipsed by a vertigo of terror. "Half the time Tom was afraid Injun Joe would never be captured; the other half he was afraid he would be." Such fears are hardly the groundless imaginings of an impressionable child. On the contrary, Tom recognizes and accepts the hard lessons of Joe's escape. Most obviously, there are forms of evil and violence that the civic institutions of St. Petersburg may be powerless to control. Worse yet, the inability to contain the half-breed is to a large extent the result of the townspeople's unwillingness to try. True, they hire an "omniscient and awe-inspiring" St. Louis detective, who "moused around, shook his head, looked wise, and made that sort of astounding success which members of that craft usually achieve." In what is a perfectly obvious refusal to admit to their own peril, or to take full responsibility for the welfare of their most favored son, the villagers rationalize their bad-faith surrender to fear in a pretense to vigilance and self-defense. All public gestures to the contrary notwithstanding, the people of St. Petersburg don't want to capture Injun Joe, they want to forget him. Mark Twain knows this, and his irony shows that it makes him angry. He notes that the detective turns up a "clew," but adds wryly that "you can't hang a 'clew' for murder." As usual, however, the brief duration of his anger is the surest sign of his veiled complicity with its object.

Tom's return to equanimity is almost as sudden, and finally just as imperfect, as Mark Twain's. Before settling down, however, Tom surrenders briefly to a mood so dark, and so desperate and extreme in its murderous implications, that we must be struck with how little it has been noted. "He felt sure he never could draw a safe breath again until [Injun Joe] was dead and he had seen the corpse." It seems quite likely that we are inclined to ignore or quickly forget this heavy shadow in Tom's characterization because it conflicts so completely with our dominant conception of him as the bright-eyed, irrepressibly optimistic American boy. To a significant degree, Tom has himself adopted this sunny, uncluttered self-image, and so readily joins in the general maneuvering to purge consciousness of all discord. Thus, while the chapter's penultimate sentence is a reminder that the detective's failure left Tom feeling "just as insecure as he was before," the conclusion is an assurance that "the slow days drifted on, and each left behind it a slightly lightened weight of apprehension" (173–74).

Such gradual recessions of fear as do occur, however, are left to our imaginations and the blank space between chapters. For the reader is next greeted with an activity not deliberately undertaken in a mood of composure, but rushed to in a haste apparently verging on panic. "There comes a time in every rightly constructed boy's life when he has a raging desire to go somewhere and dig for hidden treasure. This desire suddenly came upon Tom one day" (175). The rhetoric here ("There comes a time . . . one day") is significant to the extent that it promises escape. For Tom's sudden, "raging" enthusiasm for adventure is quite evidently a manifestation of his characteristic pattern of withdrawal from painful emotions into gaudy distractions. Quite as characteristically, Mark Twain is a willing—even a leading—party to the evasion, and Tom's audience has been perfectly satisfied to go along without comment. Having said this much, however, I should add that for Tom and Mark Twain, and to some degree for the reader, the inclination to evasive forgetfulness is more powerful than the capacity for its achievement. Thus the nearly frantic excitement that opens Chapter 25 may be viewed as a resurfacing of the emotional energy that is pressed out of consciousness, but not completely buried, at the end of Chapter 24. This is the first of many signs that the fear in *Tom Sawyer,* like the guilt that precedes it, goes underground, where it works subliminally as a major strand in the organization of the novel's third movement. This process commences in Chapters 24–25; it ends in Chapter 33, when Tom sees Injun Joe's corpse at the mouth of the cave. "His pity was moved, but nevertheless he felt an abounding sense of relief and security, now, which revealed to him in a degree which he had not fully appreciated before, how vast a weight of dread had been lying upon him since the day he lifted his voice against this bloody-minded outcast" (220).

IX

The plotting of the third division of the novel arises out of the imperatives of Tom's character as they are molded and driven by Mark Twain's creative imagination. Chapters 24–31 complete Tom's education by bringing him face to face with the kind of terror that gives rise to, and might even be said to justify, the tacit but virtually unanimous social acquiescence in bad faith. The first two movements of the novel reveal the dynamics and major consequences of gamesmanship; the third affords us a glimpse of its utility and what might be called its historical necessity. The leading inference to be drawn from these later chapters is that fear of Injun Joe as intense as Tom's cannot be successfully repressed or ignored. Rather, the brute upsurge of the emotion causes it to bleed into the outward face of events, and to draw its possessor, almost as it would a passive agent of its own energy and design, back to a confrontation with its source. More concretely, Tom's fear—in combination with his character and circumstances as they are formed by his maker—easily subdues all resistance, and brings him rapidly and irresistibly to a reencounter with Injun Joe. He is drawn back to the source of his guilt in much the same fashion, but his coming to terms with Muff Potter seems leisurely when it is compared with the hectic pace of his return to Injun Joe. Thus, though fear and guilt appear to obey some of the same psychological rules, it is also evident that fear is the much "hotter" and more headlong state of mind. This may mean that fear, in some imagined history or myth of bad faith, is the more primary phenomenon.[25] Primal, existential terror, one might speculate, originally sets in motion the processes of psychological adaptation that eventually lead to the development of social bad faith as we recognize it in St. Petersburg. If some such history lies buried in Tom Sawyer, then several of its key and recurrent elements emerge for recapitulation in the treasure hunt that commences in Chapter 25.

It seems clear that Tom undertakes his new adventure in order to empty his consciousness of fear. If he wants at some level to forget about Injun Joe, however, at another level he wants even more to be on familiar terms with varieties of terror. It is the dark strategy of Tom's fear to make him seek exciting distractions, only to restore him—suddenly, and in the very midst of his diversions—to the source and object of his terror. Thus before long the treasure hunt leads to talk (with Huck, who has joined the fun) of witches, furtive midnight outings, a discussion of dead people and ghosts, and, finally, the decision to visit a haunted house. Given this fatal inclination toward darkness and death and spooks, it comes as little surprise (to the reader) when Injun Joe turns up with the treasure in the abandoned mansion. Indeed, so apparently inevitable is this meeting of boy and villain that the plot seems to bend itself out of shape to hasten its occurrence. Thus when the boys overhear Injun Joe's announcement that he will meet his evil confederate at "No. 2," Tom draws the quite implausible conclusion that a back-room at the "Temperance Tavern" is intended. In fact, a hiding place in McDougal's cave, later discovered by the boys, is what Joe has in mind. No matter, though; for reasons that are never clear, the half-breed turns up at the Tavern to terrify the boys, and to lead them on. Conscious choice is simply not an issue here; rather, such plot-wrenching coincidences reinforce our sense that Tom is impelled toward his nemesis by forces too numerous and powerful to be controlled. One such force is the boys' quite unmistakable greed. On more than one occasion their fear of Joe gives way temporarily to their lust for gold.[26] For the most part, however, the determinants of Tom's strange attraction to his dark opposite work behind the scenes, in the recesses of his mind, in the paradoxical projections of his maker, and in the resistless forward thrust of the novel's plot. These apparently disparate elements overlap one another at the submerged pole of Tom's (or Mark Twain's, or the novel's) ambivalence toward Injun Joe; in turn, the pull along this axis is a manifestation of the structurally polarized, inherently paradoxical design of bad faith itself.

The delicate equipoise of Tom's ambivalence is perhaps nowhere more evident than in his mingled reaction to the discovery of Injun Joe, and to the fleeting vision of Injun Joe's treasure, in the haunted house. At the surface of his consciousness, Tom is frustrated when circumstances prompt Joe to take his plunder with him, rather than leave it behind to the greedy pleasure of the onlooking boys. This disappointment resurfaces on the morning after the adventure, when Tom arises to the memory of dreams in which

> he had his hands on that rich treasure, and four times it wasted to nothingness in his fingers as sleep forsook him and wakefulness brought back the hard reality of his misfortune. As he lay in the early morning recalling the incidents of his great adventure, he noticed that they seemed curiously subdued and far away—somewhat as if they had happened in another world, or in a time long gone by. Then it occurred to him that the great adventure itself must be a dream!

But no sooner has this trend established itself than its opposite takes over. Now "the incidents of his adventure grew sensibly sharper and clearer under the attrition of thinking them over, and so he presently found himself leaning to the impression that the thing might not have been a dream, after all" (188).

As the most ready and reliable means of resolving his uncertainty, Tom seeks the guidance of his accomplice and friend, Huck Finn. First, however, the narrator speculates that Tom's doubts about the veracity of his dream are the natural result of boyish innocence and awe. Mark Twain assures us that

> the quantity of coin he had seen was too vast to be real. He had never seen as much as fifty dollars in one mass before, and he was like all boys

of his age and station in life, in that he imagined that all references to "hundreds" and "thousands" were mere fanciful forms of speech, and that no such sums really existed in the world . . . If his notions of hidden treasure had been analyzed, they would have been found to consist of a handful of real dimes and a bushel of vague, splendid, ungraspable dollars.

In a perfectly ironic reversal, however, it soon becomes clear that the only ingenuousness conspicuously at work in the situation is the nearly palpable naivete of Mark Twain's confident, condescending sermon on Tom's alleged childishness. In fact, we behold here yet another instance of our narrator's failure to fully penetrate the subtlety of his own characterizations. For when Huck makes it clear that his companion's dream is faithful to the facts of the incident at the haunted house, Tom's response is hardly one of awe and incredulity. He offers no resistance to Huck's lament that if it hadn't been for wayward circumstances, "we'd 'a' got the money. O, ain't it awful!" Instead, he reacts with a vague and quite uncharacteristic wistfulness. "'Tain't a dream, then, 'tain't a dream! Somehow I most wish it was. Dog'd if I don't, Huck" (188–89). Quite obviously, Tom's reluctance to accept the truth of his dream is not the result of an inability to conceive of a vast "quantity of coin." Rather, this initial inclination to disbelief is an oblique acknowledgment of fear. If the adventure and the treasure and the haunted house are real, then so is the terrifying threat of Injun Joe. As he focuses momentarily on that dark strand in his memory, Tom permits us a rare—because rather direct—view of the underside of his consciousness. For a brief interval we are witness to the side of his mind that distracting adventures usually hold in abeyance, but very occasionally betray. After all, while the treasure hunt is unconsciously designed to put fear out of mind, it also leads Tom straight to Injun Joe. That Mark Twain furnishes us with this unmistakable clue to Tom's repressed fear, but then overlooks his own subtle lead in favor of a more benign (or, if you like, a more simpleminded) line of analysis, merely confirms the strong impression that our narrator's blind spots quite frequently coincide with Tom's. At one further, by now familiar, remove, we may be willing to acknowledge that a century of critical blindness to this clue is a version—on a much broader historical and cultural base—of the same myopia. With Tom and Mark Twain, we are culturally disposed to want to wish Injun Joe out of consciousness—to join Tom in his regret that it "'tain't a dream."

But, of course, Injun Joe is not a dream and he is not about to go away. Given this much, it may appear an encouraging sign when Tom breaks off his wishful sighing and rather manfully squares himself up to the reality of his enemy. When Huck complains that he has "had dreams enough all night—with that patch-eyed Spanish devil going for me all through 'em—rot him!" Tom replies, "No, not rot him. *Find* him! Track the money!" (189). But to the extent that it is an oblique expression of fear, Tom's wistful mood is a glancing acknowledgment of his deepest feelings about Injun Joe. In abandoning that frame of mind, and in seeming to take on courage, the boy is in fact simply pressing his resurgent terror out of consciousness. It may strike us as curious or even faintly ironic that the key to Tom's success in this evasive maneuver is greed, an impulse apparently remote from fear in all important respects save in its formidable potency. By displacing the image of the vengeful murderer with one of fabulous riches, Tom activates a materialistic drive adequate to the temporary silencing of his terror. And chasing after money, in the St. Petersburg scale of values, is quite evidently respectable. Like the treasure hunt before it, however, this dauntless pursuit of "the money" has the distinct disadvantage of drawing Tom closer and closer to the object of his very real, if submerged, terror. When the opportunity presents itself, then, it is little wonder that the self-deceived and deeply frightened boy readily abandons the trail of riches for less threatening diversions.

In this case, as it happens, opportunity presents itself in the person of Becky Thatcher. To some extent, of course, Tom is attracted to Becky, just as, in some measure, he is susceptible to the lure of money. But the deeper appeal of romance, like the evident but unstated attraction of treasure, resides in its power to overtake and fill consciousness, and thus to liberate Tom's mind from its bondage to terror. As an additional feature of local bad faith, it appears that when materialism becomes too perilous, it gives place to romance as the most effective, socially acceptable means of dealing with fear. This general principle is clearly in evidence in the opening sentences of Chapter 29. "The first thing Tom heard on Friday morning was a glad piece of news—Judge Thatcher's family had come back to town the night before. Both Injun Joe and the treasure sunk into secondary importance for a moment, and Becky took the chief place in the boy's interest" (194). True, Tom's thoughts wander to his adventure with Huck, but not for long. "The sure fun of the evening outweighed the uncertain treasure; and boy like, he determined to yield to the stronger inclination and not allow himself to think of the box of money another time that day" (195). To insist that this seeming preference for amorous pleasure is in fact a veiled concession to fear is not to deny that the citizens of St. Petersburg are capable of getting and spending and courting and coupling in unencumbered ways. Still, if we use the text of *Tom Sawyer* as evidence, then amorous and acquisitive motives, though apparently autonomous, are upon close scrutiny often found to be alternatives in consciousness to the more potent, but the more painful, emotions of guilt and fear. Nor would I argue that love is for Tom a less perilous sentiment than greed. To the contrary, so long as his fear is unacknowledged and therefore unresolved, all of Tom's impulses will spring obliquely from fear, and they will all lead him back to its source. Thus the romantic pursuit of Becky Thatcher leads inevitably to McDougal's cave, the labyrinthine lair of Injun Joe, and the dark site for Tom's final lessons in bad faith.

X

As if to reinforce our appreciation of the terrifying reality of Injun Joe, the interval between Tom's discovery of Becky and their actual entry into the cave (Chapters 29–30) is given to an account of Huck's heroic exertions on behalf of the widow Douglas. Infatuated as he is with the idea of treasure, Huck follows Joe and his accomplice to a dark hillside near town, and there overhears the half-breed's revengeful scheme to mutilate the widow. He overcomes his fear long enough to alert a neighboring and friendly Welshman to the widow's plight, but then succumbs to a mysterious affliction that keeps him bedridden, enfeebled, and unable to endure the excitement of visitors until long after Tom's escape from the cave. As the reward for his courage and honesty, Huck earns temporary admission to respectable St. Petersburg society. But such welcome and comfort as he receives come too late to protect him from his totally debilitating encounter with Injun Joe. Huck's collapse, in other words, is a timely reminder of the physical and psychological defenses enjoyed by insiders to St. Petersburg culture. Local citizens recognize that Injun Joe is a threat, but they have the means (both institutions and comforting bad-faith illusions) of putting him out of mind. For a marginal figure such as Huck, however, the lack of these defenses can mean vulnerability to panic of nearly hallucinatory intensity.

If Huck's encounter with Injun Joe earns him access—admittedly belated—to local society, then Tom's evasion of the half-breed commences with decisions that cut him off from the comforts and security of St. Petersburg citizenship. First, he persuades Becky that there is no harm in misleading Mrs. Thatcher as to her daughter's whereabouts on the night of the picnic. Second, he surrenders to thoughtlessness and inflated self-confidence in leading Becky deep into McDougal's cave. In both cases, Tom takes the initiative in actions that remove him and Becky from the safe inner circle of family and community. As the concomitant of such inadvertent alienation, Tom and Becky stumble more and more deeply into the perilous territory of Injun Joe.

According to anthropologist Victor Turner, *rites de passage* characteristically first conduct neophytes to a marginal or "liminal" state between childhood and adulthood. Thus temporarily suspended "betwixt and between" identities, the initiand is especially receptive to instruction in the rites and rewards of solidarity with the community. On one side, the initiation demonstrates that compliance with law and custom "is to live satisfactorily"; on the other, it is emphasized "that ways of acting and thinking alternative to those laid down by the deities or ancestors are ultimately unworkable and may have disastrous consequences." In this vein, Turner gives special emphasis to the thematic opposition of the processes of dissolution and death with those of "growth, transformation, and the reformulation of old elements in new patterns." Logical oppositions of this sort are often resolved into the same symbol, and the "coincidence of opposite processes and notions in a single representation characterizes the peculiar unity of the liminal: that which is neither this nor that, and yet is both."[27]

If we return to Tom and Becky with Turner's description in mind, it soon becomes clear that their perilous journey to the underground includes many of the key elements of a typical initiation. Injun Joe's simultaneous powers of attraction and repulsion obviously fit the mold, and will come up for much more detailed discussion later on. Meanwhile, the cave is at once the site for, and the symbol of, opposed notions and processes. Initially, it is the place where Tom and Becky go to pieces, where their identities as children begin to dissolve, and where, in various ways, they "die." Later on, it is the place where they begin to reintegrate themselves as individuals, where they take the first steps in the transformation of their social roles, and from which they are reborn to their new personal and social identities. In short, the cave is at once a grave and a womb.

Entry into this ambiguous place, and into this "betwixt and between" state, has as its first condition the total separation of the neophytes from their community. This sudden and complete severing of physical ties is followed almost immediately by a rapidly escalating feeling of isolation and vulnerability. As their initial apprehension arches sharply upward toward total panic, the children become acutely aware of the immeasurable value of the social supports that they have, until now, taken for granted. For a few moments Becky urges Tom to cry out for help. But her resistance to the terror of isolation is quite thin, and before long her encouragement gives way to hopelessness. "Tom, Tom, we're lost! we're lost! We never never can get out of this awful place! O, why *did* we ever leave the others!" Hopelessness in turn threatens to become total physical and mental collapse. "She sank to the ground and burst into such a frenzy of crying that Tom was appalled with the idea that she might die, or lose her reason" (211). So rapid and complete is the girl's breakdown that we must suppose hopeless solitude and alienation answer some dark expectation in the remote corners of her nature. Indeed, we may go further and note that in losing consciousness Becky betrays an inclination to heed the soft lure of oblivion. The threat of death that seems to loom up out of the darkness has its counterpart in a seductive beckoning toward dissolution that emerges from within. When Becky awakens, Tom is gratified that she has rested and assures her that they will "find the way out." She replies: "We can try, Tom; but I've seen such a beautiful country in my dream. I reckon we are going there" (212). Becky's dependency on the physical and psychological support of the community and its culture could not be more graphically evident. Once deprived of that context, she surrenders rapidly to a vertigo of terror at imagined menaces from without, and to the subtle life-threatening impulses ready to surface within herself.

The tenuousness of Becky's resistance to fear, and her concomitant readiness to seek relief in oblivion, are qualities that she shares with Mark Twain himself, and with some of his leading characters. Becky feels, as her maker felt from time to time, that the imagined serenity of death is preferable to certain varieties of emotional suffering. And though his apprehension is of a rather different kind than hers, Huck Finn responds to fear, as Becky does, by wishing he could die.[28] Against this background, the echo of *Paradise Lost* in Mark Twain's description of the children's deflated spirits—"They rose up and wandered along, hand in hand and hopeless" (213)—is especially poignant and significant.[29] For if Tom and Becky are to overcome the perils that threaten them, they must leave the garden of childhood innocence and enter the fallen world of adult society and adult consciousness. The threshold to that transformation of consciousness is the cave, where the children are forced into an awareness of their vulnerability to a host of unsettling and even life-threatening forces. In turn, this unpleasant revelation impresses them with their desperate need for union with the larger human community. They first respond to this need by turning to each other for help. In huddling together, consoling one another, and sharing scant resources, Tom and Becky acknowledge the precariousness of their "unaccommodated" individual conditions, and their utter dependency on each other for physical and psychological survival. As the symbolic culmination of their entry into this rudimentary social dyad, the children divide and consume a piece of cake as part of a brief marriage ceremony. Becky is quite clear and direct about the significance of the ceremonial meal: "It's our wedding cake, Tom," she says. "I saved it from the pic-nic for us to dream on, Tom, the way grown-up people do with wedding cake" (213).

Though Tom and Becky react sharply to common fears, and though their reactions incline them both to value and to seek the sanctuary of group alliances, it would be wrong to suggest that their behavior in the cave is similar in all ways. To the contrary, as a major part of their experience in the cave the children face circumstances which tend to enforce "practical" compliance with role behavior based on culturally sanctioned perceptions of sexual difference. To the very considerable extent that it involves deception of self and other, such compliance with gender-related behavior patterns may be located within the larger framework of bad faith. When Tom and Becky deceive themselves and each other in the cave, they do so not merely as individuals, but as the representatives of a specific culture. The children betray a marked aptitude for the assimilation of gender roles in earlier "courtship" chapters of the novel. To a very considerable extent, this "playing" with romantic roles consists of varieties of posturing, dissembling, pretense and tergiversation. Matters are much more culturally in earnest when Becky comes across the picture of a naked human figure in the schoolmaster's anatomy book. No sooner has she glimpsed the fascinating image than she becomes aware of Tom watching her. "Becky snatched at the book to close it, and had the hard luck to tear the pictured page half down the middle" (154). For themselves, Tom and Becky agree—immediately, without discussion, as if by reflex—*not* to discuss the precise nature of Becky's offense. This silence permits them the illusion that Becky's error was to have invaded the teacher's privacy and torn his book, while in fact they both know—and quickly forget—that her only serious lapse was the apparently inadvertent one of seeing the anatomical illustration. Obliged by their culture, and enabled by bad faith, the children simply deny to themselves, and by implication to the world, that there is anything at all remarkable about what Becky saw. For similar reasons, but also for others perhaps more peculiarly his own, the schoolmaster complies with the cover-up by neglecting to specify the volume's content when he angrily inquires, "Who tore this book?" (156). But since Tom and Becky both still know at one level what they have denied at another, and since they recognize the same doubleness in Mr. Dobbins, it emerges as a necessity that Tom take the blame for tearing the book. While it is not acceptable to anyone that Becky should have seen and "known" the picture, it is acceptable, apparently appropriate, and possibly even culturally desirable, that Tom should have. By incriminating himself, Tom spares Becky the humiliating exposure to Mr. Dobbins's judgmental eye. At the same time, Tom's "confession" signals to Becky in a dramatic and conclusive way his determination to deflect public attention away from the real truth, both as a way of hiding it, and as an aid to forgetting it. In short, Tom acts on the principle that it is easiest to forget what no one else can possibly know, or even suspect. Thus, by a series of rather complex and subtle adjustments, the fact of Becky's sexual "knowledge" is overlooked, then absorbed by Tom, and finally dissipated in a publicly validated illusion about the nature of the misdeed and the identity of the misdoer.

Mark Twain's plotting of the elaborate maneuverings involved in the preservation of Becky's "innocence" is rather rich in implication. For one thing, it gives us a window on the way the children's ready compliance with their culture's demands rapidly deepens their immersion in culturally prescribed roles. More specifically, in assuming their parts in the crisis of Becky's sexual consciousness, they at once adhere to, express, and substantially reinforce their commitments to highly (though rarely) articulated sexual identities. It becomes clear, as well, that their mutual participation, conscious and unconscious, in a variety of deceptions, serves to bind the children together around a carefully guarded cluster of secrets. We may go further and note that Becky is more fully bound than Tom by their union in bad faith. This is so because the deepest of their shared secrets is the unacceptable truth about Becky's sexual "knowledge." In a way that dramatically illuminates the surrounding social context, Becky is in thrall to Tom for the preservation of a sexual identity that is at once totally a cultural construction and nearly as essential as air and food and sleep to her sense of well-being. It does not follow that Tom is somehow to be faulted for possessing or exploiting the power that his knowledge might seem to confer. Because bad faith has worked to obscure what consciousness has found unacceptable, Tom is hardly aware of what he knows about Becky and the anatomy book. The leading Son of St. Petersburg, he is hard put to see or remember for long what his culture has decided to put out of sight and mind.

Nor are Tom's neighbors his only companions in this marked tendency to forget. Readers and critics have for decades glanced with Tom and Becky at the anatomy book, and they have then joined without comment both in the children's deception of one another and the world, and in the world's apparent readiness to be deceived. This willingness to see and forget, to join passively in the bad faith, has from the beginning enjoyed the silent support of the novel's narrator. Most obviously, Mark Twain seems quite as ready as Tom and Becky and their neighbors and audience to overlook embarrassing details. But a much deeper complicity in the general bad faith is evident in what we know of his molding and manipulation of the story before it was published. In an early version of the episode at Mr. Dobbins's desk Becky is brought to the verge of emotional collapse by the discovery that Tom has been watching her. "O, what shall I do, what shall I do! I'll be whipped, and I never was whipped in school—But that ain't anything—it ain't *half*. You'll tell everybody about the picture, and O, O, O!" The worst of her offense, Becky acknowledges, is to have been caught looking at, and by clear implication "knowing," the image of the naked person. It is perfectly in keeping both with the perceived gravity of her error and with its subsequent concealment that Becky would fail to find words for, or the will to say, precisely what it is she has done wrong. It is as though the act of verbal acknowledgment would confer upon the deed more reality than Becky, or the culture that works through her, can tolerate. Just so, Mark Twain joined in the pervasive bad faith when he elected not to include Becky's frantic reaction in the published version of *Tom Sawyer*. The same cultural impulse prompted him to suppress the following passage, in which Tom edges toward an outright declaration of what he finds wrong in the picture, and in Becky's having seen it:

> But that picture is—is—well, now it ain't so curious she feels bad about that. No . . . . . . No, I reckon it ain't. Suppose she was Mary, and Alf Temple caught her looking at such a picture as that, and went around telling. She'd feel mighty bad. She'd feel—well, I'd *lick* him. I bet I would. Well, of course I ain't going to tell on this little fool, because that's a good deal too mean.[30]

What we see here more nearly expressed than anywhere in the published text is Tom's initial squeamishness, and the process by which it is transformed into high-sounding bravado. What Tom fails utterly to recognize, of course, is that his own culturally based notions about gender and propriety are at least as well served as Becky's by his apparently magnanimous resolution to conceal the truth. At the same time that he pleases Becky by taking her blame, Tom has the very evident male pleasure of acting as virile protector ("I'd lick him. I bet I would."). And while it is gratifying in itself, this happy round of role-playing achieves its deeper bad-faith objective of distracting the children from the truth they have collaborated to conceal and forget.

Mark Twain's decision to excise these materials from his novel is the precise cultural recapitulation of the act of suppression that the materials dramatize. He was obviously as reluctant as Tom and Becky to acknowledge the culturally unacceptable implications of the episode with the anatomy book. In the opinion of John C. Gerber, editor of the Iowa/California edition of *Tom Sawyer,* this truncation of the novel is a "real loss" because it cost us "the one scene in which the author allowed himself to show the fascination and fear that the subject of sex had for Victorian children."[31] But in assigning the "fascination and fear" exclusively to the children, and thus failing to recognize the same sentiments in Mr. Dobbins and the other St. Petersburg adults, or in Mark Twain himself, or in the novel's audience, Gerber's remarks must seem to participate in the culturally induced myopia, or bad faith, of the text it proposes to analyze. In fact, Mark Twain's removal of these passages from the final copy of *Tom Sawyer* was an act of impeccable consistency and verisimilitude. To have included Becky's overwrought reactions and Tom's muscular rationalizing of his own motives would have revealed what the text, and the context, seem bent on concealing. Culturally speaking, then, it is entirely meaningful that these passages were excluded from *Tom Sawyer* and are now virtually buried and forgotten in a remote special collection noted in passing in a remote scholarly edition. Like Mr. Dobbins's fascinating and fearful book, they are now just where the culture wants them: locked up, out of sight, and apparently out of mind.

This protracted excursion into the classroom should help to prepare us for what goes on between Tom and Becky in the cave. They have, we know, a clear if rudimentary grasp of the roles, rooted in gender and defined for the most part in terms of the limits and responsibilities of consciousness, assigned to them as individuals, and as a potential social dyad. As a key element in this accession to adult identities, the children are forced by their exposure to Mr. Dobbins's book to substantially deepen their shared commitment to bad faith. Having strayed briefly into tempting but forbidden territory, Tom and Becky withdraw to prescribed sexual roles that demand, as the price of social and psychological security, a drastic narrowing of sexual consciousness. At the same time that it affords us a clear measure of their culture's authority in their lives, the children's ready acquiescence in such social bad faith is also the absolutely essential final phase of their preparation for a descent into the cave. For in wandering further and further outside the safe limits of the known and familiar, Tom and Becky drift more deeply into the dark orbit of energies and impulses that are at one level unknown and unfamiliar to them, but at another as proximate to their lives and minds as Injun Joe himself. In approaching this close encounter with their culture's nether side, one that St. Petersburg has chosen to cast out or press down or forget, the children are thrown back on models for behavior brought with them from the bright security of the upper world. In effect, Tom and Becky earn their survival by successfully withdrawing to the safety of these roles.

For Becky, as we have seen, the acknowledgment that she is lost makes her prey to crippling fear, and ultimately to the complete loss of consciousness.[32] The irresistible message of this experience is that when a female is alone and separated from the security of her culture, she is unable to protect herself from fears and forces that threaten from every side. In short, Becky's collapse clearly illustrates her deep, culturally induced dependency on men in general, and on Tom in particular. Her evident acquiescence in this virtually obligatory posture entails much more than simple physical helplessness. Becky is also deeply dependent on Tom for what little psychological security she enjoys in the cave. Once she is cut off from known and familiar circumstances, Becky's consciousness descends rapidly toward despair and oblivion, and is temporarily restrained and buoyed up only by Tom's injections of encouragement and hope. The pattern and the terms of this precarious dependency are clear from the moment that Becky accepts the possibility that they may be lost. She allows that it would be "awful," and then "shuddered at the thought of the dreadful possibilities."

> They started through a corridor, and traversed it in silence a long way, glancing at each new opening, to see if there was anything familiar about the look of it; but they were all strange. Every time Tom made an examination, Becky would watch his face for an encouraging sign, and he would say cheerily—
> "Oh, it's all right. This ain't the one, but we'll come to it right away!"
> But he felt less and less hopeful with each failure, and presently began to turn off into diverging avenues at sheer random, in the desperate hope of finding the one that was wanted. He still said it was "all right," but there was such a leaden dread at his heart, that the words had lost their ring and sounded just as if he had said, "All is lost!" Becky clung to his side in an anguish of fear, and tried hard to keep back the tears, but they would come. At last she said:
> "O, Tom, never mind the bats, let's go back that way! We seem to get worse and worse off all the time."
> Tom stopped.
> "Listen!" said he.
> Profound silence; silence so deep that even their breathings were conspicuous in the hush. Tom shouted. The call went echoing down the empty aisles and died out in the distance in a faint sound that resembled a ripple of mocking laughter.
> "Oh, don't do it again, Tom, it is too horrid," said Becky.
> "It is horrid, but I better, Becky; they *might* hear us, you know;" and he shouted again.
> The "might" was even a chillier horror than the ghostly laughter, it so confessed a perishing hope. The children stood still and listened; but there was no result. Tom turned upon the back track at once, and hurried his steps. It was but a little while before a certain indecision in his manner revealed another fearful fact to Becky—he could not find his way back!
> "O, Tom, you didn't make any marks!"
> "Becky I was such a fool! Such a fool! I never thought we might want to come back! No—I can't find the way. It's all mixed up."   (210–11)

From the very beginning Becky views Tom as a source of support, and he correspondingly takes it as his responsibility to provide what she seeks. But in turning to Tom, Becky is emphatically not seeking a considered and frankly realistic assessment of their circumstances; rather, she adopts the posture of passive dependency assigned to women in distress, and thus implicitly appeals for, and possibly in a sense even demands, "an encouraging sign." It is clear, in other words, that Becky is willing, and under certain conditions, even anxious, to be lied to. Despairing of what she perceives in her circumstances, Becky's state of mind wavers between the comforting but fragile illusion that Tom's superior vision will fall on happier vistas, and the fear that the apparent factitiousness of the encouragement he provides will exhaust her will to be deceived. On one side, then, Becky's tenuous psychological equilibrium rests on her capacity for rather gross self-deception; on the other, it rests as well on Tom's willingness and ability to meet her implicit but emphatic appeal to be deceived.

Of course Tom rushes to Becky's aid. After all, the same cultural assumptions and impulses which prompt Becky to seek his support prompt Tom to give it. Thus while he is quite evidently concerned to come up with a realistic assessment of their objective circumstances, he is equally clearly determined to provide her with all possible encouragement. In short, he collaborates immediately, completely, and without being asked to, in the bad-faith maneuvers that culture and circumstance require. His success in deceiving Becky about the true nature of their situation rests to a large extent on his ability to conceal his inner fears behind a carefully guarded exterior. Tom knows that in response to his every move "Becky would watch his face for an encouraging sign." Thus he is completely in earnest when he applies his gamesman's mastery of face to the business of giving nothing away. But while this rite of passage forces the children to exercise their bad faith to the limits of its versatility and refinement, it also forces them into an awareness of the drastic limits of their unaided power. Try as he may, Tom is helpless to disguise the "leaden dread at his heart," and Becky's ear cannot fail to pick up the hollowness in his words of hope. When he cries out in response to an imagined sound, Becky catches the element of fear in his voice and then shrinks in horror from its echoing reverberations. She is thus primed to seize on the "perishing hope" that Tom unwittingly betrays in assuring her that "they *might* hear us." This *faux pas* triggers a reaction so extreme that Tom fears for Becky's sanity and life. He responds by "blaming and abusing himself for getting her into this miserable situation." This sudden shift in approach is the result, I must believe, of an extraordinarily shrewd, culturally telling, intuition. Tom's offer to accept blame steers Becky into a positive frame of mind by at once anticipating and blocking her impulse to assign that blame to him. Finding that the rather dark pleasures of righteous denunciation are closed to her, Becky settles instead for the equally righteous, but much more sanguine pleasures to be derived from magnanimity. "She said she would try to hope again, she would get up and follow wherever he might lead if only he would not talk like that any more. For he was no more to blame than she, she said" (212).

Buoyed up, as Tom seems to have imagined she would be, by the spectacle of her own selflessness and pluck, Becky enters a brief period of revived optimism. Before long, however, when Tom prudently economizes by extinguishing a candle, his gesture points to a reality that Becky cannot accept. "Words were not needed. Becky understood, and her hope died again." For a while longer the children cling to such shreds of optimism, patched together by bad faith, as remain within their grasp. For example, they refuse to acknowledge the growing weight of their fatigue, but instead press onward in the tacit agreement that "to sit down was to invite death and shorten its pursuit." But when weariness finally forces Becky to a standstill, and when all of Tom's "encouragements were grown threadbare with use," the onset of sleep appears a blessing. "Tom was grateful" (212); but he is also soon made aware that the blessing of sleep is at the very best a mixed one. For the other side of peaceful oblivion is the misery of the return to the harshness and darkness and hopelessness of the cave. Sleeping does not restore Becky's spirits; rather, it hastens their erosion by highlighting the painful contrast between waking reality and what she calls the "beautiful country in my dream." Once this contrast is fully established in her consciousness, Becky is more completely than ever outside the range of Tom's well-meaning deceptions. She is so removed in space and time from the security of familiar social constructions that she has lost hope of their retrieval. Desperately, but also in conformity to the cultural expectations that attach to her gender, she gives up on consciousness as a potential habitat of comfort and turns instead to the imagined solace of oblivion.

It may surprise us at first that Becky is as easily undone by adversity, and as ready to resort to extremes, as the narrative says she is. But her headlong collapse illustrates perfectly what rites of passage are designed to make clear to the initiand—that rapid mental deterioration and physical death await on the other side of the boundary that separates the inside of the social and cultural enclosure from the outside. For a short while Becky is on the wrong side of the line. Much more than ever before, the routines of ordinary life must seem dear to her now. She will not stray to these perilous margins again, nor will she strain and grow restive in the traces of her adult identity.

Aside from differences rooted primarily in gender, Tom endures a similarly ruthless and effective socialization. In witnessing Becky's rapid decline, and in being forced to confront and accept the limits of his once proud power as a gamesman, he is also led briefly to the perimeter of the cultural circle. Like Becky, he gives way to oblivion, though his retreat is not as determined, and his loss of hope not as complete, as hers. To the very end, Tom struggles manfully to meet his responsibilities as the strong, vigilant keeper of sanity and conscious hope. As we have seen, the constant bad-faith reinforcement of Becky's wavering morale is the core and absolutely essential ingredient in Tom's role as male partner. Ordinarily he attempts to meet this demand by mediating and ameliorating Becky's perception of their circumstances. At the nadir and apparent destination of their dark journey, however, when they come face to face at last with Tom's nemesis and the concentrated embodiment of all that their culture most fears in itself and the world, it is Tom's task not merely to improve on reality, but to conceal it altogether. It is a matter of inner psychological necessity that Tom confront Injun Joe, just as it is indispensable to the children's rite of passage that they descend to this dark underworld of chaotic energies and bloody-minded impulses. But if it is necessary that Becky pass in view of the dread half-breed, it is equally necessary that she fail to consciously recognize what it is she has almost seen. For as Tom well knows, Injun Joe is quite literally beyond Becky's ken.

As the narrative would have it, the children are separated when Injun Joe suddenly appears to Tom's horrified view. The boy is naturally relieved when Joe takes to his heels, but no amount of security will permit him to betray his terrible secret. Indeed, the narrator is very simple and direct and, for that, very final in declaring that Tom "was careful to keep from Becky what it was he had seen" (215). The situation requires no comment or elaboration; it is assumed that the reader will join immediately in the tacit approval of Tom's manly decision to protect his companion from an upsetting revelation. In fact, however, Mark Twain's brevity and our ready compliance make it possible to ignore the deeper implications both of what Tom has witnessed and of his decision to keep it to himself. Becky's carefully guarded ignorance about Joe's appearance in the cave is culturally of a piece with her carefully preserved ignorance in the matter of the anatomy book. Tom knows immediately and for a certainty that knowledge about Injun Joe, in anything like its full range of implication, is incompatible with Becky's culturally defined "innocence." His unthinking self-assurance on this score is perfectly in keeping with the large measure of bad faith in the town's rejection of Injun Joe. The citizens of St. Petersburg are uniform and vigorous in their banishment of the half-breed, but the original reasons for their harsh disapproval are never articulated, and— again in keeping with bad faith—are undoubtedly lost to memory. I will have more to say on this in the next section. For now, it is perhaps enough to say that the term "half-breed" is freighted with the suggestion of vague and unspeakable sins for local folk, and that this cultural reflex is at work in Tom when he decides to conceal the fact that he has seen Injun Joe. For her part, and thanks to cognate cultural operations, Becky is virtually incapable of entertaining knowledge about the local pariah. We may be fairly sure, in other words, that Tom's silence spares Becky an encounter with a reality so alien and ominous that her consciousness would withdraw immediately from its contemplation. Confronted directly with Injun Joe, Becky would undoubtedly shriek with horror and pass out. Still, it is a culminating moment in this rite of passage when Tom, without pausing to reflect, steps confidently into his role as male guardian of the purity of Becky's mind.

In readily adopting an attitude that is the perfect cultural complement to Becky's, Tom joins his apparently destined mate in a rudimentary form of social union. Clinging to each other in fearful, fragile interdependence, the children form a point of intersection for the assumptions and values and institutions of their culture. Cut off from all that is familiar and comfortable, bereft and literally buried in darkness, exposed to the deepest fears of their community and cast for sanity and safety into new roles and upon each other, Tom and Becky are now ready to emerge from the liminal gloom. Meanwhile, Mark Twain and his audience, quite evidently impressed with the manly propriety of their hero's gesture, pause no longer than Tom does over its essential bad faith.

Once the dark destination of their journey has been reached, and Tom and Becky have been aligned and confirmed in suitable relationships to each other and their world, the outward phase of the rite of passage draws to a close. Henceforth it is a relatively simple matter to bring the children, now subtly but profoundly transformed by their descent, back home. Hunger and fatigue rapidly take their toll, and though Tom is manfully "willing to risk Injun Joe and all other terrors," Becky moves toward an equally extreme and seemingly perilous verge of her gender role. She "was very weak."

> She had sunk into a dreary apathy and would not be roused. She said she would wait, now, where she was, and die—it would not be long. She told Tom to go with the kite-line and explore if he chose; but she implored him to come back every little while and speak to her; and she made him promise that when the awful time came, he would stay by her and hold her hand until all was over.
>
> Tom kissed her, with a choking sensation in his throat, and made a show of being confident of finding the searchers or an escape from the cave; then he took the kite-line in his hand and went groping down one of the passages on his hands and knees, distressed with hunger and sick with bodings of coming doom.   (216)

Becky has passed beyond hope and, characteristically, has found a measure of peace in preparing herself for death. Tom is nearly as hopeless, but he is nonetheless—and also quite characteristically—still able to make "a show of being confident." Thus firmly bound up in their new identities and in each other, Tom and Becky descend for the last time as children into the oblivion of sleep. On the other side of their terrifying liminal dream they will be reborn as young initiates to the mysteries of St. Petersburg culture.

XI

Mark Twain seems to have been aware that the emergence of Tom and Becky from McDougal's Cave marked an important crux in his narrative. As he puts it in his "Conclusion," "So endeth this chronicle. It being strictly a history of a *boy,* it must stop here; the story could not go much further without becoming the history of a *man.* When one writes a novel about grown people, he knows exactly where to stop— that is, with a marriage; but when he writes of juveniles, he must stop where he best can" (237). The oddly stilted "endeth" and the failure to specify with any precision what properly ends a juvenile story may well be signs of Mark Twain's uncertainty about the type of narrative he had written and the type of audience he had written it for. In fact, while *Tom Sawyer* does not cross the line into the adult domain of marriage, it nonetheless concludes with a brief survey of what awaits the children at the conclusion of their rite of passage. The novel's third movement, in which Tom and Becky confront isolation and darkness and Injun Joe, and in the process achieve mastery of their adult social roles, forms the essential background to this glimpse into the world of "grown people." Its fourth movement, which I have called the coda (Chapters 32–35), recapitulates many of the principal elements that have figured in Tom's education as St. Petersburg's leading gamesman, and that will continue to figure in what promises to be his triumphant ascent of the village social order.

The patterns of past and future successes overlap completely in Tom's continuing role as St. Petersburg's leading source of amusement and excitement. The village is "sad and forlorn" when it appears that the children will not be found, and feverish with festive exhilaration when Tom, accompanied by Becky, makes his second return from the dead.

> Away in the middle of the night a wild peal burst from the village bells, and in a moment the streets were swarming with frantic half-clad people, who shouted, "Turn out! turn out! they're found! they're found!" Tin pans and horns were added to the din, the population massed itself and moved toward the river, met the children coming in an open carriage drawn by shouting citizens, thronged around it, joined its homeward march, and swept magnificently up the main street roaring huzzah after huzzah!

"It was the greatest night the little town had ever seen" (217), certainly because the children have been found, and also because their emergence from the cave results in an animated affirmation of social and cultural unity. If this "resurrection" is somehow more momentous than Tom's return from Jackson's Island, it is undoubtedly because the town now opens its arms not to a trio of wayward boys, but to a heroic new leader and his mate. To the earlier affirmation of unity, there is now added the promise of its continuity. It is characteristic of Tom in this already familiar situation that he should parlay apparently disastrous circumstances to the dramatic enhancement of his social power. Nor are we surprised to find that his triumph over adversity lands him squarely in front of "an eager auditory" breathlessly attentive to the unfolding of his "wonderful adventure," and prepared to believe everything they hear, "striking additions" (217–18) and all. In sum, *Tom Sawyer* ends by completing what it began, a portrait of the rise to pre-eminence of a master gamesman. Tom's developing control of social forms, his intuitive grasp of the subtleties of cultural play, his power to create plausible and gratifying illusions, his genius for manipulation, his ability to rule his face and to land on his feet, his voracious hunger for power and his concomitant relish for center stage—these are the staples of the hero's future authority, just as they have been the terms of his education, in the culture of bad faith.

In the midst of this pattern of continuities, the relationship between Tom's plotting and the narrative plot takes a familiar but significantly modified form as the novel draws to a close. In the early and middle chapters of *Tom Sawyer,* the hero's apparently autonomous scheming gives life and obliquely perceptible direction and coherence to the episodic portrayal of his education in the finer points of local bad faith. As the novel moves forward, however, we have the gathering impression that Tom's schemes are embedded in and defined by a dense, stable, and constraining social fabric. His autonomy seems to narrow as his initiation progresses. Finally, with the descent into McDougal's cave and the encounter with Injun Joe, Tom is quite passive in his relationship to the developing action. Circumstances in the cave are well beyond the reach of his powers of manipulation and deception; as the result, his best laid plans collapse in futility around him. Where he had earlier seemed to be the independent maker of action, Tom is now the instrument of a design that at least temporarily exceeds his comprehension and control. My point here is simple enough. The exhilarating autonomy that Tom appears to enjoy at the outset is gradually revealed to be a familiar variety of social play rooted in and defined by the local culture of bad faith. *Tom Sawyer* may be plotted by the plotting of its hero, but young Tom's schemes are themselves determined by the roles and rules, informed and enforced by guilt and fear, that the social reality of St. Petersburg sets in his path. Indeed, we may go even further in this vein. For if the culture of *Tom Sawyer* is Tom's because it is the town's, then it is the town's culture because it is Mark Twain's; and it is Mark Twain's because he shared it with, and profoundly articulated it for, his audience. In a very important sense, then, we are all—Tom, the townspeople, the narrator, and an American audience of several generations—embedded in the deeply plotted web of culture that informs the text of *Tom Sawyer.* This common and intimate embeddedness may well explain the *déjà vu* often experienced by adults reading the novel for the first time, and the feelings of proprietary familiarity with the young hero experienced by many Americans who have never read his story.

At the same time that *Tom Sawyer* records the molding of an immediately recognizable social type, it also sets forth the narrative of Tom's heroic defense and reaffirmation of the values and conventions of his culture. To be sure, the American everyboy and the American superboy are not always readily distinguishable. But the hero in Tom is perfectly manifest in the mock-resurrection, where he provides spurs to faith and fellow-feeling and fuels a revival of communal pride. We are witness to more of the same at the trial, where Tom acts as a potent agent of justice in the liberation of Muff Potter. It is equally obvious, however, that Tom's heroic potential awaits for its fullest exercise the dark underworld encounter with Injun Joe. Here Tom appears rather in the manner of Theseus, the demigod whose great career as a military and political leader took rise from his triumph over the monstrous Minotaur. Just as Theseus surfaces from the Labyrinth a hero of civilized order in its combat with passion and perversity, so Tom's emergence from the cave and his instrumental role in the death of Injun Joe seal him as the civilized embodiment of order and restraint, and as the resourceful adversary of all that threatens purity and innocence. It is neatly symmetrical with the classical story that Judge Thatcher should reward the young hero's exploits with a pledge "to see Tom a great lawyer or a great soldier some day" (233).

At one level, then, the descent into the cave is the final stage in a process of socialization and self-mastery that renders Tom the leading citizen and gamesman in his community. At another, clearly related level, Tom's triumph over Injun Joe is a more public and a thoroughly heroic exploit in which he appears to master for the community those forces which, as model citizen, he may seem to have mastered in himself. Sexuality in general, sexual aggressiveness in particular, vengefulness, deceit, greed, varieties of perversity and violence and the resistance to social restraint—these are the kinds of energies and impulses which the town fears, and which it attempts to cast away from itself and to control by heaping them on Injun Joe. The clearly implied social construction has it that all irremediable antisocial forces are traceable to the darkness in the half-breed; such forces are present in a threatening way only when he is present, they are gone when he is gone, and, consistency would seem to demand, they are dead when he is dead. In effect, of course, the townspeople make oblique acknowledgment of their own portion of darkness by failing to pursue their scapegoat with any energy, by petitioning the governor for his pardon, by directing tourists to stand in awe at the site of his death ("first in the list of the cavern's marvels"), and by flocking to his funeral "in boats and wagons from the town and from all the farms and hamlets for seven miles around" (221). They allow that the arch villain is dead, but something in them warms to his memory and refuses to believe that his spirit has departed.

In their inadvertent admission of an affinity for Joe, and in bending on occasion to an impulse to forgive him, the citizens of St. Petersburg recognize in a glancing way his authority with them, and give expression to the vague intimation that the half-breed is permanently their own. Indeed, the community's cultural blindness, its inability to see clearly and consciously that Joe is a kindred spirit, is at once a leading symptom and a primary cause of its bad faith. So long as the townspeople fail to recognize Joe as their fellow equal, the alien half-breed will continue to flourish in their midst, and bad faith will continue to require that he be kept out of sight and mind. McDougal's Cave is thus not merely an underground place suitable for habitation by the likes of Injun Joe; it is also a remote "place" in the mind where threats to consciousness and community are held in uncertain exile. Indeed, Mark Twain's description of the cavern might serve as well as the description of the unacknowledged capacity of the mind to hide from itself and others. It is "a vast labyrinth of crooked aisles that ran into each other and out again and led nowhere. It was said that one might wander days and nights together in its intricate tangle of rifts and chasms, and never find the end of the cave." It is perfectly appropriate that the party of village neophytes should be transported to the entrance of this hellish place, invited to explore its margins, introduced in a vague sort of way to its mysterious perils, and warned away from its interior. As he sets the scene and draws the children forward, Mark Twain settles on language that once again invites us to view the cave as a figure for the unconscious and the repressed. "No man 'knew' the cave. That was an impossible thing. Most of the young men knew a portion of it, and it was not customary to venture much beyond this known portion." Not customary, that is, unless like Theseus and countless other heroes you have a calling to descend to the underworld in search of the enemies of your people. This is quite evidently Tom's vocation, and thus it is fitting that from the outset he "knew as much of the cave as any one" (196).

Tom's privileged "knowledge" of McDougal's Cave, clearly the corollary of his uniquely intuitive grasp of the mechanisms of bad faith, is a profoundly mixed blessing. The boy's penetrating insight into, and rapid mastery of, the submerged dimensions of his culture are the avenue to great social preeminence and material security. The reward for the mock-resurrection is public acclaim; just so, Tom's exploits in the cave earn him the mantle of a hero and more money than anyone in the village "had ever seen at one time before" (231). But the special privileges that accrue to Tom because of his "knowledge" are at least partially offset by the liabilities that he falls heir to as an expert gamesman. As we have seen, virtual blindness to the existence of bad faith is characteristic of most of the actors in *Tom Sawyer,* and it goes a long way toward accounting for their optimism and equanimity and general readiness to be pleased. For Tom himself, however, the condition of blissful myopia is subject to the rather constant threat of a lapse into the awareness of essential, pervasive duplicity. To be sure, Tom is blind to his own scheming and maneuvering most of the time. Were he more fully or regularly conscious of the submerged rules of the social game, he would be much less successful as a gamesman. Heightened acuity would result for Tom, as it does for Sid, in the loss of his peace of mind, his sleep, and the respect of his family and peers. But Tom's intuitive mastery of bad faith, and its adjunct, his acumen in the matter of caves, make him vulnerable to occasional awakenings to the reality of his situation. This almost happens when he begins to glimpse the personal implications of what he has seen in the graveyard, but the oath with Huck serves as a stopgap to full awareness. In the sequel, however, the knowledge of his predicament presses painfully upward against consciousness, especially when he visits Muff in jail, and later on when he seeks distraction in courtship and adventure, and finally and most frantically when he succumbs to the measles. Tom cannot close his eyes completely, nor can he forget. Thus he is finally unable to put Muff's innocence from his mind; and, unlike his neighbors, who forget the half-breed once he is out of sight, Tom is powerless to avoid a decisive reckoning with his dread of Injun Joe. Quite evidently, then, the price that Tom pays for accelerated social mobility and the adulation of a hero includes the more or less permanent apprehension that a painful measure of fear or guilt will suddenly intrude upon his state of mind. Moreover, at intervals he must in fact succumb to that painful invasion as the submerged realities of bad faith, embodied in such marginal figures as Muff Potter and Injun Joe, surface in his consciousness.

To adopt this general perspective on Tom Sawyer is to be reminded of the terrific intensity that he brings to his youthful experience. Tom's interior life is conducted at a very high emotional pitch, and it is virtually always focused, either directly or obliquely, on guilt or fear. Given such extremes of emotional content and duration and intensity, we may be puzzled with the narrator's repeated assurances that Tom, and children generally, are much readier than adults to forget their troubles. This is so, he argues, not because Tom's "troubles were one whit less heavy and bitter to him than a man's are to a man, but because a new and powerful interest bore them down and drove them out of his mind for the time—just as men's misfortunes are forgotten in the excitement of new enterprises" (42). Children are not only easily distracted, the narrator assures us; they also enjoy much greater emotional resilience than adults. Thus even though they know they are lost in the cave, the children's "hope made a show of reviving—not with any reason to back it, but only because it is its nature to revive when the spring has not been taken out of it by age and familiarity with failure" (212). In fact, Mark Twain's insistence on the relative emotional buoyancy of children is in direct contradiction to the evidence provided by his own narrative. The adults in St. Petersburg quite readily ignore or rationalize or forget their mistreatment of Muff Potter; and while they register fear of Injun Joe, and even hire a detective to find him, they suffer no apparent anxiety when the half-hearted search comes up emptyhanded. For Tom, on the other hand, the flight from guilty knowledge about Muff proceeds from varieties of nagging anxiety through psychosomatic illness to public confession. And far from forgetting about Injun Joe, Tom is more than ever overcome with terror after the arch villain escapes from the courtroom. The boy now sees that the local authorities are as incompetent to hold the killer in custody as they are powerless to recapture him once he has slipped from their grasp. Worse yet, Tom must sense that the adults of St. Petersburg secretly welcome Joe's escape because it seems to free them from the necessity of facing their nemesis. Tom knows better; he knows, in a deeply unforgettable way, that his life will be in peril so long as Joe is alive. Thus just as he was earlier compelled to a resolution with the object of his guilt, so now, as the sequel to that encounter, he is unconsciously drawn to a confrontation with the object of his fear. The emergent irony is a familiar one. For if it is the first condition of embarking on his heroic journey that the young gamesman enjoy extraordinary command of bad faith, then it is the final condition of arrival at his goal that he endure, quite unwillingly, the failure of bad faith to shelter him, as it shelters his neighbors, from the awareness of the most active threats to their peace of mind. At the price of great pain to himself, Tom sees in order that others may be blind.

Tom differs from most of the other children in St. Petersburg in both the frequency and the intensity of his ventures into consciousness beyond the safe boundaries of bad faith. Other children also step outside the limits, but their suffering on this account is gradually reduced as they grow older and adapt themselves to adult modes of consciousness. Early in adolescence, the narrative suggests, the youngsters are exposed to liminality along the margins of the cave, and react by retreating to join the adults within the warm mantle of bad faith. Thus the children grow progressively more adept at avoiding in consciousness what the adults have long since put from their minds, but what Tom, as hero, must continue to endure. This analysis helps to explain why the inner lives of children, as they are represented in *Tom Sawyer,* are more intensely and protractedly dark than the inner lives of adults. Moreover, it casts some light on Mark Twain's repeated claim that just the opposite is the case. For if we are struck with the narrator's failure to properly assess the mental anguish that he has so plausibly portrayed in Tom and, to a lesser extent, in Tom's juvenile peers, then we must recognize that the misconstruction is one that he shares with most of the adults in his story and in his audience. It is a case, at all levels, of the refusal—indeed, the inability—to grasp what culture has proscribed from consciousness. To have acknowledged the extent of Tom's emotional pain would have brought Mark Twain closer than he wanted to come to a recognition of the personal anguish, half buried in memory, that fueled and formed his art. At the same time, however, the simple fact of the existence of *Tom Sawyer* is testimony that while the novelist shared the strong, general cultural tendency to forget, he also participated fully in his young hero's incapacity to surrender quietly or for long to the somnolence of bad faith. Thus while the boy is drawn back to the secret sources of his guilt and fear, the novelist obeyed a blind impulse to return, again and again during his long career, to the site and time of his formative years. *Tom Sawyer* is one of the first of these imaginative journeys home, and it sets the pattern for the major published versions that follow in insisting, against the evidence of memory, and in spite of the difficulties that gathered up and obstructed the telling, that boyhood was a fine, free, innocent time of life, after all.[33]

The adult actors in *Tom Sawyer* share the narrator's blindness to the emotional troubles of the children in their midst, and they share as

well—in a less complicated form—the history of acculturation that
has resulted in their common shortsightedness. Something of the same
may be said for the generations of readers who have been as irresistibly
drawn to the story as they have been unmindful of its darker intimations. Mark Twain's authority with us derives in good part from the
fact that in telling and retelling this strangely beguiling story he gives
voice to an important chapter in our national story—our myth.[34] As I
have tried to show, the plotting of the story, the dynamics of its narration, and our way of listening, are all deeply embedded in our culture
of bad faith. The novel's great popularity with Americans over the years
is an index to the striking intersection of Mark Twain's obsessive memories of childhood and the nation's ways of thinking and feeling about
its own past. At one level, this very ambiguous fable tells us that the
good times were the old ones when, as individuals and as a people, we
were children. At another level, *Tom Sawyer* suggests to us what life
might be like if we were as defenseless against memories of guilt and
terror as Tom is. The novel's power, inseparable from its characteristic
bad faith, derives in good part from the fact that it sets us before this
bifocal perspective on the past in such a way that we are unaware of
precisely what we have seen. Beneath the image of blissful childhood
innocence is a much darker impression, one only barely accessible to
consciousness, which operates subliminally to deflate nostalgia and at
the same time to reinforce the impulse to blinking forgetfulness. We
are content, in the upshot, to join the narrator in his cool, amused
detachment from the childhood past. Viewed from this superior, thoroughly adult point of view, *Tom Sawyer* fosters acquiescence in bad faith
by quietly assuring us of our good fortune in being just what and where
we are.

I suspect that the pleasure adults take in reading *Tom Sawyer* to children may have a partial source in our remote recognition that the story
is at once a consolation and a threat. For the adult reader, the reminder
of a fall from childish innocence to the urbane maturity personified in
the narrator is softened quite considerably by the happier comparison
between the reader's own sophistication and what he takes to be the
bumbling of the grownups in the story. In effect, the perceived foolishness and hypocrisy of the citizens of St. Petersburg permits the adult
reader, with the implied approval of Mark Twain, to accept the loss of
Eden with a measure of equanimity. Adult acquiescence is substantially
reinforced by the novel's subliminal reminder that childhood was more
torment than play. At this level, the narrative sets forth the juxtaposi-

tion of a haunted, furtive childhood past with the serene good humor of the adult present. This is the story as it is apt to fasten on the consciousness of children, warning them of the perils of their youthful estate. Failing to recognize that this darker strain in *Tom Sawyer* is invisible to the bad faith whose emergence it records, the children in the audience may be puzzled at the adult reader's evident pleasure in the novel.

The remarkable, really mysterious power of this slender novel resides in its compressed and comprehensive recapitulation of a range of mingled perspectives on the past and the present, youth and growing old. The source of the power is mysterious, and will remain so for most readers—who will persist in the view that *Tom Sawyer* is primarily "suitable for children"—because concealment is as obligatory in our representations of bad faith as blindness is virtually inevitable in their reception. The freemasonry may be as self-conscious as Melville's in *Moby-Dick,* or as unconscious as Mark Twain's in *Tom Sawyer.* Differences in authorial intention notwithstanding, however, the interposition of obstacles to ready understanding is in both texts the index to a prior, deeply shared obsession with deceit and deception in all their polymorphous variety. In both instances the manner of telling recapitulates the theme of bad faith; but since the theme of concealment must remain concealed, the story can never be satisfactorily brought to a conclusion, the obsession never fully raised and laid to rest. Thus *Moby-Dick* gives way to *Pierre* and "Bartleby" and "Benito" and *The Confidence-Man,* variations in form and content on the familiar—finally the only—theme. For Mark Twain, albeit much less consciously, there was a similar pattern of return to the unforgettable "matter of Hannibal." In returning with him, Mark Twain's enormous American audience has assented to his authority with them as the interpreter and guardian of their deepest cultural selves. *Tom Sawyer* lends credence to this surmise. After all, when Tom returns from his escapades in graveyards and on rivers and in caves, he is always greeted not so much by a community as by an audience, breathless for amusement and ready to believe anything. In no setting is Tom more clearly the child of his maker's imagination than this one, when he takes it as his final pleasure and obligation as hero to perform as bard for his people, and to tell them, in terms they can accept, what they are.

PART TWO

The Grand Evasion
Huckleberry Finn and the Later Works

W HEN the duke insists that it is "blame foolishness" to risk the harsh consequences of being exposed as fraudulent claimants to the estate of Peter Wilks, the king replies: "Hain't we got all the fools in town on our side? and ain't that a big enough majority in any town?" (228) The argument is perfectly plausible, of course; the townspeople in *Huckleberry Finn* are as perpetually ready to be deceived as the residents of St. Petersburg in *Tom Sawyer.* Armed with this knowledge, these comical, utterly unprincipled charlatans enjoy virtual immunity from detection and great material benefit in the confidence games they play on unsuspecting bumpkins along the Mississippi. It has been noted more than once that Tom Sawyer's possession and exploitation of the same knowledge is a key ingredient in his kinship with this pair of humbugs. When Huck warns that the plans for Jim's escape are much too easily detected, Tom replies that the Phelpses and their neighbors are all "so confiding and mullet-headed they don't take notice of nothing at all" (332). Such self-assurance is well founded in the world of *Huckleberry Finn,* where improbable claims of all kinds earn ready credulity. Citizens in river towns spend money on manifestly bogus entertainments and cures, make large donations toward the conversion of pirates in the Indian Ocean, and settle estates on thinly varnished frauds. Jim believes that he has dreamt when, quite obviously, he has not. Uncle Silas is persuaded that he filled the rat-holes with tallow, though he can't remember when; aunt Sally believes that Huck is Tom, and Tom is Sid; and the boys "let on" endlessly in their play, and in laying their plans for Jim's escape.

This is not to suggest that widespread belief in the unbelievable is simple, wide-eyed gullibility. In both novels, the readiness to be deceived is an integral component of the culture of bad faith, in which credulity is almost always in the service of unacknowledged, often unconscious ends. Prominent exploiters of bad faith, such as the king and the duke, and Tom, and, as we shall see, Huck, are enabled in their manipulations by an intuitive penetration into this ulterior dimension of the readiness to believe. They recognize that the tolerance for varieties of deceit is roughly proportional to the benefits that derive from being deceived. As in *Tom Sawyer,* there is a premium on pious false-

hoods, and it is evident that the religious and legal establishments ac-
commodate themselves quite readily to a host of social delusions, some
harmless, some full of mischief. Those intrepid successors to Sid Sawyer, who perceive the gross deceptions in their midst and attempt to
expose them, are characterized as abrasive, physically unattractive kill-
joys and are either silenced or ignored.

But if the mechanisms of bad faith are virtually identical in the two
novels, the contexts in which those mechanisms operate, and the manner of their presentation—and, therefore, of their reception—differ
significantly. *Tom Sawyer* explores the dynamics of bad faith within a
rather narrowly defined social reality. It verges on the mythic in its
deliberate, step-by-step exposition of the hero's education and final initiation into the mysteries and obligations of his calling. At the same
time, the narrative is admirably thorough in its implicit analysis of the
creation and maintenance of a complex social system. But while the
pattern of deception of self and other running through the cultural
fabric is everywhere in evidence, and while the training of its master
manipulator is centrally dealt with, the novel never engages in or seriously invites an explicit, sustained challenge to the values of the unfolding scheme of things. As I have shown, such hushed acquiescence
is testimony to the cultural authority of bad faith not only with the
citizens of St. Petersburg, but with the novel's narrator, Mark Twain,
and with generations of readers as well. We may go further in this vein
and argue that the potency and continuity of the social scheme are manifest in the very narrowness of the social reality envisioned by the novel.
Tom Sawyer is a comic novel because of the relative ease with which it
overcomes obstacles to the assertion and confirmation of its social order;
but this relative ease is in turn inseparable from the readiness of actors
and audience to settle for the narrative's construction of reality. In fact,
Tom Sawyer successfully conveys the illusion that all experience is ultimately reducible to entertainment. Murder, grave-robbing, the with-
holding of life-saving evidence, impulses to suicide, simulated disas-
ters, numerous close brushes with death, the violation of sanguinary
oaths, wrenching fear and guilt, and numberless suppressions of the
truth and miscarriages of justice are all transformed, through masterful
orchestration and narrative control, into entertainment. The relationship between the principal agent of comic transformation and his audience within the fictive world of the novel is mirrored rather precisely
in the relationship between Mark Twain and his audience without.
Both function, in parallel spheres of influence, as master gamesmen,

heroic artificers, cultural impresarios, to fabricate in language an image of experience that is at once immediately identifiable as our own, warmly gratifying to our cultural prepossessions, proof against the revelation of its essential bad faith, and therefore as bountiful a source of entertainment for us as it is for our kin in St. Petersburg.

In good part, then, we settle for the comic illusion—the entertainment—of *Tom Sawyer* because of the novel's complex narrative manner. Quite inevitably, however, our smiling acquiescence is also tied to the matter of the story. As I have already pointed out, *Tom Sawyer* is notable for its success at turning grave developments to festive ends. Success in this area is the more remarkable for the fact that the novel's endless chronicling of extreme, painful emotions, and its deep drift toward catastrophe, are little or long noticed by most readers. Yet it is also the case, as the example of *Huckleberry Finn* well illustrates, that the apparently resistless comedic thrust of *Tom Sawyer* is hardly invulnerable. For the sequel is cut from the same cultural cloth as its predecessor, and it is no more burdened with violence and suffering; yet it is immeasurably heavier in tone. Differences in narrative point of view notwithstanding, we can begin to account fully for this affective disparity only when we recognize, and properly emphasize, the omission of black people and— what is the same thing, given the time and setting of the story—slavery from *Tom Sawyer*. Once observed, the omission is immediately recognizable as conspicuous; but that recognition in turn draws attention to the paradox that the omission is notable not only because it is conspicuous, but also because it generally goes unnoticed.

Black people and slavery are virtually nonexistent in *Tom Sawyer* because they are utterly incompatible, for Mark Twain and his audience, with a comic perspective on that world. It is the very essence of the bad faith of this omission that it is not experienced as a distortion or a lack—indeed, that it is not consciously experienced at all. Yet the absence of slavery where its presence is properly, if subliminally, anticipated, makes all the difference in the reception of the novel. We happily endure the painful realities of *Tom Sawyer* because of the much greater woe that the fiction implicitly threatens, and then defers. Our readiness to join Mark Twain in submerging this constituent social and historical reality, and our difficulty in recognizing the omission for what it is, are an index to the painful confusion that attaches to this tragic national legacy, and the urgency of our impulse to mitigate its impact on consciousness. It is, as *Tom Sawyer* may serve to suggest, something we are strongly inclined to exclude from our happiest cultural self-portraits, something we would prefer to keep from our children. Slavery and racism are so absolutely counter to America's proudest ideals that the vast majority of attempts to deal with them—whether to justify, explain, repudiate, or ignore—almost perforce involve recourse to varieties of bad faith. And since the deceptions of self and other on this score usually serve in some fashion to rationalize or renounce or eclipse from consciousness what has been, by our own standards and admission, a crime against humanity, the bad faith involved may well be integral to the problem.

If *Tom Sawyer* is symptomatic, by its conspicuous omissions, of our culture's bad faith in its most severely pathological form, then *Huckleberry Finn* is a direct, anguished meditation on the affliction iteself, the environment through which it spreads, and the tortuous pattern of its operation in the minds of its agents and victims and witnesses. To be sure, the world of the novel is everywhere informed by Huck's way of seeing it; but it is equally the case that Huck's point of view is heavily influenced by the world he surveys. That world is virtually identical to Tom's in its values and social organization, though Huck's marginal point of vantage affords him a wider but culturally much less mediated perspective than his privileged friend's. Thus Huck expresses himself in a blunt, unwashed vernacular that bespeaks a broad but uneven immersion in St. Petersburg culture. He has notions about Providence and propriety and style, but they overlap very imperfectly with accepted views on such matters. His departures from correct form and his intermittent chafing at the manifold contradictions of Christian civilization serve to focus attention, often in an inadvertently humorous light, on the clear if generally unobserved boundaries that separate what is culturally "in" from what is culturally "out." Tom, on the other hand, operates from within a much more correct, and therefore much narrower, range of experience. His culturally mediated point of view takes expression in the carefully modulated voice of an urbane, literate, rather smug adult who has occasional brushes with village bad faith, but quite readily absorbs them into his own. Tom's mobility within the field of respectability seems almost unlimited because attention falls almost exclusively on the apparent freedom of his social play, and not on the sharp boundaries that he at once observes and helps to reinforce.

While Tom experiences a measure of freedom, and looks free to most observers, this is because he conforms, usually without reflection, to a rigid, elaborate, often contradictory social code. In fact, his freedom is

largely the lack of abrasion that results from a near perfect "fit" between
the contours of his aspirations and their social mold. This snug coex-
tension between personal and cultural boundaries accounts for the vi-
sual transparency of the numerous constraints on Tom's consciousness
and behavior. By comparison, Huck is much freer from the pressure of
social forms, but he is also much more alert to and constrained by the
bad-faith contradictions of those that he does feel. Paradoxically, then,
Tom's relative freedom and contentment are the result of his submission to the heavy informing hand of his culture, while Huck's sense of
constricted discontent issues directly from the relatively free play of his
restless resistance to the same forces. The paradox begins to unravel
when we recognize that the awareness of culture as an aggregation of
constraints on individual autonomy diminishes as the process of acculturation advances. The sense of pressure and contradiction grows less
acute as surrender to the contradictory deepens. Thus Huck's discomfort with the weight and inconsistency of St. Petersburg respectability
decreases as he shapes his behavior to the widow's civilized regimen;
and Tom grows less vulnerable to crippling attacks of guilt and fear as
the gamesman's mantle settles on his shoulders. But Huck's immersion
in village culture is abruptly terminated when Pap takes him forcibly
in tow, while his friend's is well advanced by the beginning of *Tom
Sawyer,* and complete to perfection when he emerges from McDougal's
cave. The numerous and far-reaching implications of this prominent
disparity are nowhere more consequential than in the attitudes that the
boys bring to slavery. Tom's gathering mastery and equanimity in the
local culture of bad faith are inseparable from his blindness to the inhumanity in his midst. As I have noted, the consciousness of *Tom Sawyer* is a virtual blank on the score of slavery; and Tom responds to Jim,
when circumstances bring them together in *Huckleberry Finn,* as an object to be purchased for play. In all of this, of course, the young hero
conforms to the view, adopted at least consciously by most of the actors
in both books, that the institution of slavery is essentially right. Tom's
acculturation renders him as insensible to Jim's suffering and peril as
he is to the bullet that lodges in his calf when the escape goes awry,
and that he wears around his neck in triumph once the strange entertainment is over. Indeed, by the closing chapters of *Huckleberry Finn,*
Tom is so exultant in his mastery of the field of play defined and sanctioned by his culture's "authorities" that he is virtually invulnerable to
pain, his own or anyone else's.

For Huck, on the other hand, restive, humorless discontent is deeply rooted in an expanding awareness of slavery, and in gathering, agonized intimations of its hypocrisy and cruelty. As incompletely proof against such anguish as he is imperfectly initiated into the dominant culture of bad faith, Huck's mental suffering grows more painfully acute as increased proximity to slavery draws his irreducible ambivalence into bold relief. Huck's references to blacks in *Tom Sawyer* are few, though they indicate that he is much more aware of and sensitive to slaves than mainstream white people in the book. When Tom asks him where he is going to sleep, for example, Huck replies:

> In Ben Rogers's hayloft. He lets me, and so does his pap's nigger man, Uncle Jake. I tote water for Uncle Jake whenever he wants me to, and any time I ask him he gives me a little something to eat if he can spare it. That's a mighty good nigger, Tom. He likes me, becuz I don't ever act as if I was above him. Sometimes I've set right down and eat *with* him. But you needn't tell that. A body's got to do things when he's awful hungry he wouldn't want to do as a steady thing.   (193)

Evidently enough, Huck's humble social station and destitution bring him into company with slaves. To be sure, there is a measure of racism in what he has to say, though the final, apologetic appeal to the demands of survival has a false ring to it, both because it implicitly falsifies his enormous resourcefulness, and because it contrasts so sharply with the sentiments that immediately precede it. After all, Huck begins with blandly unqualified deference to Uncle Jake's authority and liberality, and with the unblinking admission that he works for the black man when he is asked to. There may be hunger here, but there is much greater respect. Indeed, the first half of the passage is clear evidence that Huck and Uncle Jake are friends, and that their relationship is as affectionate and reciprocal as any Huck enjoys until the advent of Jim on Jackson's Island. The racist sentiments that follow are also integral to the young speaker's consciousness, though they surface belatedly, as though Huck intuits that his declarations of friendship for a slave have grown too warm, and may threaten to provoke Tom's suspicion or ridicule. Huck is by circumstance and inclination deeply in touch with the humanity of the slaves in St. Petersburg; at the same time, he is attuned to the unthinking racial cruelty of the dominant white culture. That division in his psyche sets him apart from his neighbors, black and white, and forms the center of all his woe.

The wide disparity in the boys' awareness of slavery is faithfully mirrored in the books bearing their names, both as those narratives represent the experience of an American community, and as they have been received by a large American audience. *Tom Sawyer* at once dramatizes and evokes the equanimity that issues from the bad-faith omission of the culture's leading contradiction. *Huckleberry Finn* at once dramatizes and evokes the agonized ambivalence that the consciousness of slavery can provoke, and the varieties of deception of self and other that relief from that consciousness may entail. With the obvious exception of Huck and Jim, the major figures in both novels seem perfectly comfortable with their peculiar institution. In *Tom Sawyer,* the work of bad faith is so complete that slavery rarely intrudes upon consciousness. In *Huckleberry Finn,* on the other hand, the inhumanity of the institution seems to dominate the foreground; yet members of the white community are untroubled by moral questions, and attend to slavery only when it is profitable, or forced by circumstance into their consciousness. Huck is unique, of course, both for the dividedness of his feelings, and for the painful intensity of awareness that his uncertainty gives rise to.

If it gives us pause to reflect that Huck is alone among the citizens of St. Petersburg in his conscious uneasiness over slavery, then we may be quite struck with the fact that the critics in Mark Twain's audience were initially slow to identify Huck's concern, and to allow that they shared it with him. The large majority of early reviewers of *Huckleberry Finn* were hostile to the novel because of its alleged irreligion and vulgarity. The general tone was set by the Concord, Massachusetts, Library Committee, which excluded the book, declaring it "rough, coarse, and inelegant, dealing with a series of experiences not elevating . . . It is the veriest trash." In Springfield, Illinois, offended gentility recoiled with the charge that "Mr. Clemens . . . has no reliable sense of propriety."[1] The response focused almost entirely on the novel's lapses from accepted standards of morality and taste. Mark Twain's vernacular art was rarely assessed, while Huck was viewed as a bad moral example for the nation's impressionable youth. Nowhere in the reviews, not even in the occasional favorable responses, was there any attention to the novel's conspicuous preoccupation with slavery. Perhaps the reviewers took the institution so for granted that they perceived no necessity to emphasize its prominent place in the novel. Much more likely, the novel's treatment of slavery came as an unwelcome reminder that the Civil War and Reconstruction had failed utterly to ease racial prejudice and to reduce its attendant hatred and violence. Viewed in this light, the contemporary critics' disproportionate attention to alleged lapses from respectable standards may be seen as an indirect acknowledgment that *Huckleberry Finn* was too painfully current for comfort. There was, in short, a measure of bad faith in their righteous outrage.

This is not to suggest that the early reviewers were singular in their myopia, and that we have now completely overcome the inclination to shrink from the novel's racial implications. To the contrary, modern critics have rediscovered the meaning of *Huckleberry Finn* only to partially resubmerge it in debates which focus too narrowly on the propriety or consistency of Huck's, or the novel's, response to the central, admittedly vexing, problem. Such discussions bear the suggestion that the narrative somehow *contains* within itself all that is necessary to its proper comprehension. In fact, of course, we find *Huckleberry Finn* profoundly meaningful, and we readily acknowledge its cultural authority, because it continues to speak directly to our condition. To read it is to be made mindful of the unbroken legacy of racial discord in America; of the persistence and pervasiveness of prejudice; and of our readiness, out of guilt and frustration and fear, to submerge the novel's most challenging implications in a tempest of esthetic dispute.

We are drawn to and fixed by *Huckleberry Finn* because it thrusts our fondest cultural self-image, an innocent—"natural," rootless, unlettered, preadolescent—boy, into direct contact with our most crippling cultural contradiction. We suspect, perhaps, that a proper understanding of the relationship between the innocent white boy and the enslaved black man will throw light on our problem. To the extent that Huck and Jim are perceived to love and care for one another, I suppose we are enlightened. But there is abundant trouble between them, too, and it appears that in lighting out Huck is as much in flight from Jim as he is from the civilization that shackles them both. Uncertainty on this vital question may help to account for our disinclination to reflect on the source of our interest in *Huckleberry Finn*. Rather than confront directly the uncompromising cultural lesson held out to us, we have been inclined, quite understandably I believe, to turn the novel back on itself, and to insist that the problem it dramatizes is Huck's, or the ante-bellum South's, or Mark Twain's, or the text's. At the same time, however, it is precisely its ambiguity that has secured *Huckleberry Finn* its place as the leading popular expression of America's self-image when it comes to matters of slavery and race. We return to the novel, and we read it to our children, because it gives us a bearable perspective on what continues to be an almost unbearable but absolutely unavoidable

problem. For the critics, ambiguity has seemed to necessitate the retreat to narrow, comfortably manageable "textual" considerations. For
the great mass of admiring readers, because Huck and Jim are friends,
and because Jim is finally emancipated, the novel's ambiguities are
simply dissolved in an overflow of relief and warm fellow-feeling. In
either case, *Huckleberry Finn* continues to be our favorite story about
slavery and race because it gives us no more of this reality than we can
bear.

It remains to add that *Huckleberry Finn* does more than merely facilitate our bad-faith prevarications. Like *Tom Sawyer,* but in more direct
and comprehensive ways, it provides us with models for the management of our shrinking disposition to the dilemma that it poses. *Tom
Sawyer* demonstrates that contradiction and inhumanity can be
wished—by actors and audience alike—out of sight and mind. *Huckleberry Finn* bears the suggestion that, for Mark Twain at least, consciousness could not repose indefinitely in such gross delusions. But at
the same time that the sequel surrenders to the irrepressible, it does so
with considerable hesitation at a number of levels. Jim first appears in
the novel as the unwitting butt of a practical joke conceived by Tom to
expose his gullibility and superstition. Huck urges Tom to forgo the
prank; he is not amused. Neither are we. Tom's gamesmanship ceases
to be funny when it preys on the credulity of a slave. With Jim's arrival
on the seemingly enchanted St. Petersburg scene, the illusion that
childish deeds yield only childish consequences gives way to a much
more ominous tone. The subsequent drift into disenchantment is gradual, and apparently as irresistible as it is unpremeditated. Mark Twain
seems to have been baffled and dismayed with the adverse flow of his
narrative. The halting rhythm of the composition of *Huckleberry Finn,*
clearly echoed in the uncertain movements of the published novel, is
marked by major pauses at recurrent crisis points in the relationship
between Huck and Jim. These are generally followed by intervals of
separation, followed in turn by reunion and renewed drift toward crisis.[2] As the price of deliverance from this melancholy cycle, Mark
Twain was obliged to restore Tom Sawyer to the foreground, and to
revert to the strangely compromised, furtive comedy that somehow
overtook him at the outset. His ambivalence toward his refractory material—the unfinished manuscript of *Huckleberry Finn* was no more easily completed than forgotten—is faithfully mirrored at the level of narration in Huck's final sentiments on the score of authorship. "There
ain't nothing more to write about, and I am rotten glad of it, because

if I'd a knowed what a trouble it was to make a book I wouldn't a tackled it and ain't agoing to no more" (362). And with that, he announces his imminent departure for the Territory.

This pattern of uncertainty and ambivalent retreat has been a decisive influence on the general contours of audience response. With Mark Twain and Huck Finn, readers have no doubt been subliminally attuned to the incompatibility of slavery with a sustained and plausible comedic perspective on America. We have shared their deep cultural reluctance to directly acknowledge this enormous obstacle to laughter. Instead, we have been inclined to withdraw along paths that the novel opens up to us. We may follow Mark Twain's example and submit to the alternating currents of a blindly irresolute ambivalence. Or we may surrender the novel's management to Tom Sawyer, and settle for nervous laughter at what he aptly calls the "evasion." As a leading element in this approach, we may wish civilization upon Huck, trusting that the proper training will help to settle the trouble in his mind. Alternatively, we may align ourselves more positively with Huck in the immemorial delusion that the return to Nature will somehow heal the wounds of all God's children and restore us to a peaceable kingdom. Of course we may, with Huck, simply close our eyes and run away. Or, finally, in moments of desperation we may be tempted to emulate in spirit the example of Mark Twain at the first terminal of composition in Chapter 16, when man and boy, black and white, raft and all, go down under the sweep of an enormous, avenging Leviathan. To Hell with it!

But even the apocalypse is inconclusive. Nothing is resolved or revealed; the raft turns up in workable repair and the perilous drift southward is resumed. This is, I take it, the novel's deep meaning. Over and over, one way or another, the seemingly inescapable tragic consequences of the journey are glimpsed and then blinked, skirted and then somehow averted, directly encountered only to be wished away. Audience participation in this process is of course vitally constitutive of meaning so construed. The imperishable currency of *Huckleberry Finn* is part and parcel with its almost ritual authority as a rite of passage. It carries us further into our culture's heart of darkness than is compatible with equanimity; far enough so that we will retreat quite willingly from the dark center to one of the bad-faith perspectives that the novel opens up and validates. This passive, ambivalent, malleably complicit relationship to the narrative finds a striking parallel in the Bricksville crowd's reaction to the murder of Boggs. The people are entertained by the old man's drunken rampages, and they take no action to prevent him from endangering himself, or to interfere with Colonel Sherburn's revenge. In effect, the slaughter of Boggs occurs, public laws and codes of honor notwithstanding, because the people of Bricksville permit it. The episode, I will argue, seems to answer a need arising from the circumstances of their lives. The reaction to the murder tends to confirm this view. The putative claims of justice are subordinated entirely to the craving for spectacle when Sherburn retires unchallenged while the crowd, Huck included, turns its attention to the next act in the exhilarating show. "They took Boggs to a little drug store, the crowd pressing around, just the same, and the whole town following, and I rushed and got a good place at the window, where I was close to him and could see in." There is plenty of competition for the good seats, and people grow impatient, "squirming and scrouging and pushing and shoving to get at the window and have a look." When those in front refuse to move aside for others, the mob surges forward amid appeals to human rights and the spirit of fair play. "Say, now, you've looked enough, you fellows; 'taint right and 'taint fair, for you to stay thar all the time, and never give nobody a chance; other folks has their rights as well as you" (187).

The pious resort to principles of equity and fair play is in perfect bad faith, for the absurd clamoring over audience rights serves to draw attention away from the villagers' complicity in the much heavier injustice that has befallen poor Boggs. The large Bible that is placed on the chest of the expiring victim, and that seems to press the last breath out of his failing body, is richly emblematic of the epidemic of paradoxes at large in the village culture. Public professions of piety and righteousness are not simply hollow and harmless; rather, they are silent but very substantial contributors to much that is unholy in Bricksville. Cruelty and violence are staples of the local diet, yet the citizens of Bricksville are no more willing or able to acknowledge the reality of their condition than they are to avert the murder of Boggs. To do so would entail a very painful recognition of the contradictions in their lives; and it would mean an end to the fun. Instead, they have contrived to indulge their weakness for spectacles of lawless violence and at the same time to persist in the delusion that they are a just, righteous people.

In the most general terms, the reader response to *Huckleberry Finn* and the Bricksville response to the murder of Boggs are parallel in the sense that both involve an audience and an entertainment. More specifically, in both the spectacle dramatizes the cultural condition of the audience, but in ways that ease ambivalence by enabling bad-faith evasions; and in both the audience settles quite readily for the relatively composed perspectives that the spectacle seems at once to invite and exemplify. In both, moreover, audience and entertainment are integral to each other, all of a piece, so that the meaning of the drama is neither in the spectacle nor in the response taken separately, but in the collaboration of audience and actors in the fabrication of a complex, dynamic cultural self-image. The absolutely indispensable element in this paradoxically short-sighted yet penetrating mimesis is, of course, bad faith. It releases the impulses that give rise to the spectacle and determine its content, but at the same time it accounts for the fact that the yielding to lawless violence is never so narrowly scrutinized as to threaten the audience's self-esteem. The citizens of Bricksville have collaborated in the creation of the show, but they have collaborated as well in turning a blind eye to its leading implications.

Meanwhile, as members of the larger, framing audience of *Huckleberry Finn,* we have ourselves been rather slow to grasp the bad faith dynamics of the Boggs murder. This is so, I believe, because the analysis of the cultural reflexivity of the fictional episode leads almost inevitably to the disclosure of a similar dynamic in the relationship between the reader and the novel. The seeming reluctance to come to critical terms with Bricksville may thus be seen as a manifestation of a prior, deeper reluctance to explore fully the implications of our involvement with *Huckleberry Finn.*

II

A culture committed simultaneously to the principles of human freedom and equality, and to the forcible degradation of black human beings to chattel, is quite obviously in the grip of an explosive contradiction. When practical resolutions to the contradiction have been tacitly abandoned as unworkable, the chronic tension that results may necessitate the resort to extreme measures. In good health and in bad, cultures depend for their equilibrium on the liberal application of bad faith. A healthy culture submits to self-deception, generally unacknowledged, in ways that reduce tension, enable free play, and at the same time affirm and reinforce leading systems of value and belief. The mock-resurrection in *Tom Sawyer* fits this pattern. So deployed, bad faith would seem to be indispensable to the maintenance of cultural stability. The deception of self and other ceases to be culturally constructive, however, when it functions to reduce tension and to enable free play in ways that are incompatible with leading systems of value and belief. The Bricksville "evasion" falls into this category. When major disjunctions develop between practice and belief, action and consciousness, in areas of central cultural concern, then bad faith may be said to have entered a pathological phase. It is just such a phase of development that *Tom Sawyer* and *Huckleberry Finn* open for analysis.

The root of this cultural sickness, it bears repeating, is slavery. The bad faith it entails is manifest at several levels in both novels. *Tom Sawyer* may be said to spring from, exemplify, and reinforce a cultural impulse to eclipse the facts of racism and slavery from consciousness. *Huckleberry Finn* may be said to illustrate, again at several levels, the virtually insurmountable problems that issue from the bad-faith acquiescence in racism and slavery, and the evasive maneuverings (*Tom Sawyer* among them) that result. In both novels, the major examples of what I have defined as pathological bad faith may be understood as symptoms, direct or oblique, of this primary cultural disorder. At the same time, however, the books are hardly analytical in any sustained or self-conscious way of the issues they open for critical scrutiny. To the contrary, *Tom Sawyer* and *Huckleberry Finn* derive their popularity, and thus their great cultural authority, from the fact that they simultaneously enact and enable the recapitulation of the bad-faith dynamics they centrally portray. Later on in his career, Mark Twain came to a much fuller conscious understanding of the ways in which racism and slavery spread, like a disease, through the rural American experience that he was compelled, again and again, to remember and to write about. Most especially in *Pudd'nhead Wilson*, he was able to hold at arms length what Henry Nash Smith has called "the tragic theme of slavery, with all it implies of hereditary but constantly renewed guilt and of perverted social conventions distorting human fact. . . . The society of Dawson's Landing imposes upon slaves and masters alike the fictions which sustain the institution of slavery."[3] There is nothing of uncertainty or ambiguity in Mark Twain's assault on the "fiction of law and custom"[4] which makes Roxy and her child black and therefore chattel. Indeed, one of the most mordant of his many ironic thrusts is his analysis of the bad faith that Roxy must resort to in order to save her son.

> With all her splendid common sense and practical every-day ability, Roxy was a doting fool of a mother. She was this toward her child—and she was also more than this: by the fiction created by herself, he was become her master; the necessity of recognizing this relation outwardly and of perfecting herself in the forms required to express the recognition, had moved her to such diligence and faithfulness in practicing these forms that this exercise soon concreted itself into habit; it became automatic and unconscious; then a natural result followed: deceptions intended solely for others gradually grew practically into self-deceptions as well; the mock reverence became real reverence, the mock obsequiousness real obsequiousness, the mock homage real homage; the little counterfeit rift of separation between imitation-slave and imitation-master widened and widened, and became an abyss, and a very real one—and on one side of it stood Roxy, the dupe of her own deceptions, and on the other stood her child, no longer a usurper to her, but her accepted and recognized master.
>
> He was her darling, her master, and her deity all in one, and in her worship of him she forgot who she was and what he had been.[5]

It is unlikely that a more detailed, penetrating analysis of the mechanics of bad faith, and of its spread in a culture of extreme contradictions, can be found in Mark Twain's works.

Yet the gain in conscious clarity brought with it a concomitant loss in popular appeal. *Pudd'nhead Wilson* has been less popular than *Tom Sawyer* and *Huckleberry Finn,* I suspect, because it is relatively more direct and unequivocal than the earlier novels in its portrayal of the hopelessness and inhumanity of slavery. There are no conspicuous omissions here, and the ending does not open up avenues of retreat from a painful encounter with hopeless injustice. Rather, the novel is sparely, relentlessly diagnostic. The narrator is nearly as remote and coolly ironic in his attitude toward his story as David Wilson is to his variously ridiculous neighbors. Both seem to find the matter of Dawson's Landing irresistibly fascinating, and yet both settle rather guardedly into detached perspectives on it. They puzzle over the spectacle they behold, and they at once "solve" it and "distance" it by construing it in mechanical terms. The withdrawal to a mood of clinical detachment, complete with fingerprints, cynical determinism and imperial, almost mechanistic ironies of plot and characterization, is quite evidently the essential correlative of a direct reckoning with this most tragic strain in American history. As in *Tom Sawyer* and *Huckleberry Finn,* the manner of the telling is integral to the presentation of the problem, and at the same time a cue for the audience. Thus *Pudd'nhead Wilson* seems to invite us to focus attention on the complex pattern of ironies emergent from its copious doublings, oppositions, mistaken identities, contradictions, even the author's account of how he found that he was writing "not one story but two stories entangled together."[6] We are encouraged, in other words, to give our attention to the novel's structural geometry, or to ironies that seem safely contained in the narrator's tone or Pudd'nhead's Calendar. In casting ourselves as disinterested spectators to essentially technical operations, we join Mark Twain and David Wilson in neglecting to attend to our own entanglement in the drama unfolding before us. The novel's cultural significance is thus inseparable from its validation of the reader's impulse to back away from its sharp cutting edge, and to view it instead from a detached critical perspective as a diminished, rather mechanical performance.

If the controlled, relentlessly penetrating social analysis set forth in *Pudd'nhead Wilson* has enjoyed less attention than it deserves, this is so in part because the novel makes itself something we can comfortably dismiss. *Pudd'nhead Wilson* expresses its cultural authority by fostering our neglect. The same can hardly be said of *Tom Sawyer* and *Huckleberry Finn,* novels whose address to delicate social issues has been compatible with the cultural prepossessions of enormous popular audiences. At the same time, however, the earlier, "juvenile" books are very different, as I have already suggested, in the latitude of their social vision and, as a result, in their general tone. *Pudd'nhead Wilson* would seem to demonstrate that a too proximate, concentrated exposure to racism and slavery can prompt an audience retreat to safer, cooler perspectives. *Tom Sawyer,* at the opposite extreme, sets its winning festive tone against a background of seemingly effortless hegemony—"seemingly," of course, because the novel's rendering of bad faith depends for its buoyancy on what may seem, when we turn to *Huckleberry Finn,* an extreme distortion of social reality. The books are transpositions of the same social score in dramatically different keys; and the descent to the minor in the sequel is directly the result of Jim's advent. Even before the escaped slave moves into the foreground of the novel, and of Huck's consciousness, the deep social trouble that he represents begins to bleed into the fabric of the narrative. Slavery and racism are everywhere in *Huckleberry Finn;* take them away and the novel loses its center and most of its substance. The utterly intolerable obstacles to human freedom that Huck associates with civilization, and more than once rejects, are in fact shadows cast by Jim and the monstrous institution that binds him. Racism and slavery are the grand cultural progenitors of the pathological bad faith that suffuses the novel; their omnipresence helps to account for the low value placed on life, the tacit legitimacy granted to gross injustice, and the very high general tolerance for all varieties of inhumanity. The culture that engages in feuds and lynchings, that surrenders to the authority of a Sherburn, and that is entertained by perfidious humbug and burning dogs, is a culture that engages first in slavery.

The very pronounced difference in tone between *Tom Sawyer* and *Huckleberry Finn* has been frequently noted and variously explained. The comparison often takes Tom as its point of critical departure, for most readers find that the young hero of the first novel suffers a troublesome transformation in the second. Far and away the most systematic development of this line of thought appears in Judith Fetterley's essay, "Disenchantment: Tom Sawyer in *Huckleberry Finn*." As her title indicates, Fetterley believes that Mark Twain "had become disenchanted with his boy hero" toward the end of *Tom Sawyer,* and that his "disillusionment" is accountable for the unhappy transformation that occurs in the sequel. Specifically, Fetterley finds that the new Tom, unlike the old, is an aggressive, cruel joker; "a creature of delusion" whose rules have lost their former touch with reality; and a "petty tyrant" who has reversed himself and now makes play into work, and who has been obliged to replace pleasure with money as "the currency" of his social control. She observes that a thirst for glory "is nothing new to Tom," but adds that his egotism is no longer redeemed, as it was in *Tom Sawyer,* by its provision of "pleasure for everyone." Finally and rather summarily, she draws Tom into alignment with Miss Watson, arguing that they are "connected through their mutual possession of the syndrome of moralism, aggression, and hypocrisy."[7]

There is much to be said for Fetterley's essay. It addresses itself to a problem fully worthy of the very thoughtful, systematic attention that she provides. Her argument is clearly and plausibly elaborated, and it forms an essential point of departure for subsequent critical discussion. Still, the focus of Fetterley's approach, centering exclusively on Tom, is much too narrow to be fully satisfactory. While she assumes, as I do, that *Huckleberry Finn* is cut from the same cultural cloth as *Tom Sawyer,* she fails to allow for the very marked differences in perspective and tone that turn up within the larger continuity of the two novels. Tom may change, but so does the size of the cultural frame in which he appears, and the point of view from which he is observed. Huck registers no awareness of change in his friend. He is at times uneasy with Tom's jokes and schemes, but he does not suggest that his old companion has altered his ways. Nor is there any expression of deep surprise or displeasure at the Phelps plantation when Tom's "evasion" is revealed. "Look at that, now! I might have expected it" (358), exclaims aunt Polly, much more amused and relieved than upset. So far as his closest friends and relatives are concerned, then, the Tom Sawyer who dominates the closing chapters of *Huckleberry Finn* is recognizably his old self. Thus the testimony provided by the fictional actors strongly suggests that the transformation of the young gamesman in their midst is not as self-evidently complete as Fetterley finds.

To an extent, Fetterley simply overstates her case. For example, the notion that money takes the place of pleasure as a means of control—that Tom's "relationship with the world is no longer the symbiotic one of entertainer and entertained but is rather the tyrannical, aristocratic one of the haves and the have-nots"[8]—seems to ignore the rapid accumulation of Bible tickets at the beginning of *Tom Sawyer*, and the treasure-hunting at its conclusion. This error of emphasis overlaps with the insistence that Tom develops into an "unredeemed egotist" whose craving for attention ceases to be "justified" when it no longer results in pleasure for others. This claim rests on the failure to recognize that Tom's "evasion" is a perfectly characteristic scheme, involving, as he explains to Huck, plans for a climactic return from "the mouth of the river," complete "with a torchlight procession, and a brass band" (360). In overlooking this manifest intention to entertain, Fetterley fails as well to perceive that the crowd at the Phelps plantation is also an audience, summoned there by Tom to witness an exhilarating, socially affirmative spectacle. Tom is thus just as surely a successful entertainer at the end of *Huckleberry Finn* as he is at the beginning of *Tom Sawyer*.

Such exaggerations and oversights in Fetterley's argument are relatively minor distortions that follow naturally enough from the assumption that Tom in fact undergoes major character changes in the course of the two novels. As I have already suggested, however, this assumption loses much of its plausibility once critical attention is brought to bear on the context in which the hero's putative transformation occurs. In the earlier novel, Tom is observed from the point of view of a sophisticated, gently ironic, fondly amused adult. Not surprisingly, when taken in this perspective Tom's activities may seem the happy overflow of liveliness and pluck in an attractive—resourceful, imaginative, fearless—American boy. But it is surely no more surprising that Tom should seem to change when he is seen through Huck Finn's eyes. Huck is self-effacing, morally earnest, skeptical, literal, and virtually without irony or humor. Observed from his "innocent" point of view, the Tom who once seemed boyish and benign may appear cruel, aggressive, grasping, and all the rest of it.

Indeed, to frame Tom in Huck's point of view is to draw two American fables, one of success and the other of innocence, into telling juxtaposition, and to become aware of their profound incompatibility, and of a surprising disparity in their power to compel assent. But if Tom's personal qualities seem to lose their luster when viewed alongside Huck's, then his activities, his manipulative gamesmanship, must appear repellent to us when the field of play is further expanded to include Jim. Social bad faith of the St. Petersburg variety, as exemplified in the behavior of Tom Sawyer, seems benign—indeed, it is in most respects socially beneficial—so long as its dominant role in the rationalization and maintenance of slavery is kept from view. Once that connection is made, however—once the distance between Huck and Tom is transparently the measure of the latter's complicity in racism and slavery— then we recoil from our quondam hero, in part because we are shocked by the unlooked for revelation about him, and in much greater part because of what that revelation implies about us, his admirers, his close cultural kin. Paradoxically, it is precisely our kinship with Tom that prompts us to retreat from the significance of his example; sharing his bad faith, we share his disinclination, his virtual incapacity, to recognize that bad faith for what it is. This reflex self-deception may manifest itself in a variety of ways. We may take Hemingway's lead and baldly dismiss everything after Chapter 31, complaining that it is esthetically inferior. Or we may simply veer away from the troublesome implications of Tom's behavior, settling instead on the conclusion's formal proprieties. Or we may persuade ourselves that there are two Toms: one, an irresistibly good bad boy whom we lovingly claim as our own; the other, a shadow of the original, aberrant, alien, to be disapproved of and rejected. Whatever the avenue of retreat, however, the objective is always the rapid achievement of a comfortable sense of distance from Tom Sawyer. He is ignored, explained away, or dismissed.

The retreat from Tom is generally accompanied by an implicit reconfirmation of esteem for Huck. More than ever—because he seems instinctively to share the impulse to back away from Tom, and because his example may be taken as a source of consolation, and even affirmation—Huck seems one of us. As I shall argue more fully, however, this final surrender to the authority of innocence is the culminating step in the bad-faith refusal, or incapacity, to deal directly with the novel. Huck knows too much to qualify as innocent; he has been much too ready to play along with Tom's heartless game. Huck's innocence is thus the fond illusion of audience bad faith; it is an image of saving ignorance or purity of heart that we retreat to and cling to when confronted, as we are at the end of *Huckleberry Finn,* with more of our reality than we can bear. Huck is one of us not because he is somehow free from implication in what he beholds, but because he responds to a gathering sense of moral complicity by renouncing and running away from the civilization that has formed him. It is Huck's cultural bad faith, as it is ours, to imagine that he can wash his hands of his story.

This contextual dimension to what she calls "disenchantment" appears in full, clear outline just below the surface of Fetterley's argument. She insists that Tom has been transformed; but she demonstrates, without seeming to be aware of it, that the appearance of change in Tom is directly linked to the presence of Jim. Every item on Fetterley's extensive list of changes is illustrated at least once, and most often exclusively, by examples involving Jim. Tom the "compulsive practical joker" takes Jim as his victim; the same joke is offered as an instance of Tom's cruelty; the climactic example of Tom's aggression is the scheme to free an already free man; his addiction to rules, his delusions, his conversion of play into work, his tyranny, his resort to money, his egotism—all these negative qualities are most persuasively illustrated by incidents in which Jim is a leading actor. "Tom gave Jim forty dollars" for being a patient prisoner; "Tom forces Jim to work as hard as any slave in order to carry out his elaborate plans"; "Tom insists on filling Jim's room with snakes and spiders and rats"; "while Tom's plan is elegant and has gobs of style, it effectively destroys Jim's chances for freedom"; and so on.[9] But of course Tom has not changed at all; his behavior is the perfectly consistent expression of his character as it manifests itself in the company of a slave. It is not the sign of a transformation in Tom, as Fetterley suggests, that such conscience and self-perspective as he displays in *Tom Sawyer* are largely absent from his behavior in *Huckleberry Finn;* in the first novel he always appears in the company of white people, while in the second the primary object of his gamesmanship is a slave. Tom is the leading youthful representative of a society that has persuaded itself, against its proudest moral inclinations, that blacks are inferior and their enslavement is just. It is thus consistent in Tom that in his relations with Jim he should display "the self-righteousness of a character who knows exactly what is right and what is wrong."[10] When it comes to black people, Tom does not, in part because he dares not, open himself to doubts. Indeed, the inhibition of reflection on its conspicuous contradictions is integral to the bad faith of the slaveholding ideology. This virtually obligatory evasion in turn nourishes an ambivalence which surfaces in the exaggerated moralism, aggression, and hypocrisy that Fetterley observes in Tom and Miss Watson. The moralism and hypocrisy are essentially defensive reflexes, righteous posturings that serve to rationalize and extenuate the naked aggression of the slave system. But the human qualities that Fetterley isolates for comment have been perfectly evident in St. Petersburg, as they are to some degree in all societies, from the beginning. The new, really repellent ingredient is slavery, a supplement to the portrait of village social life that casts the moralism and hypocrisy and aggression into sharp relief, and that looms in *Huckleberry Finn* as an insuperable obstacle to the sense of warm affinity that most readers feel for *Tom Sawyer*.

Fetterley's neglect of the contextual factors that inform our perception of Tom may be viewed as culturally symptomatic. This is not to suggest that there is anything in the slightest wrong or wrong-headed in her very useful essay. Rather, it is to claim her perspective as our own, and to invite reflection on the ways in which her management of emphasis and implication speaks for the culture at large. The narrowing of the critical focus to the characterization of Tom is most notable in this regard. For while this approach has a cultural "cost" in the apparent degradation of the youthful hero, it amply compensates us by drawing attention and the threat of reproach away from the larger cultural frame in which Tom operates. The trouble that we sense and shy away from in *Huckleberry Finn*—a feeling, perhaps, of implication in the novel's unsettling conclusion—is labeled "disenchantment" and safely pinned on the somehow transformed and alien figure of Tom. This distancing strategy is cognate with the evasion of implication that the slaveholding society angles for in its righteous moralizing, and that Tom seems to enjoy in his respectably "authorized" playing with poor Jim. Nor does disenchantment finally deprive us of a hero. For by making two Toms out of one, and then dismissing the cruel egotist who misuses Jim, we acknowledge and dispel our uneasiness with the novel's final chapters and at the same time deliver the "good" Tom from the threat of contamination. Disenchantment is thus hardly thrust upon us. Rather, it belongs with piety that protests too much, with Tom's evasion, and, as I shall argue, with Huck's running away, as a culturally characteristic bad-faith response to the trouble that Jim brings with him into *Huckleberry Finn*.

This is not to suggest that Jim's impact on "the matter of Hannibal" is somehow confined to the transformation, actual or perceived, of the young hope of St. Petersburg. To the contrary, the comparison between *Tom Sawyer* and *Huckleberry Finn* yields abundant evidence that the addition of a black slave to Mark Twain's principal dramatis personae was sweeping in its influence on the tone of and general response to the latter novel. On one side, for example, consider that "Huck's confidence in the human race was well nigh obliterated" (173) when Tom violates their blood oath to "keep mum" about the murder of Dr. Robinson. Readers seldom pause for long over this detail, in part at least because it is offered up almost casually, and without comment or elaboration, in the midst of a long disquisition on Tom. It is quite another matter, however, when Huck appears ready to break his promise not to turn Jim over to the slaveholding authorities. The moral and legal pressure on the boys in these parallel circumstances is equally great, and the felt threat of danger is roughly equivalent. But while Tom's actual betrayal of Huck goes virtually unnoticed, the mere threat of Huck's betrayal of Jim gives rise to pages of intense, celebrated soul-searching. This puzzling disparity tells us something about differences in characterization and point of view; but at its root it speaks of our culture's deeply ambivalent disposition to race–slavery. The comparison of Injun Joe and Jim, both as they are represented and received, sheds light on the same phenomenon. Most readers of *Tom Sawyer* are prepared to recognize that Injun Joe is a victim of racial prejudice; the text makes this clear enough. It is equally notable that for most readers the novel seems to invite the absorption of racial considerations into much larger, "universal" anthropological or psychological frames of reference. Thus we are inclined to lose sight of the half-breed in the scapegoat, or in the dark bearer of society's repressed sexual energy. But the racism that figures in the abuse of Jim is not so readily dealt with. Indeed, where we witness the fear and hatred and mistreatment and death of Injun Joe with relative equanimity, we bring anxious, lingering uncertainty to a story that features long intervals of relative racial amity and that culminates in the liberation of a slave. Again, the disparity can be tied to formal differences between the novels; but it is also evidence that we grow uncomfortable with images of racism, as we do with images of human betrayal, when they are drawn into direct association with the familiar circumstances of slavery in America. When Huckleberry Finn threatens to turn Jim over to the authorities, the fantasy of interracial concord and liberation seems poised for a fall into American history.

We are most aware of the discord that accompanies slavery into *Huckleberry Finn* when Jim is present. But the burden of the tragic theme is also discernible when he has withdrawn from the foreground, even when the comic energy of the novel is most engaged. We are amused by the duke and the king, as we are always amused by flim-flam, especially when it feeds on folly and hypocrisy. But we are never fully comfortable with these resourceful frauds because Jim is one of their victims—and perhaps the only one who does not in any way deserve what he gets. Indeed, our disenchantment with the confidence men deepens precisely as they become more deeply a threat to Jim's well-being. At first, though we may share Huck's worries about their plans for Jim, we are also amused and distracted by the broad, farcical play of deception between the clowns and their audience. The laughter is dampened quite considerably when the impostors divide up and auction the slave family left by Peter Wilks, sending the sons to Memphis and their mother down the river to New Orleans. With their final betrayal of Jim, the show is over. Or, rather, the comedy is over. For the impulse to be entertained is hardly inhibited by a turn toward seriousness. To the contrary, the play of bad faith seems to intensify as the gravity of the drama deepens, suggesting that the pleasures of passive absorption in cultural play have given way to more urgent demands for distraction from the untoward exposure of the culture's darker realities. Jim's presence, especially as his suffering increases toward the end of the novel, does not stop the show; but it subdues laughter, forcing the audience to witness that in itself which causes the painful injustice, and which explains the addiction to distracting amusements. The final performance in *Huckleberry Finn,* Tom's spectacular scheme to free a free slave, simply takes this tendency to an extreme. The spectators—and of course I mean to include readers in the audience—witness the attempt to make a childish game, an amusing skit, of their history's darkest chapter, and they try, in rather desperate bad faith, to see the humor in the thing, or to dismiss it altogether from consideration.

We may observe a similar pattern in the sad conclusion to the Wilks episode. The mob that tars and feathers the duke and king imagines that it is serving justice on two guileful frauds. There is some truth in this, but there is a larger measure of bad faith. For the perfectly transparent—not to say bumbling—deceptions practiced by the false claimants succeed only because the townspeople suspend their disbelief in the service of amusement. Cooler heads warn them away from foolish gullibility—Dr. Robinson declares publicly that the king is "a fraud" and "the thinnest kind of an imposter" (218–19)—but the rank and file are hungry for pleasurable diversions, and therefore willing to be taken in. Paradoxically, then, the members of the mob are moved to violence not primarily because they have been deceived, but because they have been *un*deceived. Thus the tar and feathers figure centrally in a culturally apposite sequel to the amusement that ends when the conmen are exposed. It is a spectacle in which the audience reacts to the revelation of its self-deception by dramatically refabricating the illusion that it has been deceived. The violence of the action has little ultimate relation to justice, but simply measures the degree of inflated self-righteousness that the crowd must resort to in order to distract itself from the revelation of its bad faith.

The mob that participates in the punishment of the duke and king is composed of many of the same people who fail to intervene when the impostors heartlessly auction the slaves. The family and the community express shock, of course—the auction "injured the frauds some" (234), Huck observes—but there is no evident impulse to intervene, no willingness, apparently, to interrupt the gratifying flow of things. In human terms, the price of the amusement that the swindlers provide is greatest at this interval when movements of compassion and simple justice yield to the yearning for a show. Once again it appears that the hunger for amusement arises in good part out of an unspoken desire to mollify conscience by drawing attention away from the moral lapses it has witnessed. More specifically, the endless rage for diversion in *Huckleberry Finn* is an oblique manifestation of the culture's submerged discomfort with itself, most especially with the inhumanity of its treatment of black people. Race—slavery is the deeply inhuman strand of bad faith that gives rise to the mania for shows, and that the shows are increasingly compelled to act out. Again, we are reminded of Tom Sawyer's concluding performance.

To the extent that shows such as Tom's fail to entertain, they may be viewed as symptoms of a breakdown in the culture's mission to affirm and amuse itself in dramatic reconfirmations of its preferred self-conceptions. Laughter gives way when these illusions fail to win complete assent and credulity. Such lapses never really occur in *Tom Sawyer*. To be sure, the narrator occasionally erupts at the sight of hypocrisy, and the readers' composure may be slightly shaken at moments when the seams and wrinkles in village life come to view. But for the most part the citizens of St. Petersburg and their audience behold in Tom's adventures a series of amusing, warmly affirmative enactments of their happiest cultural prepossessions. With the appearance of Jim in *Huckleberry Finn*, however, such gratifying illusions and the equanimity they breed rapidly dissipate, and the narrative never recovers the confident, effortless comic tone of its predecessor. Jim and what he represents are the rub; but the same bad faith that enslaves him works to obscure the tragedy that it has engendered. The novel is thus instinct with darkness, yet the circumstances that give rise to the terrible trouble are never acknowledged, and the seemingly irresistible narrative surge toward catastrophe is indefinitely forestalled. In the upshot, Huck is never able to locate the precise source of his uneasiness, and of his final decision to run away; his neighbors never glimpse the fact that the violence of their diversions measures a taste for brutality unleashed by slavery; and the narrative impulse to rise to comedy never gets far off the ground.

Yet the pattern of evasion in the novel is no more pronounced than the pattern of repetition. His extreme discomfort notwithstanding, Huck responds to a need to tell his story. Though their public amusements frequently turn sour, the crowds along the river continue to go to shows. And *Huckleberry Finn* is far and away the most popular of the great American novels in spite of manifest inconsistencies of plot and tone, a conclusion that few enjoy and many ignore, and little of the sustained humor and clarity of point that generally attracts readers to Mark Twain. The third of these closely related riddles begins to open itself when we reflect that *Huckleberry Finn* is that rarest and most indispensable literary quantity, a novel about slavery that we can bear to read. This most widely read of our canonical fictions is evidence that we are culturally compelled to bear witness to the reality of racism and slavery, but powerless to view that reality directly or for long or in any save historical terms. We can bring ourselves to acknowledge Jim and some of what attaches to him, but only when he is viewed through a child's eyes, as an object for child's play, in a remote past time. Of course, the urgent mitigative impulse in all of this betrays the fact that racism and slavery are simply too much—of injustice and contradiction and suffering and fear—to handle in a direct, sustained way. Thus *Huckleberry Finn* succeeds with us because it permits us to see and not to see the same thing.

But the evasion that enables our return to this virtually obligatory cultural experience also works to distort the novel's surface, and to undermine its capacity to please. Huck's rambling, uncertain narrative is replete with vague, undeveloped intimations of trouble, and it is unsettling in its elusive challenges to leading heroes and myths. As the result, it tends to stifle laughter and festivity at what is confidently assumed to be their source. Yet we return to *Huckleberry Finn,* and we read it to our children. It is as though the cultural pathology deeply inscribed in the novel enforces a compulsion to witness periodic reenactments of its bad-faith sources and symptoms. This rending tale of drift, betrayal, violence, and injustice is viewed as a national oracle, approached in the anticipation of laughter and affirmation, experienced as something incoherent, disturbing, to varying degrees depressing, yet returned to again and again with the original expectations virtually intact.

A similar and related inclination to seek amusement in spectacles potent with disappointment and disaster is everywhere to be observed in the novel itself. The mob's response to the clown who happens into their midst after the Boggs murder is an obvious case in point. But Tom's collaboration with his audience in the putative comedy of freeing an already free man is the most elaborate example of what I have in mind, and it is quite properly and pointedly placed within the text. It is the culminating instance of the evasion of dramatic implication that is prominently a characteristic of audience response both within *and* without *Huckleberry Finn.* So long as the attempt, and the failure, to sustain a comic perspective on racism and slavery goes unacknowledged, the darkly equivocal cast of that failure is at liberty to spread, like a shadow, across the face of all that surrounds it. Thus there is no fully satisfying relief from the consequences of this pathological bad faith, since all sources of distraction are touched by the influence of the primary disorder. Instead, there is blind, unsatisfying repetition: first, the evasion that gives rise to the compulsion to be distracted; then the evasion of the failure to be distracted in the renewal of the search. For Mark Twain's admirers, this circular pattern has expressed itself in generations of telling and retelling *Huckleberry Finn.* In Huck's narrative, meanwhile, it appears as a series of attempts to find distraction and to recover laughter in an endless round of amusements.

III

The action of *Huckleberry Finn* takes rise, it will be recalled, from Huck's decision to return to the widow's house, and to respectability, as the price of membership in Tom Sawyer's gang. The novel has a point of departure, in other words, in the ambition to be amused. For most readers, as for Huck, the initial prospects for pleasure, for more of *Tom Sawyer,* seem bright. But the first prank takes Jim as its victim, and turns on the superstition and gullibility attributed to him as a black person. Huck is quite evidently uncomfortable with this game, and his initial reluctance to play along settles into a suspicion of Tom's schemes that persists after the practical joking with Jim is behind them. Subsequent adventures seem increasingly implausible and flat to him—just another "of Tom Sawyer's lies" (17)—and before long he gives up altogether on the effort to "make" fun. Most readers share Huck's disenchantment with Tom's games; they feel, somehow, that the happy brand of adventure witnessed in *Tom Sawyer* has lapsed into a strained, even false variety of make-believe. But while we are ready enough to share Huck's view that Tom's plots have "all the marks of a Sunday school" (17), we are much less likely to connect the general loss of pleasure in play to Tom's unthinking mistreatment of Jim. Our own ambition to be amused—based for many on expectations derived from *Tom Sawyer*—and a cultural aversion to encounters with the harsh realities of racism and slavery (especially in books ostensibly for children) strongly incline us to duck the implications of Tom's behavior. Characteristically, levels of bad faith mirror one another; our failure to see recapitulates Tom's (and Huck's). Yet the link between Tom's prank and race–slavery is surely there, submerged in our subsequent incapacity to be amused by childish diversions.

From the very beginning, then, the bright, unmingled pleasure promised by *Huckleberry Finn* is subverted by a brush with the historical reality, carefully held to the margins of *Tom Sawyer,* most responsible for the pathological strain in American cultural bad faith. In more ways than one, Jim spoils the fun. Once properly admitted to his place in St. Petersburg, he moves irresistibly to the foreground, displacing other business, transforming tone. He brings a mood of sadness and guilt and fear and a sense of hopelessness into that rural landscape, that garden, where national heroes and myths have flourished; indeed, he threatens us with the knowledge that those optimistic images are precious in good part because of what they exclude, because of the respite they provide from unbearable realities. Our capacity for pleasure in Tom is strained to breaking with the appearance of Jim. That strain in our feelings toward the former hero bears with it an implicit challenge to the assumption, quintessentially cultural in origin, that boys like Tom and Huck are constitutionally incapable of harm. The essential purity of preadolescent males of a certain rural, plucky, unlettered but resourceful variety, is a notion freighted with the profound cultural longing for redemption from the burden of history. In boys and in boyishness we behold a vision of how it might have been, of how it should be. But the weight of the culture that formed the history overpowers the fantasy. No sooner has Jim come to view than Huck acquiesces in Tom's mistreatment of him, and we are moved reluctantly toward the recognition that boyish bad faith is a mirror of the adult variety, and that our smiling disregard of the former is tantamount to a refusal to acknowledge the latter.

The bad-faith retreat from dramatic implication, especially as it bears on Jim, tends to work as a subtle, nameless stay on our laughter. The potential for such deflation of humorous pleasure is greatest, as I have already suggested, when Jim and Huck are alone together. This is because Huck's racism, and the cruel behavior that it provokes in him, are erosive of the cultural fantasy of racial concord that the novel awakens. We are amused and gratified in a rather special way by the "set piece" in which Huck and Jim argue about the morality in King Solomon's threat to carve a child in two. Yet this brief interlude, a favorite with audiences at Mark Twain's readings, quite subtly subverts laughter by belatedly exposing the racist assumptions woven through the fabric of the comedy. From the outset, the humor of the dialogue has its principal source in the gullibility and literal-mindedness that fall as attributes to Jim because he is black. This may seem harmless enough, especially as Jim's childish simplicity has great humanity as its implied correlative. But when Huck responds to Jim's ingenious logic with the reflection, "I see it warn't no use wasting words—you can't learn a nigger to argue. So I quit" (98), the fundamental injustice and potential for harm coiled up in the humor come suddenly and very disturbingly to view. The entire episode, the diminutive comical show, turns sour to the taste as our earlier amusement surfaces as evidence of our complicity in the racist assumptions underlying Huck's angry, imperious injustice. Huck's bad faith compounds itself later on when he contrives to confirm his conviction of Jim's mental inferiority. For the reader, meanwhile, bad faith may seize upon Huck's conspicuous prejudice as the exclusive focus of attention; or, unwilling to countenance that much mean-mindedness in the innocent boy, we may simply laugh it off and turn the page.

In due course, I will elaborate much more fully on the pattern of disenchantment as it unfolds in Huck's experience, and as it is mirrored in our own. First, however, I want to expand a bit more on the failure of amusements to amuse in the larger action of the novel. My wish here is to emphasize that the simultaneous craving and incapacity for pleasurable diversion are everywhere to be found in *Huckleberry Finn,* even when their principal cause is not immediately present to sight and mind. This general and persistent pattern recurs in the sequence of shows—some presented formally, others simply emerging as collective energies find focus, all somehow compromised, and many linked in more or less obvious ways—that commence with the appearance of the king and the duke. Virtually from the moment of their arrival Huck tolerates, and even indulges, the pair of derelict frauds, not because he is taken in by their preposterous claims, but because he wishes to preserve the peace aboard the raft, and because the newcomers are a source of amusement. The confidence men's initial angling for aristocratic preeminence is a comic masterpiece of bad faith maneuvering in which competing lies strike a prudent bad faith truce. Huck is hardly fooled by pretensions to royal "rights" (164) and titles, but he enters with ease into a posture of seeming credulity. If we sense that this much deception, however comical, cannot be a good thing, it may be because Huck's readiness to appear to be fooled has a parallel in the readiness to fool himself, and Jim. I refer here to his decision not to share what he knows about the king and duke with his friend. "It warn't no use to tell Jim," he reflects, "so I didn't tell him" (165). Huck may have persuaded himself that Jim will react with confusion or disappointment to·the truth about the intruders. But to characterize complete candor as of "no use" on such grounds is surely disingenuous. Jim would have no trouble understanding what the king and the duke are up to. And he would be disappointed with the truth not because of the collapse of a happy illusion—indeed, he recognizes that the royalty on board are pretty poor specimens—but because it would confirm his undoubted and very reasonable suspicion that the mountebanks represent a serious obstacle to his quest for freedom. Knowing what he does about the frauds, Huck cannot fail to recognize for a certainty what Jim merely senses. Yet he elects to withhold his knowledge, and thereby denies Jim the opportunity to deal with the danger in his own way. Perhaps Huck's decision not to tell is the reflex of his fear that Jim will react to the truth by running away; perhaps, too, it expresses a fatalistic surrender to the inevitable failure of the quest for freedom. Whatever the case, the "no use" that Huck appeals to cannot possibly speak for Jim, even though in declining to share what he knows Huck does just that.

Social roles established and their small audience properly disposed, the royalty next set about planning the confidence schemes that they will spring on the unsuspecting villagers along the shore. The first of these, an enormously profitable dip into the proceeds of a camp meeting, sets the tone for the shows that follow. The success enjoyed by the confidence men has its source in their genius for the detection of the motives that drive collective endeavors, but that human beings hide from themselves and each other under civilized covers of one kind or another. Generally speaking, the simple folk along the Mississippi want to think of themselves as respectable, but at the same time they hanker for diversions of an earthy, not to say barbaric, cast. The king and duke recognize this, and they know that if they can contrive to serve the crude bumpkin in the name of the God-fearing citizen, then the opportunities for exploitation and profit are virtually unlimited. In effect, that confidence game succeeds best that most faithfully mirrors the specific variety of social bad faith practiced by its audience. In the case of the camp meeting, the driving impulse is a desire for excitement and the indulgence of passionate feeling. The cover is an organized revival of Christian faith. By providing the multitude with an abundance of pleasure mantled in the barest minimum of obligatory piety, the king and the duke have the audience, and a lot of their money, in their back pockets. The king gets at the essence of the formula for success in "the missionarying line" when he observes that "heathens don't amount to shucks, alongside of pirates, to work a camp-meeting with" (174).

High culture replaces religion as the perfectly transparent pretext for crude diversions in the grand "Shakesperean Revival" that the derelict thespians rehearse next. Huck is spellbound by popular romantic selections from *Romeo and Juliet* and *Richard III,* but his most enthusiastic praise is reserved for the duke's rendering of a well-thumbed soliloquy from *Hamlet.*

> So he went to marching up and down, thinking, and frowning hor-
> rible every now and then; then he would hoist up his eye-brows; next
> he would squeeze his hand on his forehead and stagger back and kind of
> moan; next he would sigh, and next he'd let on to drop a tear. It was
> beautiful to see him . . . Then he strikes a most noble attitude, with
> one leg shoved forwards, and his arms stretched away up, and his head
> tilted back, looking up at the sky; and then he begins to rip and rave
> and grit his teeth; and after that, all through his speech he howled, and
> spread around, and swelled up his chest, and just knocked the spots out
> of any acting ever *I* see before.   (178–79)

Indeed, Huck is so impressed with what he has seen that he is moved,
as he sets off with the king and the duke for Bricksville, to describe the
theatrical extravaganza that they have rigged up as "our show" (180).

Initial prospects for success are very good. As it happens, a circus is
just about to pack up and there are lots of country folk in town primed
for a good time. So the duke rents the court house and posts bills announcing a one-time-only evening performance. To kill time before the
big event, Huck wanders through the backward Arkansas village only
to find himself, the would-be entertainer, a witness to a series of quite
arresting shows. The town is itself strangely like a set, with houses and
fences set in a row along a single street. In fact, with appropriate adjustments to paint and props, the scene served Mark Twain as a kind of
stage property, a permanent fixture in the Hannibal repertory including such works as "Old Times on the Mississippi," *A Connecticut Yankee
in King Arthur's Court, The Tragedy of Pudd'nhead Wilson,* and *The Mysterious Stranger.* In this instance, the stage is occupied by a gang of
young loafers with virtually interchangeable names and costumes who
pass the time by chewing tobacco and exchanging familiar jokes and
insults. Their own routine is so devoid of excitement that the young
toughs—"a mighty ornery lot" (181), Huck observes—find amusement in siccing dogs on a nursing sow. "Then you would see all the
loafers get up and watch the thing out of sight, and laugh at the fun
and look grateful for the noise." So culturally impoverished and utterly,
pathologically bored are these rural types that they have developed a
taste for cruelty and violence in their distractions. As Huck observes
them, they appear a small cluster of spectators at their ease on a make-
shift balcony where they await yet another development in the passing
scene. Once the terrified sow has disappeared, they "settle back again
till there was a dog-fight. There couldn't anything wake them up all
over, and make them happy all over, like a dog-fight—unless it might

be putting turpentine on a stray dog and setting fire to him, or tying a tin pan to his tail and see him run himself to death" (183).

Like the members of the camp meeting, the Bricksville loafers get precisely what they bargain for in their amusements. Spectacles of violence draw their attention away from the grinding torpor of their lives, and at the same time express the rage that those pointless lives must breed. Once again, then, the show mirrors the life of its audience, though in this case, presumably because the victims are animals, the brutalization of both actors and spectators is unashamedly manifest and seeks no excuse, no bad-faith cover. The varieties of satisfaction to be sought from the equivalent treatment of human beings cannot be so openly sought; but the dark interlude of animal torture serves nonetheless as a kind of rough index to the level of stimulation that the Bricksvillians have come to require in their amusements.

Thus the Boggs episode which immediately follows is structurally reminiscent of the spectacle that precedes it, though the pitch of excitement achieved is greater because the stakes are higher, and because the virtually inevitable denouement is viewed by the audience as a surprise. The edge of the crowd's anticipation grows sharper during a brief interval in which Huck witnesses "three fights" and "considerable whiskey drinking." Seeming to smell trouble, newcomers gather along the street. Then, as if the spontaneous outgrowth of audience expectations, entertainment materializes before their eyes.

> "Here comes old Boggs!—in from the country for his little old monthly drunk—here he comes, boys!"
> All the loafers looked glad—I reckoned they was used to having fun out of Boggs.   (183–84)

Like the dogs before him, Boggs is baited, hooked, pursued by the consequences of his own comparatively harmless folly, and senselessly destroyed. But the abundant distraction to be had in this melodrama—humor of a crude sort, then the suspense that issues from Sherburn's ultimatum, flight, and terrifying bloodshed—is virtually inseparable, as I have already indicated, from the bad-faith failure to acknowledge that the sanguinary action is silently shaped by audience design and enabled by tacit audience consent. Boggs is just fun, the spectators assure themselves. And then they stand by while he approaches and verbally assaults the predatory Sherburn; instead of removing him from harm's way, they turn the problem over to his young daughter; they offer no objection when Sherburn violates the conditions of the original, "honorable" ultimatum; and, as the crisis gathers to its climax, they draw away from the poor, foolish victim, leaving him alone, helpless, and utterly terrified before his cold-blooded murderer. By their conspicuous, fatal passivity, the spectators get precisely what they came for: violent distraction offered up in a manner compatible with the illusion of respectability.

But the bloody event that the villagers witness is theirs not simply because of the familiar, violent scenario it enacts; it is profoundly theirs as well because of its conspicuous theatricality, its development in their midst as an apparently discrete and autonomous dramatic action—a play—seeming to unfold comfortably outside the circle of their influence or responsibility. The complicity concealed in this evasive illusion comes obliquely to view in the waves of turbulence that roll through the audience. The crowding and complaining at the drug store grow increasingly disproportionate to any objective cause, and are finally so intense that Huck, "thinking maybe there was going to be trouble," withdraws to the comparative calm of the street. But there are crowds outside as well. Something is not right, they sense, and their response is a groping attempt to retell the episode in words compatible with collective equanimity.

> Everybody that seen the shooting was telling how it happened, and there was a big crowd packed around each one of these fellows, stretching their necks and listening. One long lanky man, with long hair and a big white fur stove-pipe hat on the back of his head, and a crooked-handled cane, marked out the places on the ground where Boggs stood, and where Sherburn stood, and the people following him around from one place to t'other and watching everything he done, and bobbing their heads to show they understood, and stooping a little and resting their hands on their thighs to watch him mark the places on the ground with his cane; and then he stood up straight and stiff where Sherburn had stood, frowning and having his hat-brim down over his eyes, and sung out, "Boggs!" and then fetched his cane down slow to a level, and says "Bang!" staggered backwards, says "Bang!" again, and fell down flat on his back. The people that had seen the thing said he done it perfect; said it was just exactly the way it all happened. Then as much as a dozen people got out their bottles and treated him.   (187–88)

It is noteworthy that the novel's readers, cast here once again as the framing audience to an inside audience witnessing a darkly meaningful show, have been inclined to pass this puzzling entertainment by, as Huck does, without comment. The crowd storms off to lynch Sherburn, and Huck follows. We all glimpse, I suspect, that the little drama is somehow true to our cultural condition; but we do not stay for an answer.

In any case, the "long lanky man" yields little to interpretation until he is identified as a leading figure in the cultural self-dramatization that unfolds in the village street. Evidently enough, he is an actor, a showman; indeed, he may be a clown from the circus that Huck will sneak into later in the day. But the utter uncertainty that gathers to this strange, really alien character—his identity, origins, and motives are quite obscure—combines with his expressive energy to render him a figure of mystery and enigmatic charisma. If he is a clown, then he is a clown of the transcendent variety, a figure who may quite plausibly stand in the place of his maker, as the culture's leading popular artist, spokesman, mimic, and interpreter. For it is the clown's genius, as it is Mark Twain's, and Tom's, to portray the audience to itself, to impersonate its experience and character, in a manner compatible with its ruling self-image, cultural template, or myth. The entertainer may satirize, sermonize, criticize, but to be widely heard and heeded he must return to his audience only as much of its reality as it can bear with equanimity. By instinct and training and unconscious reflex, in short, he must be the confident master of his culture's bad faith.

The clown quite clearly establishes his credentials as cultural virtuoso in his brief pantomime. He seems to intuit that the crowd is ready for a distraction from the rising tension at the drug store; and his costume is well designed to attract attention. Most vitally of all, however, he grasps the fact that his prospective audience, in its boisterous crowding and talking, is feeling its way toward a comfortable perspective on the disaster it has just witnessed. But peace of mind and social tranquility will not descend on the villagers until they find a way to blink their complicity in poor Boggs's demise and, by implication, in the lawless cruelty and violence that pervade their lives. Frustration at the failure to adequately submerge such apprehensions registers in the brittle uncertainty of the crowd's mood; in effect, the Bricksvillians need relief from an excess of their own reality. It is integral to the clown's mastery that he does not attempt to remove the source of the trouble from sight and mind. That would be too conspicuously an evasion; and it would probably backfire. Rather, he employs his art to so re-present that troubling reality that it ceases to stir ambivalence and discord. Most obviously, he mollifies crowd consciousness by presenting the murder in a way that substantially diminishes its violence and its implicit reproach. There is no blood in the pantomime, no gun, no sodden, writhing victim; and there is no daughter, "very sweet and gentle-looking, but awful pale and scared" (187), for conscience to shrink from. It is the surest index of the clown's success that the members of his audience are pleased with what they think of as the pantomime's fidelity to its origin; in fact, of course, they are pleased with its fidelity to their prepossessions. Though they consciously assent to and applaud the ostensible verisimilitude of the performance, their approval is unconsciously a response to the transformation and virtual displacement of the murder, not to its reenactment. Finally, the clown succeeds because he dissipates the townspeople's vexing intimations of complicity in the dramatic blood-letting. This deflation of resurgent anxiety results from the interposition of yet another show, a mimetic transformation of its predecessor, in which threatening implications are muted and safely folded away in a smooth, silent, coolly detached envelope of art. Freed from their unsettling sense of entanglement, the people promptly identify the villain in the piece and assign a penalty. All doubts dispatched, all righteous self-confidence restored, the audience, now quite suddenly a mob again, pauses only long enough to toast the clown and take a little courage of their own. Then "away they went," Huck reports, "mad and yelling, and snatching down every clothes-line they come to, to do the hanging with" (188).

IV

The angry townspeople who swarm "up the street, towards Sherburn's house" (189) have cast themselves as heroic protagonists in a spectacle of righteous retribution. Ironically, their energy in the pursuit of justice may be viewed as a kind of rebound from the feelings of guilty complicity that the clown has just helped them to shed. Having successfully evaded the moral burden of the Boggs murder, the townspeople now rush, quite exuberantly, to unload it on Sherburn. The lynching party serves a second, equally unacknowledged, equally ironic objective in its provision of yet more distraction—most immediately, from the lingering sense of implication in the murder; more generally, from the unbearable poverty and tedium of village life. Justice, though advanced like a banner in the mob's midst, is really quite secondary.

The hue and cry after Sherburn, like the various spectacles that immediately precede and follow it, is finally just another scene in a much
larger, virtually continuous bad-faith play.

The setting for this action is appropriately theatrical. The crowd
comes suddenly to a halt as the villain "steps out onto the roof of his
little front porch, with a double-barrel gun in his hand." As his now
strangely docile and attentive neighbors take their places at his feet,
the Colonel, apparently familiar with the script, moves confidently
into his role. First he

> run his eye slow along the crowd; and wherever it struck, the people
> tried a little to outgaze him, but they couldn't; they dropped their eyes
> and looked sneaky. Then pretty soon Sherburn sort of laughed; not the
> pleasant kind, but the kind that makes you feel like when you are eating
> bread that's got sand in it.   (189–90)

Without so much as uttering a word, the masterful Sherburn establishes both his moral and his dramatic authority. Indeed, his speechless
triumph demonstrates that in ethics, as in all things in Bricksville, the
play is paramount. That illusion which best holds and fills consciousness defines reality. Thus the mob that came to exact rough justice now
quite readily forms itself into a silent, pliant audience waiting, in effect, to be moved. For in the imperious, vengeful face that Sherburn
shows them they see not the villain they consciously expected, but a
Jeremiah, the morally outraged instrument of an angry God. The
townspeople are awed and frightened and about to be humiliated by
Sherburn, but they stay for the show. Evidently enough, he promises
to give them what their culture, as it is manifest in their behavior,
causes them to require.

In assuming the mantle of preacher to an errant flock, Colonel Sherburn delivers a sermon with a clear, blunt point. His auditors, he
thunders, are contemptible. They are all that their presence at his
house would seem to indicate; an aggregation of cowards individually
too spineless to stand behind their public codes of justice, and as a
group willing to hazard their enforcement only when lead by "half a
man," if such a rarity is to be found in their midst. Paradoxically, then,
Sherburn's most immediate and graphic illustration of his point is the
crowd's fearful failure to hang him. Furthermore, by his bold defiance
of the mob, Sherburn demonstrates that he is the only man present
with the moral fibre to take command. But if there is something plausible and disturbing in what the Jeremiah witnesses in his flock, there

is something much more upsetting in the values that his sermon bodies forth, and that his audience, by their telling silence, seem to acknowledge as their own. To be sure, the people of Bricksville lack the courage of their moral convictions; but what shall we make of that brand of fearless righteousness that expresses itself in the slaughter of helpless old men? A little reflection will show that Sherburn's implied code features an equation of virtue with a ferocious brand of individual self-reliance. Might is right, with the correlative that weakness is a species of wrong. Boggs dies not because he is morally out of line, but because he is individually out of control, contemptibly weak and defenseless. The vast majority of people, Sherburn believes, are akin to Boggs in their weakness. "The average man's a coward" (190), he insists; even worse, the average man refuses to acknowledge his cowardice for what it is. In the northern states, he has found, men hide their fear under a mantle of Christian forbearance; in the South they join their neighbors in the illusion that they are all fearless individualists. But fear of one stamp or another is as broadcast in Sherburn's America as the hypocrisy, the pervasive bad faith, that it fosters, and that he recoils from in disgust.

Sherburn's snarling assault on his audience proceeds from the implied premise that individuals are utterly incapable of standing openly and alone in the defense of their rights and values. As the result, they retreat to the safety of society. But the same fear that prompts the retreat to collective social arrangements persists as an obstacle to the efficient, consistent advancement of justice. "Why don't your juries hang murderers?" the Colonel asks, in a gesture of supreme defiance. "Because they're afraid the man's friends will shoot them in the back, in the dark—and it's just what they *would* do." The craven failure of enforcement, he goes on, leads to the formation of equally cowardly lynch mobs, who disguise their fear behind masks and darkness, and who require the leadership of "a *man*" in order to overcome the fear that rules them. Thus it is an ignominious circle of fear and hypocrisy that Sherburn beholds in his community. The cowardice that gives rise to laws also subverts their enforcement, with the result that the mass of men either surrender to criminal intimidation or adopt the methods of criminal intimidation themselves. In either outcome, however, those rare individuals who pass through life without fear are destined to assume roles of leadership in a thoroughly unjust reign of terror. For as the Colonel reiterates before commanding his auditors "to droop your tails and go home and crawl in a hole," and as the situation itself quite dramatically illustrates, "a mob without any *man* at the head of it, is *beneath* pitifulness" (190–91).

The general tone and many of the leading features of Sherburn's speech are reminiscent, as I have already suggested, of the Puritan jeremiad, a popular form of public address that has retained a remarkable cultural currency in America from the founding in New England to the present day.[11] The speaker's confident adoption of an elevated perspective on the fallen human scene, and his rapid-fire delivery of searing judgments on the heads of his auditors, are familiar elements of the genre. The same may be said of his severe Calvinistic emphasis on the general and utterly hopeless human surrender to depravity, the precarious doomsday mood that accompanies this charge, and the indication that a small group of mortals, an elect, are exempted for no apparent reason from the burden of sin. It is also quite characteristic of the American jeremiad to draw attention to the consequences of human sinfulness as they are manifest in the woeful corruption of the social order. Sherburn is properly the determinist in locating the source of Bricksville's trouble in the helpless inadequacy of human nature. The gravity of the moral predicament is many times compounded by the fact that its victims are powerless to correct it; indeed, as Sherburn clearly implies, it is part and parcel of the sinner's ignominious suffering that he is also its cause.

Sherburn's most dramatic departure from the conventions of the jeremiad is, of course, his failure to frame the tragedy of history in God's design for all time. It might be argued that this eclipse of eternity further darkens the already gloomy Calvinist scheme by removing the prospect of eternal salvation from the horizon. It seems more likely, however, that the citizens of Bricksville attend to eternity at church, or at camp meetings, and that the conspicuous theological cast of Sherburn's sermon does nothing to alter its fundamentally secular thrust. Viewed in this way, as disengaged in all save rhetoric from the cosmic drama that they echo, Sherburn's remarks begin to take on a rather sunnier cast. Most obviously, the absolutely crushing threat of Calvinist determinism, as brandished by the likes of Jonathan Edwards, has been lifted. What remains is the formal juxtaposition of a towering, fiery orator and a silent, profoundly attentive audience, a mood electric with anticipation, and a script guaranteed to stir all comers. The sermon, in short, has become a performance. In fact, it is one among many performances in Bricksville, and its sequel, as I have already noted, is not audience retirement for repentant reflection, but the circus.

As performance, as an essentially social event, the sermon in Sherburn's hands serves ultimately social ends. Like his Puritan forebears, the Colonel gives emphasis to the determined fixity of human defectiveness, and therefore to the virtual inevitability of declension. But he does not follow them in using this image of mortal helplessness as a point of departure for exhortations to seek guidance and eternal consolation in the movements of the divine will. He does not mention God, and there is no evidence that he anticipates change. But there is a social virtue of sorts, and a lure to audience assent, buried in this portrait of grinding necessity. For if there is no hope for change, then there can be no point in seeking it; and thus the status quo, for all its shortcomings, is implicitly confirmed. Indeed, upon reflection it seems clear that the element of bleak inevitability in Sherburn's portrait is in fact the servant of an impulse, shared by speaker and audience alike, to affirm the world as they find it. This subcurrent in the proceedings surfaces for inspection in Sherburn's insistence that "the average man don't like trouble and danger. *You*," he continues—and we can imagine him thrusting his quivering arm out over the rapt audience—"don't like trouble and danger" (190). This is a clear, perfectly ironic, exaggeration. Sherburn's listeners are subject to fear, as all humans are; but they are also quite identifiably human in taking pleasure from periodic flirtations with "trouble and danger." In fact, such virtually danger-free immersion in the destructive element is precisely what the Bricksville citizens cultivate in the Boggs murder, pleasantly recover from in the mime, and reenter in the jeremiad. Like the murder, the sermon brings the assembled multitude close enough to trouble and danger to distract them from the torpor of their lives, and thus to amuse them, but not so close that more than a clown or a circus is required to restore them to equanimity. Thus Sherburn's exaggeration of his neighbors' cowardice serves to confirm a social order which they profess to deplore, but from which they in fact take just enough trouble and danger to satisfy their needs and desires.

In effect, then, the Jeremiah tells his people what they want to hear: that they have no alternative to the ostensibly errant course that destiny has charted for them. Their contrite acknowledgment of helpless subjection to sin has the quite paradoxical effect of excusing, and even legitimating, the varieties of error that they fall heir to. Mortal necessity holds out this virtue to the citizens of Bricksville, as it has held it out to generations of Americans, especially as the secular thrust of our national errand has become more manifest. Of course, in covertly addressing itself to the worldly interests of the congregation, the jeremiad also advances the interests of the preacher. Thus Sherburn's emphasis on the cowardice of his audience has its correlative in the magnification of human fearlessness as it very occasionally appears in heroic individual men. Such "a *man's* safe in the hands of ten thousand of your kind," he snarls, "as long as it's daytime and you're not behind him" (190). Sherburn quite obviously qualifies, by his own definition, as a man of this unique breed. But we may be sure that his enjoyment of the social preeminence and legal exemption that come with his exalted status are conditional on his continuing to provide his neighbors with the varieties of exhilarating "trouble and danger" that they have come to expect from him. So long as their submerged, reciprocal goals are met, the predatory gamesman and his willingly deceived audience will persist in their bad-faith alliance.

It is an alliance we have witnessed before, in much more benign circumstances, in *Tom Sawyer.* Moreover, the essential structure of the relationship between Sherburn and his neighbors is familiar to us as it is endlessly duplicated in "formula" westerns and mystery stories. Such predictable fictions feature a solitary, fearless, naturally superior male whose grudging service to a fallen, cowardly, utterly hypocritical social order rewards him with occasions for the more or less legitimate release of his titanic rage and violence. This juxtaposition of a volatile, predatory male hero with a contemptible multitude expresses no hope for positive social change, but it nonetheless forms the backdrop to outbursts of righteous violence. The man gets to do what the man's got to do because his neighbors deserve it and, much more significantly, because his audience enjoys it. Thus while we may join the hero in his acquiescence to the status quo, that ostensibly dismal prospect may in fact obliquely express the culture's resistance to social change, and at the same time virtually guarantee that the show will go on. Culturally speaking, we get pretty much what we ask for.

This digression into popular expression casts some light, I believe, on the failure of the critics of *Huckleberry Finn* to pause for long over Colonel Sherburn. Far and away the most common response to Sherburn's sermon is to dismiss it on esthetic grounds. As Leo Marx puts the case in his familiar, informally "definitive" note to the Bobbs-Merrill edition, "Colonel Sherburn's speech places greater strain on the credibility of the narrative method than any other passage in the novel. Because it is difficult to believe that Huck is reporting the entire speech verbatim, the author's point of view seems to penetrate the first-person mask."[12] While there is undoubtedly some truth in these remarks, their most significant critical consequence is to effectively disqualify the passage from further scrutiny. This outcome, I want to suggest, is hardly accidental. Rather, it betrays an unwillingness among readers—which mirrors the unwillingness of Sherburn's auditors—to reflect at length on the sermon's implications. I would venture that we witness the jeremiad as somehow our own; the form is familiar, and the circumstances and subject matter are an arresting variation on an immemorial American theme. Yet we retreat from the episode, I believe, because it provides us with no comfortable foothold on its proceedings. We may sympathize with the impulse that moves the crowd to Sherburn's house, but we must allow that they richly deserve the treatment they receive once they have arrived. Thus such initial kinship as we may feel with the crowd grows increasingly awkward. Meanwhile, Sherburn is forceful and fearless and apparently on the mark, but our inclination to swing to his side is blocked by his arrogant elitism, by the memory of Boggs, and by the counter-inclination to line up with his audience. In the upshot, the unfolding action is doubly subversive of the expectations it arouses. First, it seems to demonstrate that the social order is literally made out of bad faith, but only *after* it has drawn us into sympathy with the townspeople's objectives. Second, in revealing that the fearless, self-reliant Sherburn is first a lawless predator brimming with contempt for civilized ways, it lends disturbing confirmation to D. H. Lawrence's characterization of the American hero as a righteous, solitary, murderous psychopath. Thus we retreat from the implications of the episode, just as the fictional audience does, because in bluntly assaulting our comfortable stock responses it gives us more "trouble and danger" than it initially promised.

But there is another, deeper dimension, perhaps, to the irony of declaring that Sherburn's speech imposes a "greater strain on credibility than any other passage in the novel." I have argued that what Leo Marx calls audience incredulity is the symptom of a bad-faith incapacity to deal with the awkward implications of the Sherburn speech. We have preferred not to look for long through this window on our culture—on our heroes, myths, and on what their possession may entail. It remains to go further in exploring this "strain" on our "credibility" by asking what it is about this passage that inclines Marx, speaking for a large body of readers, to complain that "the author's point of view seems to penetrate the first-person mask." This is not to object that the speech merely lapses from verisimilitude. Marx makes the perfectly reasonable claim that "it is difficult to believe that Huck is reporting the entire speech verbatim." But then he goes further, and speculates that what is implausible coming from Huck should be attributed to Mark Twain. A number of questions follow from this suggested attribution. For example, does the detection of "the author's point of view" amount to an equation of the Colonel's appraisal of the mob with Mark Twain's? If so, what are we to make of the fact that the author's sentiments have a bloody-minded murderer as their dramatic vehicle? One response to this awkward implication is to separate the Colonel's words from his character, linking the first to Mark Twain and ignoring the second. But by adopting this strategy we solve one problem only to uncover another; specifically, we spare the author guilt by association, but we also display a cultural readiness, noted so shrewdly by Lawrence, to ignore the predator in the fearless hero. Alternatively, we may infer that the attribution of the Colonel's sentiments to the author is offered as a clue to an especially savage streak in the Lincoln of our literature. But this line of analysis is unpromising both on prima facie grounds, and because it credits the note with a more searching assessment of Sherburn than it deserves. In either case, however, the seemingly innocuous discovery of an affinity between Mark Twain and Colonel Sherburn betrays either an exceedingly dark view of the author, or an extremely naive understanding of his suggested alter ego. Indeed, the very failure to recognize these implications is itself an index to the weight of the bad faith that figures in our response to this episode.

Marx is prompted to yoke the author and his fictional actor in this way, I believe, because Sherburn's words are elsewhere to be found upon his maker's lips. Specifically, in "The United States of Lyncherdom," which he composed in late August 1901, Mark Twain assails the human race for its "commonest weakness," the

> aversion to being unpleasantly conspicuous, pointed at, shunned, as being on the unpopular side. Its other name is Moral Cowardice, and is the commanding feature of the make-up of 9,999 men in the 10,000. I am not offering this as a discovery; privately the dullest of us knows it to be true. History will not allow us to forget or ignore this supreme trait of our character. It persistently and sardonically reminds us that

from the beginning of the world no revolt against a public infamy or oppression has ever been begun but by the one daring man in the 10,000, the rest timidly waiting, and slowly and reluctantly joining, under the influence of that man and his fellows from the other ten thousands.

He insists, in confirmation of what we have observed in Bricksville, that humans secretly recognize their cowardice, but nonetheless contrive in bad faith to submerge it in the social order, or in the leadership of "one daring man." On one side, Mark Twain bends to the view that people in the North and the South are generally "right-hearted and compassionate"; they prefer to take their trouble in moderate doses, and flock to lynchings only because "public approval seemed to require it." On the other hand, however, he is appalled at the mounting frequency with which lynchings occur, and thus recognizes that there is no shortage of moral cowards to go along for the show. "No mob," he insists, "has any sand in the presence of a man known to be splendidly brave." But where the mechanisms of law and order are controlled by the majority of spineless hypocrites, the rare men of courage are quite likely to turn up on the other side. Thus while there are two sheriffs and "a brave gentleman" in his gallery of heroes, they appear alongside Savonarola; "a noted desperado"; a "plucky man" who robs trains on his own; and "the half of a brave man" who does the same with stagecoaches.[13]

The elements of this general view of human nature are to be found scattered through the increasingly pessimistic pronouncements that Mark Twain produced during the final decade of his life. In no other text, however, do we find anything approaching the striking similarities in topic, tone, analysis, language, and example that we come upon in "The United States of Lyncherdom." In effect, the brief, bitter assault on American cowardice and hypocrisy was formed out of ideas that had been fully developed and articulated nearly twenty years earlier. Thus it lends signal confirmation to Marx's suggestion that Sherburn's sermon expresses the views of Mark Twain. At the same time, however, it forces us toward the rather uncomfortable recognition that the murderous Jeremiah's actions may also speak for the novelist. The contempt for the mass of mankind that overflows from both texts certainly points in this direction. So does Mark Twain's perfectly manifest, perfectly unblinking respect for the bold criminals who surface in "The United States of Lyncherdom." We are understandably reluctant to bend with the gathering weight of such evidence, both because it indicates that a murderous dimension had begun to unfold in Mark Twain well before the years of his creative decline, and because the barbs of his contempt have their target in cultural impulses toward pleasure and rough justice that we are intermittently inclined to acknowledge as our own. Indeed, this awkwardness in the alignment of Sherburn with Mark Twain has undoubtedly figured in the seemingly paradoxical readiness with which readers have accepted the assignment of "the author's point of view" to the jeremiad. For in submitting without question to the putative justice of the unsupported critical complaint we seize an opportunity to dismiss from further scrutiny a disturbingly ambiguous and potentially compromising interval in the novel. In testing Marx's judgment by going in search of support for his claim, on the other hand, we squander a perfectly comfortable evasion; and, what's worse, we run the risk of confirming the unpleasant suspicions that make the evasion seem so tempting and reasonable. Little wonder that we have been inclined to nod our assent and light out, with Huck, for the circus.

There are other, equally challenging implications to be glimpsed in the connection between Colonel Sherburn and Mark Twain. Working our way backward from the social sermon on lynching to the jeremiad embedded in *Huckleberry Finn,* we find ample reinforcement for the view that Sherburn's conception of human nature is incompatible with the sort of reform that his angry outburst would seem to call for. Mark Twain falls into the identical contradiction in many of the social polemics that he composed in the years around the turn of the century. The contempt for the species which informs many of these texts absolutely undermines their ostensible reformist thrust. "Really," observed his old friend, Joseph H. Twitchell, in early 1901, "you are getting quite orthodox, on the doctrine of Total Human Depravity anyway."[14] Such implicit despair for social amelioration is clearly emergent from Mark Twain's suggestion, toward the end of "The United States of Lyncherdom," that the intrepid American missionaries in China be brought home to face down the murderous mobs. The irony in this proposal is perfectly intentional, and quite as transparent. For the missionaries whom he professes to venerate are elsewhere—in such contemporaneous writings as "To the Person Sitting in Darkness" and "To My Missionary Critics"—represented as sanctimonious purveyors of civilized barbarity. Mark Twain's optimism is thus an ironic pretense, an oblique, cynical mockery of the naive impulse to reform.

Equipped as he was with such cast-iron contempt for human nature, it is reasonable to ask why Mark Twain raised his voice as frequently as he did. As a first step toward an answer, it seems equally reasonable to suppose that he failed to recognize the incompatibility between his assumptions about "the species" and his ostensible objectives as a social critic. This failure, in turn, appears to have been the servant of his primary ambition, which was to be in the spotlight, to be heard and heeded, to enjoy the heady sense of power that came to him in his capacity as fearless, outspoken moralist to an enormous, often admiring, always attentive audience. The role of righteous iconoclast suited the quondam comedian perfectly. It provided him with an avenue of expression for his gathering impatience with the human condition; it satisfied his lifelong ambition to preach; and, above all, it came close to satisfying his voracious entertainer's appetite for attention. Mark Twain responded to the unexampled fame and notoriety that came to him as a social critic with all the exuberant energy of a newcomer to the public eye. According to Hamlin Hill, "He wrote, he spoke at political rallies, he dashed off letters to the editors of newspapers with the frenzy of a demented spinster, and he paraded with glee and relish wherever the spotlight of publicity shone."[15] Grave doubts about the accessibility of his goals did nothing to dampen the pleasure that he took from being their very visible public advocate. "I have done very little work," he wrote puckishly to a friend in 1901, because I am in "hot water with the clergy and the other goody-goody people, but I am enjoying it more than I have ever enjoyed hot water before."[16]

Viewed in this light, as an element in a performance rather than as a premise in a social theory, Mark Twain's pessimism on the score of human nature begins to make a kind of functional sense. In his hands especially, it is a virtually inexhaustible source of rhetorical energy; it fuels his verbal assaults, gives his irony its sharp, satisfying edge, adds the pleasing combustibility to his sarcasm, and provides the pressure under which such concentrated dramatic gestures as "The War Prayer" are formed. The molten stuff that it gave rise to is as authentic as anything in Mark Twain, but it is therefore quintessentially the stuff of a master showman. Witness the supreme theatricality of the climactic tableau in "The United States of Lyncherdom." He invites us to "picture the scene" in our minds: 203 burning lynch victims

> in a row, allowing 600 feet of space for each human torch, so that there may be viewing room around it for 5,000 Christian American men, women, and children, youths and maidens; make it night, for grim effect; have the show in a gradually rising plain, and let the course of the stakes be uphill; the eye can then take in the whole line of twenty-

four miles of blood-and-flesh bonfires unbroken . . . All being ready, now, and the darkness opaque, the stillness impressive—for there should be no sound but the soft moaning of the night wind and the muffled sobbing of the sacrifices—let all the far stretch of kerosened pyres be touched off simultaneously and the glare and the shrieks and the agonies burst heavenward to the Throne.[17]

This, I would suggest, is a powerfully upsetting performance. If we feel punished by the passage, it may be because it fixes us in the role of spectators, witnesses not merely helpless to intervene, but apparently expected to assume, without discomfort or protest, a passive relationship to the scene before us. The irony in this gesture is not lost on us, perhaps; but its force is at least initially diminished by the clear suggestion that the speaker imagines an enormous, passive, American audience not simply, or even primarily, as part of an oblique social comment, but because as an entertainer he needs one. This does not eclipse the irony at our expense; rather, it renders it more elusive, and more damaging. For the more bitter thrust is in the ultimate absence of irony in Mark Twain's view of us as passive witnesses to this spectacle of barbarity. Our incapacity to ameliorate the dreadful condition we behold is simply taken for granted. Mark Twain does not expect that we will respond, any more than he expects that the missionaries in China, for whom this imaginary human bonfire is lit, are willing or capable of answering his appeal. "O kind missionary," he intones, "O compassionate missionary, leave China! come home and convert these Christians!"[18] They will not hear him; and even if they did, as the shock troops of "the Blessings of Civilization Trust," and thus leading symptoms of the culture's pathology, they could only add fuel to the terrible fires. Mark Twain knows this, of course, just as he knows that the Christians, the members of the human throng that he has imaginatively convened, are incorrigible. He may intend to confront his audience with its moral incapacity; in any case, the very assumption carries a sting. But the assumption in turn betrays Mark Twain's supreme confidence that his auditors are what as an entertainer he most wants them to be: a willing, attentive, appreciative audience seeking distraction from their bad-faith inertia, not a program for social change.

The implicit despair of reform reduces the dramatic climax of "The United States of Lyncherdom" to mere spectacle. Mark Twain's proffered apocalypse simply confirms the impotence of actors and spectators at the same time that it demonstrates the cultural authority of the cynical showman. The potential moral weight of the scene is swallowed up in the shadow of its maker, whose oblique assault on bad faith sends an exhilarating charge through his audience, but hardly challenges them to alter the status quo. They listen and applaud because he gives them what they came for. In all of this, "The United States of Lyncherdom" mirrors the secular jeremiad in *Huckleberry Finn*. The social text is also comparable in certain very telling respects with the brilliantly orchestrated pyrotechnics of the bloody, world-shattering Battle of the Sand Belt that concludes *A Connecticut Yankee in King Arthur's Court*. Throughout the novel there is for most readers a discernible, unsettling tension between Hank Morgan the bearer of progress and the Hank who indulges his showman's vanity while the world goes to Hell. In demonstrating the extent to which "Hank Morgan *is* Mark Twain," Justin Kaplan observes that "Both are showmen who love gaudy effects," and that "Their revolutionary, humanitarian zeal is tempered and at times defeated by their despairing view of human nature."[19] The perfect planning and staging and timing of the novel's spectacular denouement demonstrate yet again the extent to which the cynic and the showman merge in the secular Jeremiah. Hank's final, apparently incoherent wish to return to Arthurian England, to the hopelessly backward civilization he has contemptuously detonated, makes perfect sense when viewed as the nostalgia of an inveterate entertainer for the best audience he ever had. Hank's most characteristic response to what he describes as life's "sad pilgrimage, this pathetic drift between the eternities,"[20] is to capitalize as a bitter showman on the absurdity of the world. All of Hank's productions reveal the utter inconsequentiality of history save as show, spectacle, a moment's distraction from life's sullen fixity. And while the Battle of the Sand Belt, effectively a reduction of the apocalypse to a punitive technological extravaganza, is certainly his most spectacular statement in this vein, it is not quite his last. Hank's death is the occasion for his final production. "With the first suggestion of the death-rattle in his throat," Mark Twain reports, "he started up slightly, and seemed to listen; then he said: 'A bugle? . . . It is the king! The drawbridge, there! Man the battlements!— turn out the—' He was getting up his last 'effect;' but he never finished it" (447). For Hank, then, as for Colonel Sherburn before him, and for Mark Twain the social critic in both of them, the role of Jeremiah is more social and theatrical than spiritual or moral, and though deeply in earnest, less conspicuously a divine vocation than a transcendent variety of gamesmanship.

Finally, and most vitally, it remains to comment in more detail on the nature of the social and cultural issues that bring out the wrathful

Jeremiahs in America's premier literary humorist. The grave problem that prompts Mark Twain to imagine the simultaneous incineration of 203 human beings is the terrible epidemic of lynching that accompanied the emergence of Jim Crow policies in the late nineteenth century. The resurgence of racial conflict on a broad national basis in the decades just before and after 1900 bore with it the awful suggestion that the Civil War had done little in practical terms to improve ante-bellum conditions. The persistence of racism and an alarming gravitation to lynch law combined to render blacks as legally defenseless as they had been as slaves. Nothing, it seemed, had changed. Indeed, the illusion that mob violence could be morally justified might have appeared to some as more pernicious than the statutory racial injustice of the days gone by. After all, under the old scheme all Americans had to accept some technical responsibility for the terrible abuse of black people. After the war, once the laws had been changed and, for a period, enforced, it became possible, and understandably quite tempting, to respond to the persistence of profound racial discord by simply wishing it away. Whether he intended to or not, it is this comparatively sophisticated post-bellum racial bad faith that Mark Twain dramatizes in "The United States of Lyncherdom." For while the social sermon acknowledges and bitterly deplores the violence and injustice that it portrays, it also effectively removes the problem from the realm of audience influence, both by placing the lynchings at a great geographical distance, and by strongly suggesting that unchanging human cussedness makes such injustice inevitable. In the upshot, as I have shown, the spectacle of racial hatred is transformed into a spectacular show in which the secular Jeremiah, the gamesman, earns the acclaim that he craves by serving as minister to his culture's illusions.

The long narrative approach to the Battle of the Sand Belt marshalls the same array of historical and "philosophical" and theatrical elements into the service of the identical cultural program. From the moment at the very beginning of the novel when Hank discovers that "hogs roamed and rooted contentedly" in the streets of Camelot, we recognize that the dream of Arthurian Britain is formed out of memories of the ante-bellum South. Before the midpoint of the story has been reached, it is clear that the main cultural link between the sixth century and the Hannibal of Mark Twain's childhood is slavery. Hank declares that "The blunting effects of slavery upon the slaveholder's moral perceptions are known and conceded, the world over," and that "a privileged class, an aristocracy, is but a band of slaveholders under another name" (239).

With the optimism of a late nineteenth-century democrat, however, he makes the confident prediction that the day will come when "a man will be his own property, not the property of magistrate and master" (331). Rather more ominously, however, Hank discovers that the desire to free slaves is far from sufficient to the task of human liberation. He finds that the ordinary folk in Arthur's kingdom have grown insensitive to the brutality in their midst. When a young slave mother is savagely whipped, the Christian pilgrims with whom Hank is traveling "looked on and commented—on the expert way in which the whip was handled. They were too much hardened by lifelong every-day familiarity with slavery to notice that there was anything else in the exhibition that invited comment." For these pious souls, as for the vast majority of their countrymen, legalized violence is an "exhibition" to be observed, not an outrage to be corrected. Hank's initial impulse "to stop the whole thing and set the slaves free" is promptly modified: "If I lived and prospered I would be the death of slavery, that I was resolved upon; but I would try to fix it so that when I became its executioner it should be by command of the nation" (199–200).

As the novel goes on to reveal, it is only as "executioner" that Hank is able to act on his resolution, and even then his efforts are entirely in vain. For what he learns in the course of his adventures is that Arthurian Britain is as indifferent to slavery as human beings are by nature prone to subordinate and enslave their fellows. Even worse, he discovers that members of the peasant classes are so fully acculturated to their inferior status that they serve their masters as lynch mobs when rebellion breaks out.

> This was depressing—to a man with the dream of a republic in his head. It reminded me of a time thirteen centuries away, when the "poor whites" of our South who were always despised, and frequently insulted, by the slave lords around them, and who owed their base condition simply to the presence of slavery in their midst, were yet pusillanimously ready to side with the slave lords in all political moves for the upholding and perpetuating of slavery, and did also finally shoulder their muskets and pour out their lives in an effort to prevent the destruction of the very institution which degraded them.

Hank attempts to minimize the grim paradox emergent from his analogy by insisting "that secretly the 'poor white' did detest the slave lord, and did feel his own shame." That, he concludes, "was enough; for it showed that a man is at bottom a man, after all, even if it doesn't show on the outside" (297).

This slender shaft of faith in human nature is doomed, of course. Hatred and shame, as Hank will learn, and as Mark Twain knows, are not nearly "enough." In fact, the Yankee betrays his deep personal immersion in the cultural conditions he professes to abhor in the episode that immediately follows his pronouncements on the essential dignity of man. He encounters a mechanic named Marco whose secret hatred of his oppressors confirms Hank's view that "A man *is* a man, at bottom" (300). But he reacts to this ostensibly affirmative discovery not by cultivating the seeds of justice, but by systematically undermining them. The occasion for this puzzling development is a sumptuous dinner party that Hank arranges for Marco's friends. Before the meal is served, Hank adroitly seduces one of the guests, a blacksmith named Dowley, into an exhibition of personal vanity and pride in his accomplishments as a "self-made man." The boasting goes on at painful length, until, at last, the inflated Dowley smiles "around on the company with the satisfaction of a god who is doing the handsome and gracious thing, and is quite well aware of it" (316). With that, the opulent feast is brought out, and Marco and his wife assume the smug feeling of superiority once enjoyed by the now crushed Dowley. But the joke is on all the guests, for it exposes their awe of wealth and the social status that comes with it, and their boundless ambition to rise above their fellows. Thus Marco's putative manhood, his secret bridling under oppression, is not the principled resistance to injustice, but fierce resentment at not being on top.

This conspicuous craving for power and preeminence is not nearly so surprising as the evident care and single-mindedness that Hank brings to its exposure. It is the self-serving oppressor, the slaveholder in Marco and his guests, that his scheme draws out, and even cultivates, not the idealistic advocates of human equality. Hank appears determined to expose unprincipled selfishness where he had once seemed gratified to discover "a man." His response to the success of his elaborate practical joke gives eloquent testimony to this apparent perversity. "Ah, well," he gloats, "it was immense; yes, it was a daisy. I don't know that I ever put a situation together better, or got happier spectacular effects out of the materials available" (319).

Hank's gloating pleasure in the embarrassment occasioned by his joke betrays that the outcome affords precisely the perspective on human nature that he had anticipated and desired. But his delight in his "spectacular effects" is evidence that the progressive political activist sits rather oddly alongside the showman in his personal makeup. In fact, Hank's dream of human liberation, and the new life that it takes from the example of Marco, is quite obviously in tension with his relish for the creation of elaborate spectacles, which display his personal power at the same time that they reveal the inferior human gifts of others. The energy and imagination that he brings to the satisfaction of the latter, much deeper impulse, betrays the fact that his idealism is the profoundest self-delusion. Hank has even less enthusiasm for equality than Dowley; his avowed esteem for general human dignity is in conflict with his pronounced counter-tendency to discover true manhood only in aristocrats—"the king was a good deal more than a king, he was a man" (352). His ambition for personal power—he revels in being the "Boss" and acknowledges "a base hankering" to be the "first president" of the emergent political order—sits awkwardly with his republican rhetoric; and his egocentric compulsion to mastermind extravagant entertainments inclines him to regard his fellows as passive witnesses to his personal grandeur, not active, independent, self-governing democrats. Thus the megalomaniac showman exults in the dramatic subversion of the manhood that the idealist declares the hope of the species. It is perfectly ironic, of course, that Hank's bad-faith enslavement to his own titanic ego should predispose him to discover and condemn the identical bad faith in human nature generally. This irony is fruitful of several others. It amounts to a declaration of the inevitability in human history of the slavery that Hank professes to deplore, but which in effect enables and justifies the production of one spectacular entertainment after another.

Thus human enslavement to the deception of self and other is at once the condition, theme, and objective of the would-be liberator's performances. Hank has no desire to free Dowley of his delusions; rather, he seizes upon the blacksmith's folly as justification for a second practical joke in which his objective is "to drive him into the earth—drive him *all* in—drive him in till not even the curve of his skull should show above the ground" (324). The little show backfires when the victims of the joke pursue Hank and the King into slavery. But the net result is to confirm yet again Hank's sentiments on the score of human nature, and to create the occasion for what he later celebrates as "one of the gaudiest effects I ever instigated." For when the emancipation of the slaves takes place, only Hank and the King are numbered among the free. The other slaves are hung before Sir Launcelot arrives with "five hundred mailed and belted knights on bicycles!" to save the Boss and the King. As the assembled multitude drops, at Hank's command, to their knees, it is not freedom and human dignity that the liberator celebrates, for these are hardly paramount in the scene. Rather, he revels in the spectacle that he has engineered. "The grandest sight that ever was seen. Lord, how the plumes streamed, how the sun flamed and flashed from the endless procession of webby wheels!" (379–80).

The figure that we behold in this fabric of contradictions is, of course, the secular Jeremiah, the righteous showman who assures his audience that the conditions of life in a fallen world are remote from mortal influence and utterly resistant to change. This may seem to be bad news; in fact, in a culture of bad faith, it is doubly gratifying. For it subtly ministers to the audience's deep cultural commitment to the status quo, and at the same time it strongly suggests that acquiescence in things as they are is evidence of commendable Christian virtue in the face of inscrutable divine necessity. Moreover, the sermon, when well brought off, nourishes the audience craving for entertainment. For the Jeremiah, meanwhile, the reward for such moral leadership is enormous prestige and authority; the price is ever-deepening contempt for the participants (including himself) in this elaborate social delusion. Hank departs from this familiar pattern only in his tenacious pursuit of his republican ideals. But this departure is more apparent than real, for his determination to refashion medieval culture turns all England against him. This confirms both his sense that unregenerate human nature defies progress, and his view of himself as a member of a righteous elite, as "a man" surrounded by gross inferiors. Precisely because it arises out of what he views as the final, emphatic demonstration of human perversity, this apparent confirmation of Hank's superiority is deeply rewarding to him. It allows him to undertake, with all the righteous energy of an agent of God, the spectacular detonation of Arthurian Britain. This, we sense, is the outcome he has secretly hungered for from the beginning.

Which brings us back to Colonel Sherburn, and to the perfectly evident lines of continuity between these seemingly disparate portraits of sixth-century England, ante-bellum Bricksville, and America at the turn of the century. Judging from these texts, Mark Twain's root assumptions about human nature underwent little change during the nearly two decades before 1901. The same may be said of his conception of human society as he surveys it over a span of 1400 years. Nothing changes. The human and social realities that Hank encounters are, so far as we can tell, virtually the same as those to be found in Bricksville in about 1840 and in "The United States of Lyncherdom" sixty years later. The key constants are pathological bad faith and the varieties of conscious and unwitting enslavement that the pervasive deception of self and other entails. In all three settings the leading social activities involve extraordinary excesses of violence leading to climactic outbursts of lynch law. In all three settings the implied valorization of human dignity and equality is undermined by the manifestly extreme selfishness, cowardice, and social irresponsibility of ordinary people. The ostensibly good, respectable citizens, the prospective or presumptive democrats, are always discovered to be complicit in the degraded behavior that they might be expected to deplore and combat; either they form the mobs whose indulgence in violence fills the dramatic foreground, or they stand by as passive, secretly gratified spectators of equally repellent activities. In either case, the gross hypocrisy of the social majority gives rise to a fretful, guilt-laden uneasiness which in turn fuels an addiction to crude, often violent public amusements. It also forms the essential social and psychological background to a characteristic and symptomatic form of entertainment, the jeremiad. The Jeremiah, the most adept, perhaps the most tortured practitioner of his culture's bad faith, is "a man" whose singular exemption from the common lot is manifest in his social, moral, and theatrical preeminence. The "man" always occupies a socially elevated position, even when such distinction conflicts with his professed egalitarianism; his moral authority is measured in audience acquiescence to his severe judgments; and his success as entertainer derives both from the energy and color of his delivery, and from the core of consolation that his public seems to find in his dark teachings.

Having summarized all of these significant similarities, and thus demonstrated the essential continuity of Mark Twain's assumptions on major issues over a period of many years, it remains to acknowledge the perfectly conspicuous, all-important exception to the emergent rule. I refer, of course, to the absence of slavery in the foreground, or even in the immediate frame, of the Sherburn episode. This is a crucial difference; for it is slavery that most graphically exemplifies the pathological bad faith of ancient Britain, just as it is the specter of antebellum racial injustice that rises with the victims in "The United States of Lyncherdom." But to suggest that slavery is missing in *Huckleberry Finn* where it is elsewhere, under similar circumstances, centrally featured, is to recognize almost immediately that slavery is integral to the meaning of Sherburn's sermon and to the entire Bricksville episode, even though slaves are not mentioned. The institutionalized inhumanity in the midst of this society explains much that would otherwise be extraordinary: the general disregard for human life; the taste and tolerance for violence; the pervasive, irrational fear; the compulsive round of crude distractions; the shuffling readiness to be condemned coupled with the tacit consent to the status quo. If we add slavery to this portrait, the pathology begins to make sense. But *add* slavery we must. For it is surely appropriate to argue—taking a lead from what we have learned about *Tom Sawyer*—that the absence of slavery may in fact signify its concealed but emphatic importance. All that is wrong in Bricksville, and especially the extremity of all that is wrong, points to slavery. It is the unforgivable sin whose attempted concealment, or denial, or rationalization, totally corrupts and enervates this avowedly Christian, democratic culture. Quite obviously, it is the element in the social order that the citizens of Bricksville are least willing to change. In collaborating to ignore the slave at the center of their fear and violence and furtive mob rule, they have left a vacuum, an absence, which, because it is conspicuous, implies the presence that is later acknowledged in *A Connecticut Yankee in King Arthur's Court* and "The United States of Lyncherdom."

V

I opened the discussion of Bricksville on the premise that the village addiction to shows betrays a desire, never adequately filled, to be diverted from the unbearable reality of daily life. At the root of this bottomless craving for entertainment, I have argued, is slavery, the bad-faith inhumanity that is present as conspicuous absence, as the thing at once expressed and evaded, in the endless round of distractions. Along the way I have suggested ways in which reader response to *Huckleberry Finn* recapitulates this complex cultural pattern. Enough has been said, I think, to provide a detailed understanding of some of the major elements in the recurrent behavior I set out to describe and analyze. This is not to suggest that the materials bearing directly on this critical issue have been exhausted. *Huckleberry Finn* is the sum of parts virtually all of which involve the bad-faith amusements and evasions emergent from a culture of race–slavery. But even if the discussion is confined to Bricksville, Sherburn's sermon is hardly the end of the show. The circus provides temporary relief from the attempted lynching, though the comedy gives way quite abruptly when a drunk man tries to join the bareback riders. It is Huck's error to suppose that with this unexpected development "the whole show come to a standstill." In fact, it is just the beginning of the kind of fun the audience likes best. "A lot of men begun to pile down off of the benches and swarm towards the ring, saying, 'Knock him down! throw him out!' and one or two women begun to scream." This sudden transformation of the crowd into a mob is the obvious sequel to a tale told by Colonel Sherburn.

The ringmaster restores the angry crowd to order when he agrees to let the drunken man attempt to ride; the prospect of bloodshed brings the spectators back to their seats. Of course, it is the Boggs episode all over again—except that the circus rewards its audience with the "pleasure and astonishment" of a surprise instead of a murder. The people are "just crazy," Huck reports, as the performer gradually emerges from his drunken disguise. Huck goes on to sympathize with the ringmaster, who appears to have been fooled "by one of his own men" (192–94). In this Huck betrays a good heart, and an uncertain grasp of the line that divides appearance from reality. But he is hardly alone in being confused. After all, he is the spectator to a profoundly bad-faith audience which is itself witness to an act that delights spectators precisely because it successfully deceives them. Confusion is pervasive, even among the members of the audience outside the novel; indeed, confusion seems deeply to be the point. The clearest heads in the house belong to the ringmaster and his performers. With the Colonel, they recognize and play to the mob in their audience, but manage nonetheless to hold it at bay.

The circus succeeds, as all the shows in Bricksville succeed, because it anticipates and exploits audience bad faith at the same time that it contrives to draw attention away from its complicity in the varieties of deception that enable and impel and inform the show. In all of this, the circus is to Bricksville what Tom Sawyer is to St. Petersburg, and what Tom's novel is to the culture that embraces it. The penalties for failure in this obligatory deception of the willingly deceived can be extremely heavy, as Sherburn boldly acknowledges. The king and the duke also run very serious risks in staging their bogus performances along the river. They know this, of course; their pain and humiliation notwithstanding, they can hardly be surprised when they wind up tarred and feathered after their fraudulent posturing as the Wilks heirs. That dreadful punishment is in part the price exacted for the series of entertainments that they set in motion just after the circus. Like the drunken bareback rider before it, this act demonstrates a thorough understanding of audience bad faith. After a false start with Shakespeare—"these Arkansaw lunkheads couldn't come up to Shakspeare," the duke fumes, "what they wanted was low comedy" (194)—the resourceful charlatans come back with "The King's Camelopard," a crude stag joke that is scheduled for a limited run of three nights only. The crowd at the very brief opening performance knows that it has been "sold." But it responds, as the king and the duke must have suspected it would, not by driving the frauds from their midst, but by drawing their neighbors into the trap with them. "Hold on!" shouts a local dignitary, as the angry spectators surge toward the stage.

> "Just a word, gentlemen." They stopped to listen. "We are sold—mighty badly sold. But we don't want to be the laughing-stock of this whole town, I reckon, and never hear the last of this thing as long as we live. *No*. What we want, is to go out of here quiet, and talk this show up, and sell the *rest* of the town! Then we'll all be in the same boat. Ain't that sensible?" ("You bet it is!—the jedge is right!" everybody sings out.) "All right, then—not a word about any sell. Go along home, and advise everybody to come and see the tragedy." (197)

In hatching this triumphant scheme, the king and the duke anticipate audience bad faith at least the equal of their own, and they contrive, quite brilliantly, to exploit it. Their bold, perfectly acute perspective on Bricksville involves several implicit assumptions. They seem confident that the members of their audience will recognize that the only way to escape the public humiliation of having been "sold" is to sell all their neighbors. They assume, as their victims do, that the disclosure of the evening's events will draw attention to the folly of those deceived, not the perfidy of the deceivers. The members of the audience anticipate ridicule, not sympathy. They know that attacking their deceivers can only make matters worse, for it will serve to underscore the discomfort they feel as the result of having been taken in. Thus the king and the duke have put their spectators right where the rest of the community wants them—in the way of humiliation. The situation seems to speak of a progressive deterioration of community confidence in the collective capacity for charity and fair play. Bad faith has deeply eroded public trust, and the result is a democracy of cynics and deceivers in which the ideal of equality has been drained of its dignity as the leveling downward has progressed. Quite appropriately, it is the local judge who implicitly confirms that the only faith in Bricksville is the bad kind—the honor shared by self-convicted fools. Nor does he show any signs of reluctance or regret in his advocacy of more deception as the cure for deceit. Their momentary cries of angry disapproval notwithstanding, the putative victims are also right where they want to be. They have enjoyed the coarse little show—"it would a made a cow laugh" (196), Huck observes—and they relish their righteous denunciation of the king and the duke only slightly less than they enjoy springing the identical trap on their neighbors. Bad faith is so current in the local cultural exchange that the villagers have learned to take pleasure from the very midst of their contradictions. The entertainers know this; and for the moment at least they are well placed to profit from the bad-faith cultural drama they have entered, intuitively measured, precisely mimicked, and passed back to the actors in their audience.

The faithless plotting of neighbor against neighbor, and the sacrifice of the remnants of community integrity to the saving of a few foolish faces, may seem to have descended to a downward limit. But if a sort of bottom has been reached, it is certainly a false one. The king and the duke recognize that they are safe only so long as the members of their first audience are busy making fools of their friends. Once they are all sold, the victims will join hands in placing the blame for their humiliation on the cast of their most recent entertainment. And the show will go on. Succeeding acts of bad faith bring the local citizenry together again as witnesses and mob, audience and actors, to the third and final production of "The King's Camelopard," a play that both expresses and conceals their condition. This show, like all the shows in Bricksville, is absolutely integral to the local culture of bad faith. As such, it has no end. Burning dogs, murdering Boggs, pursuing Sherburn, the circus, "The King's Camelopard," these are acts in a continuous cultural play. Such a steady diet of distractions creates endless opportunities for charlatans like the king and the duke, master showmen in the crude round of deception, who succeed because they know how to insert themselves into the circle of bad faith, how to make the most of their opportunities on the inside, and when to get out.

But the illusion that the round of amusements in Bricksville somehow defines a limit to bad faith has its place in a much broader frame of cultural reference. For it is the deeper business of the endless shows to distract consciousness from the true depths of the culture's inhumanity to man. The faithlessness and cruelty and hypocrisy that we witness along the dusty streets are the diversions of the white members of the cultural cast; the darker players, and the much darker action, are carefully confined to the background. Such repression has enormous human costs, both those that we see in Bricksville, and those even heavier ones we can only surmise. The costs are great in good part because the repression is rigorous and complete. At the price of enduring what may seem lesser, if still considerable, social evils, the white citizens along the river have succeeded in virtually blinding themselves to the essential inhumanity of their leading institution. Slavery has come to seem benign and unremarkable because it appears, when it appears at all, in a remarkably cruel environment—an environment which the example of slavery has helped to foster and continues to validate.

Blindness and cruelty of this sort are hardly confined to Bricksville. Indeed, it is variously a source of irony that Huck and his partners in crime assume, as they hustle back to the raft, that they have left their troubles behind them. The raft seems safe and comfortable, especially when they are "about ten mile below that village." Then, Huck reports, "we lit up and had a supper, and the king and the duke fairly laughed their bones loose over the way they'd served them people" (198). But conditions aboard the raft are hardly an improvement on those along the shore. In fact, social life on the water is heavy with assorted deceits and equivocations and manipulations. The king and the duke lie with less shame and more conscious purpose than the villagers they exploit, but the relative freedom from self-deception hardly mitigates their rapacity. To be sure, the situation grows worse after the arrival of the confidence men, but the air is never as pure as we might wish. The deep source of the trouble, race–slavery, is palpably, incontrovertibly present in the person and estate of Jim. Quite appropriately, the little community finally collapses when the mean-spirited frauds serve Jim as they have served their audiences in Bricksville; only they "sell" him in deed, because he is black and a slave.

Jim is aware of the moral discord and the ominous obstacles to freedom on board the raft. For reasons that will become clearer as the argument develops, however, we must assume that Jim does not feel free to say all that he feels, even to Huck. Rather than declare his fears outright, he angles toward the center of his apprehension with a tentative, rather innocuous and noncommittal question.

"Don't it sprise you, de way dem kings carries on, Huck?"

"No," I says, "it don't."

"Why don't it, Huck?"

"Well, it don't, because it's in the breed. I reckon they're all alike."

"But Huck, dese kings o' ourn is reglar rapscallions; dat's jist what dey is; dey's reglar rapscallions."

"Well, that's what I'm a-saying; all kings is mostly rapscallions, as fur as I can make out."

"Is dat so?"   (199)

This cannot be a very satisfying interchange for Jim, as his concluding, wearily resigned question may suggest. Huck refuses to enter a discussion of the perils that their new companions bring with them on to the crowded raft. Jim ventures the quite mild suggestion that they are "regular rapscallions," but his young friend deflects the characterization, and the fears that it expresses, into a discussion of kings in general. He goes on at great length, and in comically fractured historical detail, about the infamous excesses of majesty. But his bloody examples, and the conclusion that kings are generally "a mighty ornery lot" (200), lend heavy, heavily ironic, fuel to his friend's concerns. Jim comments tentatively on both the king and the duke, and then concludes: "Well, anyways, I doan' hanker for no mo' un um, Huck. Dese is all I kin stan.'" In this, he comes as close as he can to saying what he must feel—that the newcomers are not royalty at all, but fraudulent, degraded human specimens who represent a very serious threat to his quest for freedom. In effect, Jim is appealing to Huck for confirmation of his fears, and for assistance in securing life and liberty. But Huck once again fails to take the lead. "It's the way I feel, too, Jim. But we've got them on our hands, and we got to remember what they are, and make allowances" (200–201). Huck seems incapable of penetrating beyond Jim's expression of discontent to the much graver fears that prompted it, and that he tries to convey. The boy seems to honor rank at the same time that he recognizes its characteristic defaults; what matters is that he is resigned to having the odious reprobates along. Huck does not seem to hear; thus there is nothing more for Jim to say.

We may be inclined to explain Huck's responses as a failure to attend to or properly measure Jim's legitimate concerns. But the evidence won't support this line of analysis. Huck's subsequent reflections betray his awareness of the major thrust of Jim's remarks. "What was the use to tell Jim these warn't real kings and dukes? It wouldn't a done no good; and besides, it was just as I said; you couldn't tell them from the real kind" (201). Huck's ruminations reflect his awareness that Jim's impulse is to challenge the credibility of their companions. He secretly concedes that they are frauds; but his refusal to share this knowledge with Jim betrays his resistance to the logical next step, which is to take action to control the impostors, or, more probably, to separate from them entirely. Huck hears this, but he won't go along. Instead, he has his way by refusing to acknowledge his friend's clearly implied plea for help. It may be that Huck fears the consequences of taking action against the king and the duke; perhaps he resents Jim's indirect attempt to take the initiative; quite possibly he has grown weary of the endless running away. Whatever the case, his prevarication entails a retreat to a patronizing posture toward his black friend, the deferral to the king and the duke even though they aren't "the real kind," and the perfectly arbitrary declaration that the perfidious charlatans must be indulged and endured.

The failure to take arms against the king and the duke is heavy with consequence. Its immediate result is discomfort and indignity for Jim; ultimately, of course, it leads to his sale and the final, total collapse of his ill-fated plan for escape to freedom. Jim seems to anticipate much of this. He takes both watches and stays up all night while the others sleep. When Huck awakens "just at daybreak" he finds Jim "setting there with his head down betwixt his knees, moaning and mourning to himself." Jim is restless with thoughts of home; he misses "his wife and his children, away up yonder" (201). He tells Huck that a sharp sound in the night has recalled to his mind the slap he once gave his four-year-old daughter Elizabeth when she twice ignored his request to shut the door. His discovery, a few minutes later, that the poor child's hearing and speech have been lost in a bout with scarlet fever, overcomes him with remorse and tender parental concern.

> "O, Huck, I bust out a-cryin' en grab her up in my arms en say, 'O de po' little thing! de Lord God Amighty fogive po' ole Jim, kaze he never gwyne to fogive hisseff as long's he live!' O, she was plumb deef en dumb, Huck, plumb deef en dumb—en I'd ben a treat'n her so!" (202)

Jim's intense feeling of separation from his family seems to arise and take its painful edge from his failure, the evening before, to enlist his young friend's support in dealing with the trouble on board the raft. Home seems increasingly remote as he is forced to resign himself, passively and without so much as a word of direct protest, to the inevitability of disaster. He feels as utterly alone and vulnerable as the poor child in his memory. And Jim's predicament, like his daughter's, is the result of total lapses in communication; he does not feel at liberty to speak his mind directly, and Huck fails to hear what his friend is straining to convey. This breakdown spells trouble, as Elizabeth's example well illustrates. But the night's meditations mirror and echo the day's developments only up to a point, and with a difference. Elizabeth's speechless grief ends when her father recognizes his error. Admittedly, he is woefully lacking in proper concern for a child who has recently recovered from "a powful rough spell" (201) with a disease known for its disabling effects on youngsters. No doubt this failure of consideration figures in his subsequent remorse. Still, it is an error that unleashes Jim's violence; he does not know that Elizabeth is deaf and dumb. The irony imbedded in the analogy with conditions on the raft is powerfully double-edged. On one side, Jim feels unheard in his trouble. But the parallel also suggests that he is inclined to regard Huck's failure to hear as an oversight, and to forgive it. At another level, we recognize what Jim is too generous, or too wishfully self-deceived to see: that Huck has heard, but refuses to respond to his cry for help. This is dismaying, to be sure. But the bitterest draught of all emerges from the comparison of the outcomes of the parallel episodes. Huck's refusal to hear is a major link in the chain of events that restores Jim to the hands of the slaveholders. Meanwhile, the father's perfectly reasonable error precipitates a cruel slap, but leads almost immediately to a revelation and acknowledgment of the source of the trouble, and to a tearful, comforting embrace. There is pain in the memory, but there is hope for solutions and faith in human tenderness as well.

Poor Jim! His reflections on his family, though they give him woe, are clearly, if indirectly, a retreat in consciousness from present conditions that prompt and parallel those reflections, but offer none of the consolation and comfort and human warmth that he remembers. As a father Jim is as liable to error as any man; but he is also capable of recognizing his errors, correcting them, and taking steps to repair harm. Slavery utterly perverts this apparently natural human scheme. It reduces the father to a helpless, voiceless child, remote from his family, powerless to defend himself, and bitterly frustrated in his longings for fellow-feeling, even from the child who behaves at times like his superior, but who, at others, must seem like a son to him. It is deeply telling about Jim, and about the culture in which we find him, that the most humanizing element in this poignant paternal reflection is its betrayal of a capacity for impatience and anger and sudden violence. Jim is not the harmless child that his oppressors, in their suppressed fear of slave retaliation, must fondly imagine him to be. He is their equal in the ability to inflict pain. But the confirmation of common humanity leads almost immediately to the discovery of marked cultural differences. As a slave, Jim must control and conceal his human aggressiveness in order to survive. This is a conscious form of dissimulation, however, and it does not render Jim incapable of inflicting, regretting, and repairing harm. For the citizens of Bricksville, on the other hand, the contradiction between cultural ideals and practices, as it is manifest in racism and the institutionalized violence of slavery, has issued in the submergence and denial of their consummate human aggression. This is an unconscious form of dissimulation, and it results, as we have seen, in a willing blindness to the terrible harm done, deep resistance to reform or repair, an expanding tolerance for cognate social ills, and an addiction to violent amusements that mirror the inhumanity they are designed to conceal.

Huck's failure to respond to his friend's appeal, especially as it is cast in contrast to Jim's response to Elizabeth, is a measure of his immersion in the dominant culture of bad faith. His refusal to hear, which quite literally enables the harm that it simultaneously denies, is one sure sign of his acculturation to the side of Jim's oppressors. Having said this much, however, it is absolutely essential to interpose a major qualification—to wit, that Huck's only consequential acts of bad faith, his only willfully blind deceptions of self and other, have a direct bearing on his relationship with Jim. The most prominent exception to this rule follows the mob's stunned retreat from the Colonel's house, when Huck assures himself: "I could a staid, if I'd a wanted to, but I didn't want to" (191). Such transparent self-deception is the badge of his fellowship with the cowards whom Sherburn has just contemptuously dismissed. To be sure, there is a connection between the mob behavior that the Colonel ridicules and the brutal lynching of blacks that Mark Twain condemns in "The United States of Lyncherdom." In general, however, when Huck surrenders to deception of himself and others, the link with Jim is clear and direct. When he first persuades himself, for example, that "it warn't no use to tell Jim" that the king and the duke are frauds, his declared wish to "keep peace in the family" (165) does little to conceal the racial condescension and insensitivity to Jim's predicament working below the threshold of consciousness. We will return to Huck's bad faith with Jim in a moment.

First, I want to reiterate and enlarge briefly upon the characterization of Huck's relationship to the wider culture of bad faith as it is set forth in my analysis of *Tom Sawyer*. The youngster is no stranger to deceptions of all kinds. He lies constantly, to virtually everyone, and with considerable success. He is quite masterful at the impromptu fabrication of fictional autobiographies that account plausibly for his circumstances and subtly advance his interests. He is very taken with money, and quite willing to stretch the rules when there are profits or savings to be made. As his dealings with the king and the duke demonstrate, he is willing and able to simulate credulity when it serves his purposes. Huck takes a certain pride in his readiness to be "low-down" (77). He recognizes hypocrisy when he sees it, and he is skillful at turning it to the service of his own ends. Thus he wins vital time for himself and Mary Jane Wilks by playing her sisters' belief that they have contagious mumps against their desire to travel in England. Huck is properly reluctant to tell lies, but it is clear that he hesitates more out of the fear of detection than moral scruple. In fact, in most respects the boy has about the same regard for truth as his neighbors do, and as Mark Twain does, and he knows it. "You don't know about me," he begins in *Huckleberry Finn,*

> without you have read a book by the name of "The Adventures of Tom Sawyer," but that ain't no matter. That book was made by Mr. Mark Twain, and he told the truth, mainly. There was things which he stretched, but mainly he told the truth. That is nothing. I never seen anybody but lied, one time or another, without it was Aunt Polly, or the widow, or maybe Mary. Aunt Polly—Tom's aunt Polly, she is—and Mary, and the widow Douglas, is all told about in that book—which is mostly a true book; with some stretchers, as I said before.   (1)

Huck is neither surprised nor upset by lying. It is human nature to depart from the truth, he assumes. There are times, he finds, and freely admits, when truth-telling is an invitation to trouble and danger; and there are other times when lying and human fellow-feeling go hand in hand. But while Huck lies and cheats with the best of them, he is unusual in his relative freedom from illusion about his behavior. He is generally aware of himself when he lies and cheats, just as he is shrewdly attuned to the lying and cheating of others. And to the very considerable extent that he is undeceived by his own deceitfulness, Huck is free of bad faith. In this, ironically enough, he is akin to the king and the duke. Though he has none of their predatory cruelty, he is at one with the charlatans in his social marginality, and therefore in his relatively unobstructed view of the unacknowledged terms of the dominant culture. He sees and often practices and sometimes accepts what his neighbors conceal from themselves and others. Huck's "innocence" consists not in harmlessness or ignorance or blind adherence to conventional moral rules, but in a remarkably broad and unblinking perspective on himself and his world. It is the key to his complete and quite singular freedom from self-righteousness; and it bears directly on his penchant for the inadvertent discovery of human folly, and on his own quite extraordinary lack of a sense of humor.

In his immediate and sure grasp of reality as he finds it, Huck is comparable to Tom Sawyer. It remains to add that the boys differ quite dramatically in their ways of perceiving the world, and, therefore, in the worlds they behold. These conspicuous differences between the equally acute youngsters are primarily cultural in origin. As I have suggested, Huck's marginality registers in a relatively literal, relatively unmediated accuracy of vision—a frequently baffled cultural acuity. From Huck's vantage on the social margins, the assumptions and suppressions woven imperceptibly into the fabric of everyday life appear in bold, sometimes humorous, often dismaying relief. Everyday Christian routines seem arbitrary and constructed to Huck, though they are utterly transparent to such "insiders" as the widow and Miss Watson. Likewise, mob justice and the essential inhumanity of race-slavery look especially arbitrary and cruel when witnessed from a culturally marginal perspective.

For Tom, on the other hand, departures from the admitted tedium of religious routines are fiercely resented, and such arbitrary cruelty as the social order permits is submerged in a mediating blanket of convention. As we have seen, Tom is supremely confident in his access to and control of the world as he finds it. It is also clear that his mastery is directly the result of his insider's immersion in the cultural bad faith that he intuitively grasps and exploits. Tom is blind to the blindness he masters; he fails utterly to recognize his own signature on the culturally constructed world in which he plays. Nor is he aware that the range and extravagance of his bad-faith deceptions increase markedly toward the end of *Huckleberry Finn,* when his activities bring him into direct, prolonged contact with Jim. He responds with an elaborate scheme, ostensibly conceived in the service of Jim's liberation, that includes a climactic return from New Orleans to a gaudy parade "with a torchlight procession, and a brass band"; then Jim "would be a hero," he tells Huck, "and so would we" (360). The unscheduled abbreviation of his utterly grandiose plan does very little to hinder Tom's achievement of pleasure and power, especially as those are available to him in the manipulation of people and circumstance, and as the premier entertainer to an attentive, adoring multitude. His exploits in the final chapters of *Huckleberry Finn* reach their appointed and characteristic conclusion when he expands upon them before the astonished audience that has gathered at his bedside. En route to this final, most gratifying scene, Tom has been the creator and delighted inhabitant of a world of adventure fabricated out of a handful of unpromising circumstances and a small library of popular romances. He has experienced volumes of adventures as perilous and complicated as his imagination can make them, and he has survived to tell the tale. Nor is the danger, and his heroic triumph over it, entirely in his head. The bullet on the chain around his neck could not be more real. But Tom is so deeply immersed in romantic fictions that he experiences a kind of magical immunity to mortal consequence. The bullet enters his leg, but it gives him no major fear or pain. Rather, it penetrates to the vivid center of his imaginative life, where it is received as the happy climax to his most stylish production. Tom wears it as proud, palpable testimony to the reality of his fantastic adventures, and as a token of his heroic invulnerability.

The major differences between Tom, the masterful fabricator on the inside, and Huck, the literal-minded witness along the margin, are graphically in evidence as the boys move forward in their planning for Jim's liberation. Huck opens with the perfectly practical suggestion that they free Jim on a dark night and resume their flight down the river. Predictably, Tom finds this "too blame' simple"; he insists on a plan that promises a maximum of "trouble" in the doing, and plenty of "talk" (292) once it is done. While Huck wants to free Jim as directly and safely as possible, Tom views the escape as the merest pretext for an elaborate public spectacle. "I wanted the *adventure* of it," he later explains, "and I'd a waded neck-deep in blood to" get it (357). Huck is hardly deceived; but, strangely, he readily accedes to Tom's bizarre plan, allowing that "it was worth fifteen of mine, for style, and would make Jim just as free a man as mine would, and maybe get us all killed, besides" (292).

We will come back to Huck's baffling acquiescence in a scheme that is as contradictory and dangerous as it is conspicuously indifferent to Jim's freedom. For now, however, let us follow along as he records his

friend's secret delight in having "to invent *all* the difficulties. Well,"
Tom reflects,

> we can't help it, we got to do the best we can with the materials we've
> got. Anyhow, there's one thing—there's more honor in getting him out
> through a lot of difficulties and dangers, where there warn't one of them
> furnished to you by the people who it was their duty to furnish them,
> and you had to contrive them all out of your own head.   (298–99)

Tom's evident relish for the work ahead, his remarkable anticipation in
this honorable business of contriving romantic "difficulties and dan-
gers" out of his "own head," is an index to his confidence in his ability
to "let on." "Letting on," as Tom practices it, proceeds on the assumption that experience is receptive to immediate and substantial revision
by the consciousness that witnesses it. Reality is "given," but it is also
plastic to the informing will of the participant. Letting on is thus an
individual form of reality construction, or remodeling, in which the
inhabitant of the fabricated universe is also constantly present as archi-
tect and builder in its construction. To the very considerable extent
that it involves belief in the objective existence of its own conscious
fabrications, Tom's letting on is clearly akin to bad faith. It is willing
self-deception. Tom is quite evidently aware that his stylish play involves endless make-believe, but he is also firmly committed to the
substantial reality of his willful imaginings. Having assured Huck that
"a lantern makes too much" light for safety while they are digging near
the house at night, Tom goes on to complain that even his prudence on
the score of light must be fabricated. "When you come down to the
cold facts," he laments, "we simply got to *let on* that a lantern's resky.
Why, we could work with a torchlight procession if we wanted to, *I*
believe" (299). The irony here is perfectly delicious; for while Tom
concedes that the necessity to do without a lantern is contrived, that
concession confers existence upon a nonexistent lantern and at the same
time provides an explanation for the decision not to use it.

Huck's very different, much more pragmatic approach to making
believe comes clearly to view in his running debate with Tom on
whether to use picks and shovels or case-knives in digging Jim out of
captivity. Huck favors the heavier tools; they are ready to hand, and
they will make the work light and rapid. To such eminent good sense,
Tom replies with towering contempt. Knives are used in "all the books
that gives any information about these things" (276), he insists, and

the best authorities suggest that the most heroic escapes require decades of digging. Still, with all due reluctance, Tom acknowledges that their special circumstances enforce major departures from the leading models. "By rights," he reasons, "I reckon we ought to be a couple of years; but we can't. Things being so uncertain, what I recommend is this: that we really dig right in, as quick as we can; and after that, we can *let on*, to ourselves, that we was at it thirty-seven years." In effect, Tom is perfectly, imperially, capable of having the situation both ways. On one side, he insists that there is an obligation to observe the authorities in make-believe, and then promptly ignores it; on the other, and now quite openly on his own authority, he declares that the just abandoned precedents have in fact been quite properly observed. Once again, the ostensible concession to reality forms the occasion for the pleasurable exercise of the power to undo and refashion the world.

"Now there's *sense* in that," Huck responds to Tom's recommendation. "Letting-on don't cost nothing; letting-on ain't no trouble; and if it's any object, I don't mind letting on we was at it a hundred and fifty years" (305). So long as he is able to proceed in the simplest, safest way toward his objective, Huck is satisfied. He recognizes Tom's delusions for what they are, but he simulates credulity as a harmless, practical means to his primary goal.

Before long, Tom grows weary of rapid digging with the case-knives, and insists that "we got to dig him out with the picks, and *let on* it's case-knives." Huck is delighted, of course: "*Now* you're *talking!*" he says, "your head gets leveler and leveler all the time, Tom Sawyer." Tom makes the change in plans with the obligatory reluctance. "It ain't right, and it ain't moral," he complains, "and I wouldn't like it to get out." Huck, on the other hand, is perfectly indifferent to all save practical considerations. "Picks is the thing, moral or no moral; and as for me, I don't care shucks for the morality of it, nohow." Tom replies by elaborating self-righteously on the ethical differences that Huck has drawn into the foreground.

> "Well," he says, "there's excuse for picks and letting-on, in a case like this; if it warn't so, I wouldn't approve of it, nor I wouldn't stand by and see the rules broke—because right is right, and wrong is wrong, and a body ain't got no business doing wrong when he ain't ignorant and knows better. It might answer for *you* to dig Jim out with a pick, *without* any letting-on, because you don't know no better; but it wouldn't for me, because I do know better." (307)

Tom's pious rhetoric notwithstanding, this is emphatically not a declaration of the responsibility for right action incumbent on those brought up to right thinking. Rather, the high-sounding sentiments proceed on the implicit premise that wrong-doing is often necessary, and even pleasurable. More explicitly, Tom declares—with more than a trace of envy—that wrong-doing is also the privilege of ignorance. "Wrong is wrong" for Tom only when it is a conscious departure from what is recognized to be right. Thus there is no harm, he argues condescendingly, in what he regards as Huck's ignorant departures from the straight and narrow. It follows, for Tom at least, that persons able to distinguish between right and wrong are morally obliged to persuade themselves—to "let on"—that wrong is right before pursuing wrong courses of action. Self-deception, and not adherence to rational moral principles, is the ethical imperative.

Tom is doubly self-deceived—and therefore, by his own standards, doubly successful—in his brief sermon. Most obviously, he persuades himself, immediately and without apparent strain of any kind, that picks are knives. "Gimme a caseknife," he commands. "He had his own by him," Huck reflects,

> but I handed him mine. He flung it down, and says:
> "Gimme a *caseknife*."
> I didn't know just what to do—but then I thought. I scratched around amongst the old tools, and got a pick-axe and give it to him, and he took it and went to work, and never said a word.
> He was always just that particular. Full of principle.   (307)

Tom is also self-deceived in the much more sweeping and consequential sense that he in fact regards his argument for self-induced moral blindness as the very pinnacle of right-thinking. Though morally insignificant in itself, his assurance that an ax is a knife is clear evidence that the profound moral lie at the center of his righteous bad faith is virtually proof against his own detection.

As Tom's cultural kin, we have been strongly inclined to dismiss his address to the world as child's play, as the merest make-believe. This turning away subtly recapitulates the boy's willing self-deception at the deepest level of all, for it tends to draw attention away from the morally urgent issues of race and slavery that are central to the developing action. In dismissing Tom as childish we join him in the "evasion" of the grave moral significance of his behavior. The Tom Sawyer we observe in the closing chapters of *Huckleberry Finn* is more deeply immersed in his own fabrications than ever before because the action draws him into close quarters for a prolonged period with the reality of slavery. Jim's presence triggers an impulse to "evasion" that arises out of Tom's cultural incapacity to deal directly with the terrible truth of race–slavery, and that propels him to the limits of his gamesman's capacity for manipulation and make-believe. The result is a perspective so utterly divided between right and wrong, between the proud cultural ideals of freedom and human equality and their tragic contradiction in Jim, that elements ordinarily held in tension seem to pull apart before our eyes. It is as though the absurdity of pretending to free an already free man so strains the cultural readiness to be deceived that the truth of the situation cannot be completely concealed, the proffered bad-faith illusion cannot be comfortably accepted. On one side, we are witness to a Tom Sawyer who leaps at the opportunity to free a slave, who is consummately resourceful and bold and self-sacrificing in that enterprise, who is appropriately attentive to the moral foundations of his behavior, and who takes great pride in the successful achievement of his noble human objective. This heroic emancipator seems to speak for the best in his civilization when, upon finding Jim in chains, he protests: "They hain't no *right* to shut him up! *Shove!*—and don't you lose a minute. Turn him loose! he ain't no slave, he's as free as any cretur that walks this earth!" (356).

But the Tom who glimpses a suffering human being in Jim, and who rises in fiery indignation at the abuse of a "free" black man, would collapse under the weight of unbearable guilt were it not for his bad-faith blindness to the utter contradiction in his own makeup. Tom is spared this breakdown because he comes equipped with happy illusions about what he is doing, and because his adventures consume consciousness and thereby effectively distract him from the dark drift of his activities. Just as the citizens of Bricksville are engaged in amusements that at once betray and conceal the barbarity of their lives, so Tom is never even remotely aware of the grave implications of his "evasion." Almost in the same breath with his high-minded pronouncements on Jim's freedom he acknowledges, without so much as a hint of uneasiness, that he has contrived to free the already free man simply because it feeds his craving for adventure. This is the Tom Sawyer whose ethical inquiries center on picks and shovels, issue in arguments for the necessity of bad faith, and whose pleasure in his exploits has everything to do with his extraordinary success as a gamesman and entertainer, and nothing to do with the advancement of Jim's quest for freedom. Most significantly and most ironically of all, Tom is blind to the fact that in freeing the already free black man he must first re-enslave him. He takes Jim's freedom away in order to play a game with its restoration; but the game itself nullifies its own putative outcome by demonstrating that the freedom it bestows is entirely contingent on the bad-faith whim of the giver. This is letting on in earnest, for Tom has persuaded himself that he is engaged in a gratifying drama of liberation, while in fact his adventures testify to the intractable fixity of the cultural conditions that give rise to and sustain race–slavery.

It is entirely appropriate that *Huckleberry Finn* should end with Tom Sawyer's "evasion." The conspicuous and yet totally unacknowledged contradiction and cruelty in this ostensibly childish diversion are the culminating strokes in the novel's portrayal of pathological bad faith. The virulence of the disease is everywhere to be observed: in the ease with which the essential horror of the story is reduced to child's play; in the jittery distraction from guilt that the guilty show provides; in the utter blindness to contradiction that Tom shares with his spectators; in the virtually unchallenged authority of the elaborate, comprehensive bad faith on display. Many of these elements are at work in the narrative from the very beginning; but they gather to a dark terminus in the boy's ebullient letting on to free an already free man. It is equally appropriate, and consistent with bad faith as I understand it, that we, the audience, have been strongly inclined to dismiss this final movement in *Huckleberry Finn* as esthetically flawed in one way or another. Many readers confess that they have never been able to finish the novel; others plow through to the end, but find that attention wanders and memory fails to hold details in place; still others incline to the view that the "real" *Huckleberry Finn* ends in Chapter 32, just before Tom Sawyer returns to the action. In any case, the novel's conclusion is rarely productive of much ease of mind in most readers. This is not entirely surprising. After all, this portion of the narrative is irresistibly, albeit subtly, erosive of primary American myths about boys and black men and freedom that the novel is commonly assumed to advance. Our uneasiness rises in the closing chapters because it is here that the operations of bad faith draw more plainly and painfully than ever into association with racism and slavery. The audience resistance that results is thus a recapitulation of the bad-faith recoil from implication that the action dramatizes. Tom's "evasion" exposes us to more of our reality than we can bear; but at the same time it makes that reality at least marginally bearable for most of us by permitting us to view it as less than fully real or appropriate or artistically well wrought.

But we may also resist the powerful, easeful cultural tide at least long enough to reflect on Tom's elaborate spectacle as an oblique warning on the score of evasions. For himself, Tom takes a bullet as part of the price for his flight to fiction. So complete is his refashioning of reality that he actually fails to recognize the bullet for the palpable threat that it is. In letting on that a wrong is a right and thus sublimating the guilt that attaches to membership in a Christian, democratic, racist, slaveholding civilization, he nearly gets himself killed; even more ominously, he blindly reenacts the crime that causes the guilt that in turn prompts the retreat to the life-threatening evasion. Together with his audience, and culturally on purpose, Tom learns nothing from his experience; thus he is destined to repeat it. Something of the same may be said of that virtually standard response to *Huckleberry Finn,* which avoids a full reckoning with the novel's conclusion by dismissing it as childish or misplaced or otherwise esthetically defective. Paradoxically, such a response is directly to the point precisely because it evades it; and it is bound to repeat itself, quite conceivably at its peril, so long as it continues to turn away from the unbearable spectacle.

VI

Tom's taste for the fabrication of increasingly elaborate fictions tends to confirm his leadership role in the dominant culture—a culture whose appetite for distraction grows more acute as the deep sources of its bad faith draw more fully into the foreground. Appearances to the contrary notwithstanding, there is nothing at all original in Tom's plots. Rather, he is a brilliant mimic, and his schemes, no matter how fantastic they may appear, are remarkable for their cultural fidelity. Tom's education as fabricator par excellence reaches its conclusion in the final chapters of *Huckleberry Finn,* where his resources in bad-faith reality construction meet their ultimate challenge. Tom responds with characteristic brilliance, taking the hero's part in both seeming to liberate and effectively re-enslaving an already free black man. His "evasion," which penetrates to the heart of a paramount and enduring American dilemma, is Tom's most brilliant mimetic variation on the world as he finds it, and testimony to his mastery of the bad-faith culture that more than ever defines him.

If Tom seizes on Jim's predicament as the occasion for the confirmation of his free-wheeling authority within the dominant culture, Huck views it as an obstacle to the recovery of such limited freedom as he and Jim have experienced along the cultural margins. The boys' responses serve to illustrate a clear pattern: while Tom's activities generally propel him toward the center of his world, Huck's behavior reveals a powerful inclination to back away. The impulse to withdraw from civilization culminates, of course, in Huck's decision to "light out for the Territory" at the conclusion of his narrative. But the urge to put as much space as possible between himself and the rest of the settled world grows on the boy from the very beginning of the novel.

Physical distance from civilized folk is for Huck the absolutely essential condition for the achievement of the freedom and comfort and satisfaction he so craves. To be sure, he is at his most contented in the company of Jim; and much has been made of the warm ties between the boy and the escaped slave. But Huck is also at ease with Jim because they are in flight from the same pursuers; thus Jim is acceptable as a companion, as a stay against what Huck calls "the lonesomeness of the river" (157), because he has nothing to gain and everything to lose from the betrayal of his young friend. "I was ever so glad to see Jim" on Jackson's Island, Huck recalls. "I warn't lonesome, now. I told him I warn't afraid of *him* telling the people where I was" (51). Moreover, Huck is free and easy and comfortable with Jim, as he never is with white people, because he views the black man as his inferior. Jim is no challenge to his autonomy, and hardly threatens to oppress him with superior, civilized ways. Jim is acceptable precisely because he is a fugitive whom Huck regards as less than his equal. He is a safe companion before he is a friend. And while there is evidence that Huck is emotionally attached to Jim, it is also true that he registers no regret when it appears that Jim has perished in the accident with the river boat, and makes no place for Jim in his plans for "the Territory."

Huck comes closest to realizing the ideal state of freedom, ease, and comfort on the raft in Chapter 19, just after his escape from the bloody feuding between the Grangerfords and Shepherdsons. The idyllic mood is enhanced by the dramatic contrast between the natural serenity of the river and the "civilized" mayhem Huck has just witnessed. But the mood is also vulnerable to frequent reminders of the surrounding, encroaching reality of the shore. The silence is regularly punctuated by sounds traveling across the water from passing scows and other rafts: "sometimes you could hear a sweep screaking; or jumbled up voices, it was so still, and sounds come so far." The sight of a log cabin at dawn puts Huck in mind of the "cheats" in wood-yards who pile wood "so you can throw a dog through it anywheres." A "nice breeze springs up," but fresh smells compete with the "dead fish" left by thoughtless people to rot on the banks. All of these very immediate and discordant sensory details work to disturb the natural stillness and peace of environment and mind, and they draw attention to the slender corridors of water that separate the raft from the shore. These watery margins are the key, so far as Huck is concerned, to safety and comfort. Their saving influence is gratefully confirmed for him in the sight of an "axe flash" in the morning sun, and in "the *k'chunk*" that he hears when the sound of the blow finally reaches his ear. "It had took all that time," he observes, with evident approval, "to come over the water" (156–57).

To a very considerable extent, Huck's need to separate himself physically from the people along the shore is founded on fear. At the outset, he is afraid that Pap will kill him; then, after he has staged the fake murder, he fears that his father will learn that he is still alive. But this specific source of terror seems gradually to give way to a more generalized fugitive reflex, a tense, breathless recoil from the potential threat in all humans. "Whenever anybody was after anybody," Huck allows, "I judged it was *me*—or maybe Jim" (158–59). Evidently enough, this constant verging on panic is very considerably aggravated by Huck's keeping company with a fugitive slave; fear that he will be taken for an abolitionist is part of the price that he pays for Jim's friendship.

But the world as he finds it, independent of Pap and Jim, lends abundant fuel to Huck's skittish inclination to withdraw. The simple proximity to other people is increasingly a just cause for alarm, especially on those occasions when major threats to his welfare force Huck into hiding. He last sees his father alive when Pap passes near the stand of willows in which he is hidden. "He went by so close I could a reached out the gun and touched him" (42), Huck recalls. Close human quarters equate with danger again when Huck conceals himself behind a log on Jackson's Island as the ferry-boat, crowded with townspeople searching for his corpse, noses into view.

> They all crowded up and leaned over the rails, nearly in my face, and
> kept still, watching with all their might. I could see them first-rate,
> but they couldn't see me. Then the captain sung out:
>   "Stand away!" and the cannon let off such a blast right before me that
> it made me deef with the noise and pretty near blind with the smoke,
> and I judged I was gone. If they'd a had some bullets in, I reckon they'd
> a got the corpse they was after.   (47)

Likewise, the murderers on the wreck of the *Walter Scott* come perilously close to discovering the terrified boy hidden in their midst. "I
couldn't see them," Huck recalls, "but I could tell where they was, and
how close they was by the whisky they'd been having" (83). Much later
on in the narrative, Huck relates that the king, in retrieving the Wilks
fortune from the closet in which it is cached, "come a fumbling under
the curtain two or three foot from where I was" (228) hidden. That
Huck is never caught is no less remarkable than the fact that he finds
it necessary to spend so much of his time in hiding.

Huck's fear of others, and the marked tendency to retreat that it
provokes, are both substantially reinforced by the trail of human selfishness and cruelty that runs through his narrative. When he is not
drawing back in terror, it seems, Huck is looking on in disbelief. The
memory of the Shepherdsons hounding the wounded Buck Granger-
ford and his cousin into the river, shouting "Kill them, kill them!" is
more than his consciousness can endure.

> It made me so sick I most fell out of the tree. I ain't agoing to tell
> *all* that happened—it would make me sick again if I was to do that. I
> wished I hadn't ever come ashore that night, to see such things. I ain't
> ever going to get shut of them—lots of times I dream about
> them.   (153)

Further down river, Huck finds the greedy fraudulence of the king and
the duke "enough to make a body ashamed of the human race" (210).
The spectacle of their simulated grief over the death of Peter Wilks is
just so much "rot and slush" to the boy; "it was just sickening," he
says, "I never see anything so disgusting" (212–13). He is permanently
scarred by recollections of the separation and sale of the slave family
left in the Wilks estate. "I can't ever get it out of my memory," he
laments, "the sight of them poor miserable girls and niggers hanging
around each other's necks and crying" (234). It is all quite concisely
summarized—his compassion and sensitivity on one side, and the
world's heartlessness and hypocrisy on the other—in his reaction to the

sight of the king and the duke as they are carried by, all tar and feathers, on a rail. "Well, it made me sick to see it," he recalls; "and I was sorry for them poor pitiful rascals, it seemed like I couldn't ever feel any hardness against them any more in the world. It was a dreadful thing to see. Human beings *can* be awful cruel to one another" (290).

Huckleberry Finn is not a very happy book because Huck Finn is not a very happy person. His unhappiness can be traced, as I have suggested, to immediate sources in the hypocrisy and fraud and cruelty and violence of the dominant culture, and to a deeper rootedness in race–slavery, the monstrous inhumanity which prompts Jim's flight, and which divides Huck's heart against his head. It is civilization as he finds it—a culture of bad faith grown pathological in its surrender to the gross, palpable injustice of its peculiar institution—that frightens and disgusts Huck. Grounded as it is in freedom and innocence, Huck's peace of mind is incompatible with the conditions of life he encounters in the towns along the Mississippi. Thus he is perforce an outcast, a solitary, a wanderer. This is why he is happiest when he is alone on the wide river; and this is why he ends his story with the decision "to light out" all over again.

Yet the case for Huck's happiness in "the Territory ahead" is hardly closed. There is some evidence, albeit extratextual, that other wanderers, with notions of their own about freedom, were already on the move to the West. Nor is it clear that solitude answers Huck's discontent with unmingled peace of mind. The Mississippi may be free and easy and comfortable, but it is also, Huck iterates, "just solid lonesomeness" (157). Indeed, we are not far into the novel before this association of solitude and melancholy asserts itself. In the first chapter, Huck introduces himself, describes the civilized rigors of life with the Widow Douglas, and, finally weary with Miss Watson's "pecking" at him about "the good place," withdraws to his room.

> Then I set down in a chair by the window and tried to think of something cheerful, but it warn't no use. I felt so lonesome I most wished I was dead. The stars was shining, and the leaves rustled in the woods ever so mournful; and I heard an owl, away off, who-whooing about somebody that was dead, and a whippowill and a dog crying about somebody that was going to die; and the wind was trying to whisper something to me and I couldn't make out what it was, and so it made the cold shivers run over me. Then away out in the woods I heard that kind of a sound that a ghost makes when it wants to tell about something that's on its mind and can't make itself understood, and so can't

rest easy in its grave and has to go about that way every night grieving. I got so down-hearted and scared, I did wish I had some company. Pretty soon a spider went crawling up my shoulder, and I flipped it off and it lit in the candle; and before I could budge it was all shriveled up. I didn't need anybody to tell me that that was an awful bad sign and would fetch me some bad luck, so I was scared and most shook the clothes off of me. I got up and turned around in my tracks three times and crossed my breast every time; and then I tied up a little lock of my hair with a thread to keep witches away. But I hadn't no confidence. (4)

The retreat from the pressures of civilization, at least on this occasion, results in something far worse. Alone in his room, Huck is prey to demons which spring from his imagination and crowd the solitude with terror. Remote but familiar sounds are suddenly the voices of ghosts speaking of death. Mere accidents become signs potent with doom and impervious to charms. At no point are we inclined to view Huck's reflections as a humorous riot of naive superstition. The acceleration of his terror is too immediate and authentic for release into comedy. Rather, we come away impressed with the vague but nearly palpable dread which emerges from Huck's solitude. Left to himself, he is at once fearful that his life will continue, and that it will end. Little wonder that he craves some company.

The most detailed commentary on Huck's solitary terror is offered by Henry Nash Smith. He ventures that the ghostly visitation may be the punishment Huck "inflicts on himself for defying the mores of St. Petersburg," or that it may record the "intuitive recognition that Huck's and Jim's quest for freedom must end in failure." Whatever we may choose to make of them, however, Smith argues that "these sinister images . . . develop the characterization of Huck beyond the needs of the plot."[21]

Smith goes on to note "the drastic shift in tone" that occurs in the last third of *Huckleberry Finn,* and observes that this transition commences with Huck's approach to the Phelps plantation.

When I got there it was all still and Sunday-like, and hot and sunshiny—the hands was gone to the fields; and there was them kind of faint dronings of bugs and flies in the air that makes it seem so lonesome and like everybody's dead and gone; and if a breeze fans along and quivers the leaves, it makes you feel mournful, because you feel like it's spirits whispering—spirits that's been dead ever so many years—and you always think they're talking about *you.* As a general thing, it makes

a body wish *he* was dead, too, and done with it all. . . . I went around
and clumb over the back stile by the ash-hopper, and started for the
kitchen. When I got a little ways, I heard the dim hum of a spinning
wheel wailing along up and sinking along down again; and then I
knowed for certain I wished I was dead—for that *is* the lonesomest
sound in the whole world.   (276–77)

Smith points to the evident similarity between this passage and Huck's
earlier meditation in his bedroom, adding that once again the somber
mood is "not fully accounted for by the context of the story." Despite
apparent obstacles, Huck is still quite confident that his efforts to free
Jim will meet with success. Thus his depression cannot be explained as
a conscious anticipation of failure. For lack of an adequate internal motive, therefore, Smith concludes that "the emotion is the author's rather
than Huck's, and it is derived from sources outside the story."[22] This
line of thought leads to *The Autobiography*—specifically, to a description of the farm of Mark Twain's uncle, John A. Quarles.

I can see the farm yet, with perfect clearness. I can see all its belongings,
all its details; the family room of the house, with a "trundle" bed in one
corner and a spinning-wheel in another—a wheel whose rising and fall-
ing wail, heard from a distance, was the mournfulest of all sounds to
me and made me homesick and low spirited and filled my atmosphere
with the wandering spirits of the dead.[23]

Quite clearly, as Smith points out, both the place and the emotions
attached to it form the biographical background to Huck's reflections
at the Phelps plantation. Identical elements surface in Mark Twain's
use of the Quarles farm as the model for the Mason residence in "The
Private History of a Campaign That Failed."

We stayed several days at Mason's; and after all these years the memory
of the dullness, and stillness, and lifelessness of that slumberous farm-
house still oppresses my spirit as with a sense of the presence of death
and mourning. There was nothing to do, nothing to think about; there
was no interest in life. The male part of the household were away in the
fields all day, the women were busy and out of our sight; there was no
sound but the plaintive wailing of a spinning-wheel, forever moaning
out from some distant room—the most lonesome sound in nature, a
sound steeped and sodden with homesickness and the emptiness of
life.[24]

Once again, the similarities between autobiography and fiction are perfectly evident. But the passages are linked in the additional sense that

they all record attacks of conscience. In the Mason farm episode, Mark Twain suffers for his part in a wartime "murder." In Chapter 31 of *Huckleberry Finn,* Smith continues, the traces of a "latent feeling of guilt" signal Mark Twain's admission "that Huck's and Jim's journey down the river could not be imagined as leading to freedom for either of them." In order to skirt the tragic implications of this recognition, Mark Twain removed Huck from the center of the action in the remainder of the novel, and replaced him with Tom Sawyer. This displacement of the potentially tragic by the comic is rather improbably maneuvered into the plot when Aunt Sally Phelps mistakenly identifies Huck as Tom. "We can hardly fail," Smith concludes, "to perceive the weight of the author's feeling in Huck's statement on this occasion: 'it was like being born again, I was so glad to find out who I was.' Mark Twain has found out who he must be in order to end his book: he must be Tom."[25]

Using Smith's very useful discussion as a point of departure, I want to review a number of additional passages from Mark Twain's writing which cast light on Huck's moments of solitary terror. At the outset, there can be no doubt that many of the details which appear in Huck's meditations are elsewhere to be found in association with Mark Twain's ubiquitous conscience. Curiously enough, in making this point, Smith ignores a most telling autobiographical description of the Quarles farm. Recalling an especially stormy night spent at his uncle's house, Mark Twain recounts

> how very dark that room was, in the dark of the moon, and how packed it was with ghostly stillness when one woke up by accident away in the night, and forgotten sins came flocking out of the secret chambers of the memory and wanted a hearing; and how ill chosen the time seemed for this kind of business; and how dismal was the hoo-hooing of the owl and the wailing of the wolf, sent mourning by on the night wind.[26]

Viewed in combination with the others, this passage makes it emphatically clear that recurrent descriptive details were closely associated with guilt in Mark Twain's imagination. The appearance of identical details on two occasions in *Huckleberry Finn* is strong *prima facie* evidence that guilt is also at work in the background of Huck's overt depression and fear. Yet, as Smith points out, contextual justification for an attack of conscience is not readily apparent. In Chapter 1, Huck has just rejected Miss Watson's Christian admonishments, and Chapter 32 follows in the wake of his decision to "go to hell" as the price of freeing Jim. In short, while the details of Huck's meditations dispose us to look for guilt, the fictional frame of rebellion against civilized convention leads to baseless—or at least puzzlingly extreme—expressions of fear. Nonetheless, by gathering insights from additional "sources outside the story," I want to argue that Huck's fears and death wishes and superstitious dread emerge naturally, if rather obliquely, from the text itself.

The brief passages from Chapters 1 and 32 of *Huckleberry Finn* share a number of key elements. In both, Huck is alone; in both he is lonesome; he is temporarily weary of life, even to the point of wishing to die; the tense stillness is brushed by soft, haunting sounds—of the breeze, of leaves, a spinning-wheel, insects, an owl, a dog; these oppressive sounds seem to be the voices of the dead, of ghosts trying to be heard, seeking compassion, murmuring about death; the vague voices intensify Huck's loneliness, fear, and his wish to be done with life. Both episodes augur ill, and the first includes concrete reinforcement for Huck's dark presentiments.

Some, and at times nearly all, of these elements appear in dozens of other passages scattered through Mark Twain's writing. In some instances, they serve in appropriate and predictable ways to enhance moods of loneliness, fear, and awe. Finding himself in a setting of "solitude and silence," for example, the narrator of "A Ghost Story" is overcome with "a superstitious dread." He reacts to a brush with a cobweb "as one who had encountered a phantom."[27] Ghostly presences work to like effect on the visitors to a haunted castle in *Joan of Arc*.

> An uncanny silence and solemnity ensued which was dismaler to me than the mute march past the bastilles. We sat looking vacantly at each other, and it was easy to see that no one there was comfortable. The longer we sat so, the more deadly still that stillness got to be; and when the wind began to moan around the house presently, it made me sick and miserable, and I wished I had been brave enough to be a coward this time, for indeed it is not proper shame to be afraid of ghosts, seeing how helpless the living are in their hands.   (XVII, 274–75)

Huck gives in to similar fears at a particularly tense moment in *Tom Sawyer, Detective*.

> He was thinking of that awful thing laying yonder in the sycamores, and it seemed like being that close to a ghost, and it give me the cold shudders. The moon came a-swelling up out of the ground, now, powerful big and round and bright, behind a comb of trees, like a face

looking through prison bars, and the black shadders and white places begun to creep around, and it was miserable quiet and still and night-breezy and graveyardy and scary.   (xx, 154–55)

Solitude is itself often sufficient to open the imagination to an attack of ghostly intimations. This is the case, for example, when Hank Morgan, the narrator of *A Connecticut Yankee in King Arthur's Court,* glimpses "three masses of building" in the Valley of Holiness.

They were distant and isolated temporalities shrunken to toy constructions in the lonely wastes of what seemed a desert—and was. Such a scene is always mournful, it is so impressively still, and looks so steeped in death. But there was a sound here which interrupted the stillness only to add to its mournfulness; this was the faint far sound of tolling bells which floated fitfully to us on the passing breeze, and so faintly, so softly, that we hardly knew whether we heard it with our ears or with our spirits.   (205)

Solitude is equally oppressive for the narrator of "The Enchanted Sea-Wilderness," who finds himself becalmed on a remote and desolate sea.

The stillness was horrible; and the absence of life. There was not a bird or a creature of any kind in sight, the slick surface of the water was never broken by a fin, never a breath of wind fanned the dead air, and there was not a sound of any kind, even the faintest—the silence of death was everywhere.

Meanwhile, broken in spirit, the captain "moped around again, like the rest—and prayed for death, I reckon. We all did."[28] These rather gothic interludes bear obvious similarities to the passages from *Huckleberry Finn.* Yet deeper comparison yields little. For while Huck's moments of panic strike us as anomalous intervals of dread with no immediately apparent cause, the experiences of Hank Morgan and the others arise from the manifest exigencies of plot, setting, and genre. Most especially, when viewed in the aggregate, these conventional mood pieces fail to exhibit a consistent pattern of psychological or structural integration, and thus offer no clues to a fuller understanding of Huck's enigmatic mood.

Such patterns are more evident in a group of passages in which silence and lonely apprehension function as the prelude to episodes of major, and always painful, consequence. As he approaches what he imagines to be his execution, Hank Morgan enters a "stillness . . . so profound that if I had been blindfold I should have supposed I was in a solitude instead of walled in by four thousand people" (46).[29] Virtually identical moments serve as prologues to major crises in *Joan of Arc*. Just before the Battle of Orleans,

> a mute expectancy reigned. The stillness was something awful—because it meant so much. There was no air stirring. The flags on the towers and ramparts hung straight down like tassels. Wherever one saw a person, that person had stopped what he was doing, and was in a waiting attitude, a listening attitude . . . Many people were visible—all were listening, not one was moving . . . Everywhere were these impressive petrified forms; and everywhere was suspended movement and that awful stillness.   (XVII, 340–41)

Later, as Joan is brought to trial, the narrator's heart pounds in his breast. "But there was silence now—silence absolute. All those noises ceased, and it was as if they had never been. Not a sound; the stillness grew oppressive; it was like a weight upon one" (XVIII, 142). Finally, just before Joan's condemnation,

> there was no noise, no stir; it was as if the world was dead. The impressiveness of this silence and solemnity was deepened by a leaden twilight, for the sky was hidden by a pall of low-hanging storm-clouds; and above the remote horizon faint winkings of heat-lightning played, and now and then one caught the dull mutterings and complainings of distant thunder.   (XVIII, 270–71)

A similarly deathly atmosphere surrounds a pathetic prisoner, just before her execution, in *The Mysterious Stranger*.

> It was a solitude, except that a thinly and rustily clad old woman was there, sitting on the frozen ground and fastened to a post by a chain around her waist . . . A pitiful spectacle she was, in the vague dawn and the stillness, with the faint winds whispering around her and the powdery snow-whorls frisking and playing and chasing each other over the black ground.[30]

And, appropriately enough, the mood just before the mass execution imagined in "The United States of Lyncherdom" is a familiar one.

> All being ready, now, and the darkness opaque, the stillness impressive—for there should be no sound but the soft moaning of the night wind and the muffled sobbing of the sacrifices—let all the far stretch of kerosened pyres be touched off simultaneously and the glare and the shrieks and the agonies burst heavenward to the Throne.[31]

The recurrent atmospheric elements in these passages are clear links to *Huckleberry Finn*, as is their characteristic mood of stunned silence in anticipation of death. In view of the ubiquity of death in the novel, these cognate materials lend credence to Daniel G. Hoffman's view that Huck's depressions "are an acknowledgment of the fact of death" and "an admission of evil as a positive force in the natural world."[32] Moreover, they provide support for Ray W. Frantz's contention that the spider in Chapter 1 is "the worst possible sign—the death sign,"[33] and to Richard P. Adams's linking of Huck's death wish with the fake murder he engineers in his escape from Pap's cabin.[34] These passages may also cast some faint light on Jim's superstitious and thoroughly enigmatic prediction of Huck's death ("you's gwyne to git hung") in Chapter 4. Yet in a world of frequent and often premature mortality, Huck's shrewdness and good luck add up to survival. As part of the price exacted for his life, however, Huck must endure a regular succession of simulated or symbolic deaths. Thus for James M. Cox the

> fake murder is probably the most vital and crucial incident in the entire novel. Having killed himself, Huck is "dead" throughout the entire journey down the river. He is indeed the man without identity who is reborn at almost every river bend, not because he desires a new role, but because he must re-create himself to elude the forces which close in on him from every side.[35]

The grim corollary to this deathly alienation from civilized "forces" is vulnerability to the attacks of loneliness and dark apprehension which figure so prominently in Chapters 1 and 32.

Valuable as it is in helping to account for Huck's solitary fears, Cox's analysis does not address his wish to die. Moreover, though the feeling that life has lost its value is a regular feature in the parallel passages I have cited, these materials do little to supplement our understanding of the causes for Huck's death wish. It could be argued that loneliness and fear are causes enough. George C. Carrington, Jr., insists, for example, that Huck's intervals of solitude expose him to "head-on confrontations with nature in its most frightening form—an endless, meaningless flux." In this original and quite plausible interpretation, Huck's melancholy is "an existential matter" rooted in the perception that "life . . . is not occasionally empty; it is basically empty."[36] Nonetheless, there is additional evidence, some of it already noted, that the elements which make up Huck's depressions are at other places linked to the pressures of conscience. It remains, therefore, to explore the ways in which guilt, certainly unacknowledged and perhaps unconscious, works in the background of Huck's foreboding.

VII

Henry Nash Smith admits, it will be recalled, that guilt is often associated with the elements that appear in Huck's solitary meditations, but he finds such feelings psychologically unfounded in the novel, and therefore assigns them to Mark Twain. In effect, the guilt is "laid on." Smith supports his argument by linking a passage from "The Private History of a Campaign That Failed" with the guilt that Mark Twain experienced as the result of his part in the "murder" of an innocent man. In fact, however, the elements which Smith properly identifies as the symptoms of guilt appear *before,* and not after, the commission of the "crime." The eerie description of the Mason farm is followed by the descent of an ominous mood upon the soldiers. They are "silent and nervous. And soon uneasy—worried—apprehensive . . . It was late, and there was a deep woodsy stillness everywhere."[37] The silence is then broken by the sound of hoof-beats, and the unhappy killing takes place. It is a case, in other words, of guilt emerging in advance of the event which properly gives it rise.

Such reversals of the ordinary relationship between event and emotional response are not unusual in Mark Twain's life and work. The prophecy of his brother Henry's death came to him in an anguished dream that forecast not only the details of the funeral, but the circumstances that would assail his conscience after the episode occurred.[38] Anticipatory, or proleptic, guilt of this kind is sometimes found in conjunction with the elements that appear in Chapters 1 and 32 of *Huckleberry Finn.* The episode in "The Private History," for example, has a much more circumstantial parallel in *The Mysterious Stranger.* Upon learning from Young Satan that his friend Nikolaus is fated to die in twelve days, Theodor Fischer's consciousness is flooded by memories of his mistreatment of his doomed companion.

> No, I could not sleep. These shabby little wrongs upbraided me and tortured me; and with a pain much sharper than one feels when the

wrongs have been done to the living. Nikolaus *was* living, but no matter: he was to me as one already dead. The wind was still moaning about the eaves, the rain still pattering upon the panes.   (122)

The fretful anxiety, the preoccupation with death, the solitude and the drone of ghostly sounds—the setting and the state of mind are familiar enough. Theodor's foreknowledge of Nikolaus's misfortune prompts feelings of guilt which would ordinarily arise only after the fatal episode has occurred. The intensity of Theodor's suffering is dramatically increased by his prescience, for his disproportionate guilt gathers much of its energy from the fact that he is powerless to avert the disaster. It remains to observe that Theodor's advance information derives from fanciful manipulations of plot which, if removed, would betray his foreknowledge for what it is—a wish. In thinking of Nikolaus as "one already dead," he expresses both grief and an unconscious homicidal impulse. Mark Twain was well acquainted with such divided feelings. His dream of Henry's death, I have argued elsewhere, was itself the expression of an ambivalence which had an unconscious fratricidal wish as one of its poles.[39]

In Theodor's case, the extremity of the proleptic guilt is one clue to the murderous impulse which lies submerged in his apparently helpless foreknowledge. The resolution of the episode is another. As the day of the disaster approaches, Theodor eases his own anxiety by maneuvering Nikolaus's mother into the role of villain. Thus, when Nikolaus finally dies, the poor woman "could not forgive herself and could not be comforted, and kept on saying . . . she was the cause of his death" (128). Still, though Theodor's shrewd manipulating temporarily deflects and allays his guilt, it does not really save him. As the immediate sequel to the episode he observes that people are "foolish" when "they blame themselves for anything they have done." This utterly uncharacteristic cynicism has Nikolaus's mother as its ostensible object; in fact, of course, Theodor's unwonted sentiments function primarily as a sop to his own subliminal remorse. "It is as Satan said," he concludes, "we do not know good fortune from bad, and are always mistaking the one for the other. Many a time, since then, I have heard people pray to God to spare the life of sick persons, but I have never done it" (128–29). Unable to confront the nether side of his ambivalence, Theodor decides instead that life is not worth the possessing. Viewed from this angle, of course, his unconscious impulses toward his friend appear as benefactions in disguise.

Quite evidently, the similarities between the situations of Huck and Theodor go well beyond the details of setting which prompted the initial comparison. Both boys are alone and depressed and anxious. Both hear ghostly sounds. They are preoccupied with death, and they share dark forebodings about future developments which they feel powerless to control. In the course of their reflections, both decide that life is a burden and that death is a welcome respite from intolerable suffering. For Theodor, as we have seen, these latter sentiments are the conscious reflex of repressed guilt. In Huck's case, the death wish is perfectly manifest, and there are strong suggestions that guilt somehow figures in his dark mood. Moreover, the phenomenon of proleptic guilt may well apply to Huck, for his dark moodiness (especially in Chapter 1) has no apparent cause.

Given these abundant parallels, it remains to press Theodor's example a step further, and to ask what it is that Huck's moods look forward to. What ambivalence gives rise to his spectral premonitions of disaster and death? What buried wish feeds his sense of the inevitable and explains both his premature remorse and his expiatory desire to end his own life? In other words, who plays for Huck the role that Nikolaus plays for Theodor, and that Henry Clemens played for Mark Twain? Of course, it must be Jim.

In reviewing his offenses against Nikolaus, Theodor recalls that he once failed to apologize to his friend because "I was ashamed to say I was ashamed" (121). Huck experiences similar difficulties in making his amends for a practical joke that he has played on Jim. "It was fifteen minutes before I could work myself up to go and humble myself to a nigger—but I done it, and I warn't ever sorry for it afterwards, neither" (105). To some extent, such reluctance is the result of backwardness and pride. But the boys' hesitation is also rooted in an awareness, however vague, that their apologies for specific offenses will be perfunctory so long as the well-springs of their hostility remain unacknowledged. The extremity of Theodor's guilt, and the fact that his being "ashamed" does nothing to moderate his cruelty to Nikolaus, is evidence that his ambivalence will not be held in check by mere apologies. For his part, Huck is confident that his amends redeem past transgressions and ensure future harmony. "I didn't do him no more mean tricks, and I wouldn't done that one if I'd a knowed it would make him feel that way" (105). In fact, Huck is deceived in his retrospective account of the situation. His apology, though appropriate and commendable, is woefully inadequate as a gesture of redemption, and will prove a slender stay against future lapses.

The practical joke for which Huck finally apologizes—his misleading Jim into the belief that their separation during a storm on the river has been a dream—is only the last in a series of pranks designed to expose the gullibility and superstition which manifest what is assumed to be Jim's racial inferiority. Indeed, the first of these jokes occurs in Chapter 2, and forms the immediate sequel to Huck's initial experience with ghosts and lonely depression. Ironically enough, the trick turns on Jim's belief in evil spirits ("Niggers is always talking about witches" [8]), and misleads him into the proud assurance that he has been visited by the devil.

The next practical joke occurs on Jackson's Island. It is prompted by a disagreement over the interpretation of signs. Jim insists that touching a snake-skin brings bad luck, but Huck disagrees. To make his case, and to reassert his superiority, Huck decides to expose Jim's superstitious gullibility by placing a dead rattlesnake on his friend's blanket, "thinking there'd be some fun when Jim found him there" (64). But the joke backfires. When Jim takes to his bed, the dead snake's mate bites him on the heel and nearly kills him. Once again, the irony is at Huck's expense. At one level, this close brush with death is a painful vindication of Jim's position on the proper interpretation of signs. But the episode involves more than bad luck, for it is the malice arising out of an affront to his imagined racial superiority that prompts Huck to play the trick in the first place. The more threatening serpent here, as Carrington has very astutely observed, is the much older one associated with primordial human betrayal.[40] Huck is fully aware of the gravity of his offense; indeed, like Theodor, he is too ashamed to acknowledge his shame. Instead, Huck admits, "I slid out quiet and throwed the snakes clear away amongst the bushes; for I warn't going to let Jim find out it was all my fault, not if I could help it" (65).

This decision to conceal the evidence of a fundamental moral lapse is momentous. By his own intuitive standards, Huck is wrong. He betrays no inclination to dismiss the episode as a mistake; rather, he acknowledges "fault" and admits that it is "all" his. Yet in the same breath with his admission of guilt he decides to suppress it. In refusing to confess to Jim that he has been the knowing source of his grave suffering, Huck gives evidence of at least partial complicity in the dark web of deception at the heart of race–slavery. The evidence of his involvement grows even more damaging as it becomes clear that in concealing the evidence from Jim he also succeeds in hiding the ethical lapse from himself. Thus Huck later on acquiesces without the slightest shudder in Jim's inadvertently rueful reminder "that handling a snake-skin was such awful bad luck that maybe we hadn't got to the end of it yet" (65). In the aggregate, Huck's acknowledged crime against Jim's humanity, and his subsequent concealment of that crime from Jim and himself, betray a deep immersion in the cultural pathology that his narrative describes and obliquely analyzes. He does not know this. More to the point, he does not want to know this, and he has managed, in characteristic bad-faith fashion, to deceive himself about it. Once he has thrown the dead snakes in the bushes, we hear no more about them from Huck; so far as he is concerned, they are behind him, forgotten, cancelled.

In fact, of course, Jim's surmise that they "hadn't got to the end of" the snake-skins is profoundly resonant, not only for the fugitives themselves, but for the culture that informs their lives. As the narrative clearly demonstrates, the snakes are there in Huck's future just as surely as they are present in the cultural forces that combined to shape his character. He represses the serpent in his makeup with an unthinking, virtually reflexive efficiency that testifies to long familiarity with the mechanisms of bad-faith denial, especially as they bear on black people. There is evidence as well that Huck's secret shame derives added power for harm from its being hidden, on purpose, from others and, most of all, from himself. Meanwhile, convinced that he is being pursued by spectral "bad luck," Jim fails to identify the most immediate source of his difficulty, and is thus powerless to protect himself against even greater calamities. In Chapter 14, for example, not long after his nearly fatal encounter with the snakes, Jim displays a noble heart and great common sense in a dispute over apparent trivia. But he has no way of anticipating that Huck will react to the debate by retreating into sullen, spiteful silence. "I see it warn't no use wasting words," the boy reflects; "you can't learn a nigger to argue. So I quit" (98). The immediate sequel, the separation in the fog near Cairo, provides Huck with an occasion for an indirect demonstration of Jim's imagined inferiority in matters of logic and argumentation. As we have seen, his victory is a brief one, for Jim asserts himself with force and great dignity. Huck's apology is sincere; but this halting appearance of the positive pole of his ambivalence gives way with startling suddenness to fear and resentment when Jim expresses his joy at the prospect of reaching freedom. Responding to what he half-mistakenly calls his "conscience," Huck leaves the raft with the express purpose of turning his friend over to the authorities. Just as suddenly, the rending pathos of Jim's utterly innocent farewell—"Jim won't ever forget you, Huck; you's de bes' fren' Jim's ever had; en you's de *only* fren' ole Jim's got now" (125)—inspires a complete reversal of heart and the brilliant evasion of a pair of slave hunters.

Jim overflows with relief and gratitude. But before long he surrenders to the suspicion that they have floated south past Cairo. Once again, he blames fortune for his predicament, though in doing so he unknowingly locates a more immediate, human cause for his woe. "Po' niggers can't have no luck," he laments. "I alwuz 'spected dat rattle-snake-skin warn't done wid its work." The trenchancy of the dramatic irony is hardly lost on the reader. Nor is it entirely lost on Huck, whose response resonates with the kinds of bafflement and anguish that myths are made of. "I wish I'd never seen that snake-skin, Jim—I do wish I'd never laid eyes on it." Jim replies with consolation, but all unawares he rubs a tender spot. "It ain't yo' fault, Huck; you didn' know. Don't you blame yo'self 'bout it" (129).

Huck's guilty secret does not surface directly. The accusing episode is now behind him, and his memory, pliant to the promptings of bad faith, assures him that the snake-skin itself, and not his use of it, is to blame for their troubles. But the terrific pressure of his repressed guilt finds oblique expression in the sudden advent of a steamboat which bears down on the raft. Like an avenging Old Testament Leviathan, "with a long row of wide-open furnace doors shining like red-hot teeth" (130), the monstrous boat sweeps over the forsaken raft.

Ironically, though its impact is primarily destructive, the steamboat is also an agency of relief, for it brings temporary oblivion to the deeply troubled narrative. Viewed in this way, the "accident" is no longer simply, or even primarily, retributive. Rather, it is the very dramatic, very diverting instrument of a submerged narrative impulse to be done with snakes and guilt and slave hunters and hopeless drifting—to be done, that is, with Jim, and with all that attaches to him. To the extent that it answers this unacknowledged urge to remove Jim from sight and mind, the wreck is an evasion worthy of Tom Sawyer himself. Like so much that passes for entertainment along the river, the accident is a deeply designed distraction from the painful business that fills and troubles the conscious foreground. For Mark Twain, it is well known, the destruction of the raft marked the end of the first stage of composition, and the beginning of a long withdrawal from the unlooked-for and irrepressible complications that had surfaced in his juvenile fiction. For a while at least, he drew clear of his creative drift into a full reckoning with the unbearable reality of race–slavery. For Huck, in parallel fashion, the steamboat enforces a respite from the moral vertigo of his relationship with Jim. The chapters leading up to the accident are the chronicle of an accelerating swing between the poles of an excruciating ambivalence. Placed as it is, the riverboat collision may be viewed as the outward manifestation of a psychic collapse, a breakdown issuing in a temporary retreat from the inescapable course formed by circumstance, culture, and consciousness. While it is true that the Grangerford/Shepherdson interlude brings terrors of its own, these are temporarily manageable terrors because they form an interval of separation from Jim. Not surprisingly, Huck is totally forgetful of his quondam companion during this period. Though he is a loving and admired friend, Jim has become trouble for Huck—trouble, because accompanying an escaped slave both limits and threatens his freedom, and because the personal risk involved is a constant spur to his restive ambivalence. Taken in this light, the advent of the steamboat appears a manifestation of Huck's desperate need for release from his resurgent moral dilemma. To be sure, the feuding families provide little in the way of relief or clarity; they are culturally symptomatic of the problem, not avenues toward its solution. They function for Huck as a diversion, a distracting show that fails to satisfy because, like all of the novel's bad-faith distractions, it echoes with the cultural discord it is intended to conceal. Thus this show ends, as all the others do, in an explosion of violence that drives Huck back to Jim, and to the unfinished business at the dark center of his narrative.

The gathering weight of Huck's anguished confusion is brought home to us more than once as he rationalizes his decision to betray Jim to the authorities. "I got to feeling so mean and so miserable I most wished I was dead," he complains. A bit further on he adds: "I reckoned I would die of miserableness" (124). These sentiments are clearly reminiscent of Huck's depressed feelings in Chapter 1, but his sense of the attraction and proximity of death can now be tied directly to his hopelessly divided feelings about Jim. On one side, he perceives and fears the imminent threats to his friend's freedom and well-being. On the other, he sees that he must number himself among those life-threatening forces. Craving release from this unbearable ambivalence, Huck's consciousness is drawn toward the imagined solace of oblivion.

The other elements of his earlier meditation also come into clearer focus when applied to the present context. Huck must intuitively glimpse the fact that he is as physically and psychologically alone with Jim's company as he is without it. A self-exiled alien from civilization, he is nonetheless the bearer of civilized assumptions—most prominently in matters of race—which divide his consciousness, corrupt the only really comfortable human relationship available to him, and leave him utterly bereft. Thus the haunted ambient of his room, replete with sad, doomed voices, and the reflex destruction of that companionable spider, may be seen as omens of Huck's predicament on the raft. Looking back, we may begin to understand why he feels helpless, guilty, lonely, and half in love with death.

To suggest, as I have, that Huck's initial depression specifically anticipates his dilemma with Jim may appear to strain common critical sense. After all, Huck has no way of knowing that circumstance will land him on a raft near Cairo with Miss Watson's escaped slave. On this score, one must concede Professor Smith's point, and allow that these early anticipations of subsequent developments were projections of Mark Twain's richly creative unconscious. Without being aware of it, he recognized well in advance that his juvenile romance was fraught with tragic potential. This does not mean, however, that Huck's depression is without motive or out of character. To the contrary, Huck's mood betrays the subliminal awareness that he will suffer the consequences of living on the margin. Imperfectly exiled, as imperfectly civilized, Huck will always be as uncomfortable with aliens as he is with the civilized. Huck is comfortable and satisfied on the river, but he is also lonely and afraid. He is relieved when he finds Jim, but he seems even more relieved to be rid of him. His anguished ambivalence on the raft is thus merely the extreme case of his more general moral and psychological condition. Huck is forever betwixt and between, and at some level he knows this from the start. Thus it is entirely appropriate that he should be alone at the beginning of the novel, and that he should face the future with grim foreboding.

Huck's mood at the opening of Chapter 32 is in full alignment with what we have learned of his character and situation. He has just made the heroic decision to steal Jim out of captivity, but he does so in the assurance that he will suffer eternal damnation as a consequence. In short, he is utterly divided against himself. Circumstances have conspired to enforce conscious choice, and that necessity in turn stirs his ambivalence and precipitates his second lapse into solitary melancholy and life-weariness. This time, however, the source of Huck's depression is more immediate and better focused than in Chapter 1, and so his reaction is more intense. Huck is now persuaded that the spirit-voices are talking about him, and he is straightforward in his wish to be "dead, too, and done with it all."

Appropriately enough, the source of relief is now also more extreme. In Chapter 1, Huck abandons his lonely room for adventures with Tom Sawyer. Yet he is finally incapable of losing himself in his friend's world; he sees that Tom deals in transparent fictions, and observes that his games have "all the marks of a Sunday school" (17). Ironically, too, Tom's pranks take Jim as their first target, and thus lead Huck through an oblique rehearsal of subsequent moral and psychological crises. Still, childish fantasies provide some distraction from his darker ruminations, and so, for a time, Huck submits. In Chapter 32, the requisite diversions and loss of self are much more substantial. Tom Sawyer reappears, ready as usual with grandiose plans. Once again, Jim figures centrally, and unknowingly, in the adventure. But this time, as the remainder of the novel shows, childish pranks have serious consequences. Huck is not fooled; from the beginning he sees that the game is fantastic and unnecessarily cruel. But he goes along anyway. Indeed, to the surprise and dismay of generations of admirers, he takes advantage of aunt Sally's mistake and readily permits himself to be identified as Tom Sawyer. "It was like being born again," he exults, "I was so glad to find out who I was" (282).

It is the measure of Huck's terrible mental anguish that he surrenders so eagerly and completely to this unlikely identity, and to the subsequent cruelties that it entails. We may find Huck inconsistent here; we may feel that his ready adoption of an alien personality is totally out of keeping with his true character. The real Huck Finn, we may argue, the heroic boy who risks hell in order to free his black friend, has died. In fact, however, the Huck Finn that we come to know in the first two-thirds of the novel is the victim of a wrenching ambivalence which finds its epicenter at the intersection of totally irreconcilable attitudes toward Jim. In Chapter 31, as elsewhere, something in Huck acknowledges Jim's humanity and reaches out to him as a brother. But this strand in the boy's attitude toward his friend competes with, and often succumbs to, his inclination to regard Jim as chattel. When aunt Sally asks if anybody was hurt in the steamboat accident, Huck promptly replies: "No'm. Killed a nigger" (279). At no point in his famous crisis in Chapter 31 does Huck seriously question the premise that Jim has "*got* to be a slave." True, he bridles against the Christian civilization which enforces the institution, and thus betrays an impulse to question the justice of slavery. In the main, however, he concedes the necessity and propriety of slavery, and centers his troubled soul-searching on his own sinfulness in failing to "do the right thing and the clean thing." His decision to "*go* to hell" is quite unmistakably an assertion of the justice of the system that enslaves Jim. Huck's psychological equilibrium is more precarious than ever precisely because of his heroic resolve to rescue Jim; for that decision is a conscious and manifestly consequential violation of social prohibitions which he has internalized. Thus divided against himself, the real Huck Finn—the marginal, ambivalent, guilt-haunted fugitive—falls prey to demons that arise from within his troubled mind. In this perspective, it is neither inconsistent nor surprising that he should take refuge in the comparatively unambivalent and supremely socialized identity of Tom Sawyer. As I have tried to demonstrate, this potential for death and paradoxical rebirth is certainly in character, and has been with Huck since the very beginning of the novel.

The widespread critical resistance to the Huck Finn who surfaces in Chapter 32 is at once as enigmatic and as predictable as the hero's sudden transformation. The question that Huck confronts in Chapter 31—whether to befriend or betray his black companion—is without doubt the paramount dilemma in our history and culture. Quite naturally, we warm to Huck's boldly independent and apparently successful rejection of manifestly inhumane institutions. Quite as naturally, we may fail to recognize the terrible rent in Huck's consciousness, or to allow that his resolve, no matter how heroic, may collapse under the weight of unresolved conflicts. If this is the case, then we will reject Huck's rebirth as implausible, fault the novel for lack of unity, and declare its closing chapters unrealistic. In fact, Huck's transformation, which is prepared for and anticipated from the start, is the climactic stage in a process of character development which unifies the entire novel. His rebirth and its sequel are almost unbearably realistic. The true failure of realism occurs when Huck decides that he is physically and psychologically equipped to set Jim free. In joining him in this fond wish, we betray the extent to which we share Huck's painful dilemma. Given the fact of his history and culture, it is the nearly absolute condition of Huck's survival that he die into Tom Sawyer. Paradoxically, in refusing to recognize the necessity of this transformation, we inadvertently acknowledge the full depth of our identification with this anguished American innocent.[41]

VIII

At the very beginning of *Tom Sawyer, Detective,* a sequel to *Huckleberry Finn,* Huck is overcome with an attack of what he calls "spring fever." He laments that the affliction "sets" a boy

> to sighing and saddening around, and there's something the matter with him, he don't know what. But, anyway, he gets out by himself and mopes and thinks; and mostly he hunts for a lonesome place high up on the hill in the edge of the woods, and sets there and looks away off on the big Mississippi down there a-reaching miles and miles around the points where the timber looks smoky and dim, it's so far off and still, and everything's so solemn it seems like everybody you've loved is dead and gone, and you 'most wish you was dead and gone too, and done with it all.   (xx, 126–27)

Of course, Huck has been in this setting and frame of mind before. On this occasion, however, he decides that the only cure for his woes

> is to get away; get away from the same old tedious things you're so used to seeing and so tired of, and see something new. That is the idea; you want to go and be a wanderer; you want to go wandering far away to strange countries where everything is mysterious and wonderful and romantic. And if you can't do that, you'll put up with considerable less; you'll go anywhere you *can* go, just so as to get away, and be thankful of the chance, too.   (xx, 127)

An almost identical setting and train of associations appear toward the beginning of *Tom Sawyer.* Weighed down by his troubles, Tom retires to a dense wood near Cardiff Hill.

> There was not even a zephyr stirring; the dead noonday heat had even stilled the songs of the birds; nature lay in a trance that was broken by no sound but the occasional far-off hammering of a woodpecker, and this seemed to render the pervading silence and sense of loneliness the more profound. The boy's soul was steeped in melancholy; his feelings were in happy accord with his surroundings . . . It seemed to him that

life was but a trouble, at best, and he more than half envied Jimmy
Hodges, so lately released; it must be very peaceful, he thought, to lie
and slumber and dream forever and ever, with the wind whispering
through the trees and caressing the grass and the flowers over the grave,
and nothing to bother and grieve about, ever any more . . . Ah, if he
could only die *temporarily!*

Like Huck, Tom rejects the seductions of death and decides instead to
run away. "What if he turned his back, now, and disappeared mysteri-
ously? What if he went away—ever so far away, into unknown countries beyond the seas—and never came back any more!" (87–88).

Most of the elements in these passages are by now familiar, though
the close association of death with running away and dreamy forgetfulness is something new. A similar clustering occurs in Chapter 1 of *A
Connecticut Yankee,* when Hank Morgan begins his dream of Camelot.
He finds himself in

a soft, reposeful, summer landscape, as lovely as a dream, and as lonesome as Sunday. The air was full of the smell of flowers, and the buzzing
of insects, and the twittering of birds; and there were no people, no
wagons, there was no stir of life, nothing going on.   (10)

Hank's sense of isolated well-being in this fantasy of Eden is directly
commensurate with the distance in time and space that separates him
from the bustle and human conflict of contemporary Bridgeport. For a
while, at least, Camelot is all that Hank's real world is not. Huck and
Tom, on the other hand, are surrounded and oppressed by familiar human problems, and thus long to remove themselves to a dream-world
like Hank's. In either case, however, the desired state of physical separation has its psychological parallel in the condition of dreamy oblivion. Under such circumstances—whether achieved through flight,
sleep, or death—solitude is blissful rather than threatening, for the
solitary consciousness is dead, and therefore invulnerable, to the world.
For Mark Twain, the vast Mississippi was a landscape ideally suited to
the inducement of this gradual dying away. In *Life on the Mississippi,* for
example, he records the river's impact on his initially mingled mood.

The loneliness of this solemn, stupendous flood is impressive—and depressing. League after league, and still league after league, it pours its
chocolate tide along, between its solid forest walls, its almost unten-
anted shores, with seldom a sail or a moving object of any kind to
disturb the surface and break the monotony of the blank, watery soli-

tude; and so the day goes, the night comes, and again the day—and still the same, night after night and day after day,—majestic, unchanging sameness of serenity, repose, tranquillity, lethargy, vacancy,—symbol of eternity, realization of the heaven pictured by priest and prophet, and longed for by the good and thoughtless!   (IX, 213)

The river displaces depression with serenity by emptying the mind of all content. Thoughts are not purified; they are simply washed away, leaving an easeful sense of remote imperturbability. Mark Twain drifted into an identical mood during a solitary raft voyage on the Rhône in 1891. His serenity was enhanced, he wrote to a friend, by a feeling of "extinction from the world and newspapers, and a conscience in a state of coma, and lazy comfort, and solid happiness." Gliding passively down the river, he was overcome by a "strange absence of sense of sin, and the stranger absence of the desire to commit it."[42]

Just after his escape from the feud, and just before the arrival of the king and the duke, Huck finds himself feeling equally "free and easy and comfortable on a raft." I refer, of course, to the interval of relative calm—discussed briefly, above—that overtakes the narrative in Chapter 19. The world is safely at arm's length, and for a time Huck's relationship with Jim seems free of complication. More than once the boy observes the "lonesomeness" of the river; but the solitude is easeful, and despite occasional signs of human discord along shore, his consciousness is generally as "quiet and smooth and lovely" as the setting. Clothes come off, cares drift away, and the weary fugitives surrender to the mood of tranquility. "Not a sound, anywheres—perfectly still— just like the whole world was asleep, only sometimes the bull-frogs a-cluttering, maybe." Temporarily remote from reminders of his own inner division, Huck is emptied of care and contents himself with "lazying around, listening to the stillness." Voices from a passing raft break the silence, and for a moment they sound "like spirits carrying on that way in the air." But the river's magic has relieved Huck's mind of fear and suspicion. "No," he assures Jim, "spirits wouldn't say, 'Dern the dern fog'" (155–57).

Huck's sojourn in Eden is a brief one. Soon the human world along the bank awakens fully, and the serenity gives way to an unbroken succession of conflicts and calamities. Worst of all, circumstances combine to rekindle his ambivalence toward Jim, and his sense of sin, along with the strange desire to commit it, returns with renewed intensity. The weight of his divided identity and the pressure of consciousness finally becomes so great that Huck takes flight from himself, and settles temporarily for the errors of omission which fall to him as Tom Sawyer. By novel's end, he is chastened, guarded, and quietly desperate for another, more decisive retreat from the oppressive rigors of civilization. When Jim brags that his earlier, optimistic reading of the signs has been vindicated, Huck offers no response. He is equally unresponsive when Jim explains that Pap Finn was the dead man in the house that floated past them near Jackson's Island. Huck does not supplement Jim's limited insight into the significance of snakes; nor does he point out that Jim's original refusal to discuss the mysterious dead man precipitated their quarrel about snake-skins and bad luck.[43] But the truths that he fails to mention are hard and clear ones: he and the world being what they are, Huck's survival in civilization demands that he betray his best self, his best friend, or both. In fact, Huck is hopelessly and tragically marginal. On one side, he derives scant relief from withdrawal into civilized identities. Experience and intuition give him windows on the enormity of bondage; and so long as he glimpses the absurdity of freeing a free man, he will be uncomfortable in Tom Sawyer's skin. On the other side, he is deeply entangled in that phase of civilization that mortally oppresses Jim. True, there are moments when Huck defies the system, most notably in Chapter 16 when he abruptly reverses his own course and brilliantly outwits the slave hunters who threaten to board the raft and discover Jim. The episode is fully illustrative of Huck's dividedness and marginality. He reacts with spontaneous, unmingled defiance when his friend's freedom and well-being are threatened. But this immediate, unreflecting response is in perfectly ironic juxtaposition to his considered view of the matter, which has prompted him to "paddle ashore at the first light, and tell" on Jim (125), just before the slave hunters arrive. Moreover, Huck's brilliance in anticipating and manipulating the egregious selfishness of the heartless predators demonstrates that he is in no sense innocent of the world he contrives, on this occasion, to transcend. Huck is torn between a warm, instinctive regard for Jim as a human being and friend, and the much harsher view of blacks that runs through the dominant culture. The sudden, unexpected arrival of the slave hunters leaves no time for reflection, and triggers Huck's reflexive fellow-feeling for his black companion. Much more often, however, Huck's behavior toward Jim is the product of conscious reflection, and thus bears the imprint of the civilization from which he is in flight. Huck rejects the endless varieties of bad faith deception that crop up in all phases of the civilized life he encounters along the river. But he is nonetheless a bearer of the culture's most pressing—because most contradictory and consequential—article of bad faith, its advocacy of race–slavery. On those occasions when Huck deceives himself in substantial ways about his behavior, his self-deception is always rooted in the pathological bad faith of his culturally informed attitudes on race and slavery. "I ain't agoing to tell," he assures Jim on Jackson's Island, when the black man confesses that he has "*run off.*" But Huck adds, as if to shore up a manifestly implausible claim, "I ain't agoing back there anyways" (52–53). In fact, civilization as it enslaves and pursues Jim won't stay put "back there." It is everywhere along their course down the river; and, more to the point, it is there in the dominant, though partially submerged side of Huck's attitude toward his black companion. It follows that Jim is never completely safe with Huck, and that Huck is never completely comfortable in Jim's company.

For the other characters, the conclusion to Tom Sawyer's adventure passes for a happy ending, with warmth and good feeling all around. For Huck, it is the occasion for heightened discomfort and silent retreat. He testifies to these feelings when he rejects aunt Sally's offer "to adopt me and sivilize me." "I can't stand it," he concludes; "I been there before." But we will be as deceived as Huck appears to be if we imagine that his decision "to light out for the Territory ahead of the rest" (362) will lead to the liberation and flourishing of his "real" self. In fact, the totality of Huck's "real" self, so far as we know it, is the product of his interaction with the culture he is about to abandon. He may put distance between himself and the civilized world, but he cannot get away from the civilization that he bears with him. It is the pathological strand of civilization as it informs his personal makeup, and as it has worked time and again to undermine his instinctive sense of human fellowship with Jim, that Huck "can't stand." He falls heir to his culture's most crippling prejudice, but to few of its delusions about the nature of its leading institution. Concealing the snake-skins does not work for Huck; they pass from sight and mind only to turn up again and again, suddenly, without warning. And he is much too consciously aware of bad faith as it bears on his relationship with Jim to enter at all fully or for long into the identity of Tom Sawyer. Bad faith prepares Huck for "being born again," and it explains his acquiescence in the grandiose schemes for Jim's escape; but it does not blind him, as it blinds Tom, to the essential cruelty of the "evasion." Thus in opting for flight, Huck is in fact running from the social context in which he has been prone to increasingly painful betrayals of his black companion. He is choosing to narrow rather than expand, to limit rather than free, the multiple and conflicting elements in his own makeup.

In leaving Tom and aunt Sally, Huck will undoubtedly feel little sense of loss, and some measure of relief. Leaving Jim, on the other hand, will have a more painfully mingled result. To be sure, Jim has been the unwitting source of great trouble to Huck—both the trouble that has pursued him as the companion of an escaped slave, and the much more terrible trouble that has issued, with mounting intensity, from his ambivalence. But the escape from trouble has a high price, for the separation will cost Huck his closest friend. In Jim's company, and in his alone, Huck has enjoyed immunity from "lonesomeness" and, at the same time, that easeful remoteness from civilization that leaves him feeling free and easy and satisfied. In flight from the world and separated from Jim, he will rediscover another, familiar brand of trouble; for Huck will be alone with himself, and he's been there before, too.

In fact, of course, Huck's flight is itself symptomatic of the bad faith he is aiming to leave behind. He deceives himself in locating his problem outside of himself in aunt Sally and civilization, and his self-deception on this score betrays the extent to which that problem has penetrated his interior life. Huck can learn to live with aunt Sally, just as he learns to live with the widow and Miss Watson; but he cannot live with her, or with anyone else, himself included, *and* Jim. The problem between Huck and Jim, as Huck's implied denial tends to confirm, is the bad faith within Huck himself. He is trapped, quite hopelessly it appears, betwixt and between. Unlike the vast majority of white people in his world, who approach their experience from comfortably within the culture's boundaries, Huck is intermittently subject to intimations of the inhumanity of his assumptions about black people. His bad faith is as culturally incomplete as he is, leaving him vulnerable to intervals of painful, guilt-ridden self-awareness. But while he is aware enough of his bad faith to be ashamed of its effects, he is too much the product of the dominant culture to face it for long, and thus, perhaps, to deal with it. Instead, he flees from himself, seeking oblivion in the solitude of "the Territory ahead," just as he sought it before in the concealment of the snake-skins, and again, later, in his rebirth as Tom Sawyer. Thus he concludes his narrative with a characteristic gesture, the decision to efface or terminate an aspect of his total nature. Indeed, if Tom Sawyer's plotting emplots *Tom Sawyer,* then Huckleberry Finn's retreats to fictions of himself give direction and coherence to the fiction of *Huckleberry Finn.* At the extreme, Huck artfully simulates his own murder. Much more frequently, he submerges himself in an assortment of assumed identities (of both sexes, some fictional, some "real") and fictional autobiographies. Such endless self-refashioning does not conflict with the notion of Huck as innocent and authentic because his fabrications are usually quite conspicuously in the service of his quest for freedom from civilization. In general, Huck is not deceived by his fictions of self; he inflicts no intentional harm with them; they are, if you like, the justifiable lies essential to his flight, with Jim, from the civilization whose bad faith constrains them both. On a few occasions, however—when he hides the snake-skins, for example, and when he withdraws to Tom's identity—Huck resorts to fictions of self which participate fully in the civilized sickness from which he characteristically recoils. Huck is quite willingly taken in by those fictions. Both come to light after he has joined Jim on Jackson's Island, and both have a direct bearing on Jim's welfare. Indeed, both give evidence that the most pathological strain of the dominant culture's bad faith has lodged itself in the boy's makeup. It is this bad faith sickness in himself, as it takes rise in civilization and grows acute in Jim's company, that he retreats from and conceals in his concluding fiction of self.

From the very beginning, Huck's narrative centers on his efforts to achieve personal freedom from the constraints of civilization. Once he has joined Jim, however, it becomes clear that his conception of himself as actually or potentially free from civilization is itself a bad faith fiction to the extent that it takes no account of his attitudes on race and slavery. Because he is marginal to the dominant culture, Huck is subject to periodic glimpses of this singular but all-important inconsistency in his story; for the same reason, he reacts to such intimations with prompt, unwavering denial. He refuses to face the implications of the snake-skins; his decision to "go to hell" to free Jim is the last shudder of a psyche hopelessly divided against itself and poised for a fall into Tom Sawyer; and he reacts to the revelation that he has joined Tom in freeing an already free man by implicitly denying his immersion in the civilization behind the cruel charade. Ironically, then, Huck's fictions of self, like Tom's plots, at once spring from and lead him toward the center of the dominant culture. One evasion leads to another, and with each retreat from self-awareness Huck seems to draw more deeply into the web of bad faith that his fictions reject. Like Tom, he recoils into fabrications designed to release him from the consciousness of guilt;

like Tom again, his craving for oblivion has a correlative in recurrent fantasies of death.

But here the very considerable similarities end. For when the retreat from his guilty knowledge about Muff Potter is no longer bearable for Tom, he takes relief in a disclosure that still permits the concealment of the foregoing bad faith and at the same time accelerates his rise to social preeminence. He will undoubtedly act out in bad faith again, and he will experience guilt as a result; but his awareness of his deception of self and other, and its consequences, will grow easier to bear as his acculturation deepens. Most crucially of all, as his blithe mistreatment of Jim demonstrates, Tom is proof against a conscious reckoning with the terrible reality of racism and slavery at the core of his culture's bad faith pathology.

In Huck's case, on the other hand, guilt is never easily borne, and it seems to grow heavier with each fresh assault on consciousness precisely because the diseases of racism and slavery are always conspicuously its cause. When Huck draws back in bad faith, it is always from guilty knowledge about himself in his relationship with Jim. He has no occasion and, more important, no cultural script for bad-faith dealings in Bible tickets and mock resurrections and juvenile romance. Where Tom is haunted by guilt because of what he knows about the murder of Dr. Robinson, Huck's primary response to the same knowledge is terror. This is to say that Huck's marginality exempts him from substantial involvement in the operations of bad faith *except* at the dark center of the social reality represented in *Huckleberry Finn*. The citizens of communities like St. Petersburg and Bricksville fill their lives with amusements whose curious capacity to please is roughly commensurate with their capacity to draw attention away from the unbearable fact of race–slavery. Huck does not require this steady diet of distraction because he has much less to hide and hide from—both in general, and with respect to black people in particular—than fully initiated culturebearers. Indeed, it is his relative freedom from fixed bad faith delusions in matters of race and slavery that accounts for Huck's strong inclination, on one side, to approach Jim in a spirit of human fellowship, and, on the other, to recoil in dismay from his own cruelty to Jim as it surfaces, without warning, from the branch of the cultural mainstream that flows through him. Huck's delight at discovering Jim on Jackson's Island is compounded of relief that the slave is no threat to his own freedom and, for that reason among others, acceptable as company. But as Jim gains the confidence to express his own views and desires, and as the perilous realities of flight with an escaped slave grow clearer, the harsh, nether side of Huck's deeply divided feelings about black people begins to lift toward the surface. He is evidently unable to contain these untoward civilized impulses; but he is quite as evidently without the full cultural means to persuade himself for long that slavery is somehow just or benign.

Huck's prospects are grim. Hopelessly marginal, he is just as hopelessly divided against himself. While Tom Sawyer's retreat from guilt in *Tom Sawyer* and his "evasion" in *Huckleberry Finn* draw him deeper and deeper into the envelope of his culture, Huck's stumblings into bad faith simply run him in painful circles, from unbearable moral lapses to intervals of oblivion to repetitions of the initial fall. Thus while Tom grows increasingly blind to his culture's cruelty as his initiation approaches completion, Huck's awareness of his bad faith mistreatment of Jim can only grow more acute with each stunning repetition. This, I believe, is the submerged source of his decision "to light out for the Territory." But there will be no permanent solutions in "the Territory," only a reprieve, for Huck will take some of the very worst of civilization with him as he retreats toward the new horizon. There will be more black people; and because Huck's impulse to befriend them will endure, there will also be more snakes, more withdrawals into bad faith deception, more intervals of solitary horror. To draw himself out of this vicious circle, Huck must somehow follow his instincts toward the permanent establishment of equality and fellow-feeling in his relations with black people. Yet his narrative does nothing to suggest that he is moving in this direction. Little wonder! There are no models and nothing in the way of social support for such behavior. Befriending blacks, as Huck well knows, is perilous business. It is hardly surprising, then, that the impulse to smother his best self in bad faith withdrawals to oblivion seems stronger than ever at the novel's conclusion. Huck backs away from white civilization, he says, because it limits his freedom. He also withdraws from Jim's company, and though he says nothing about it, he does so because the civilization in himself places extreme limits on Jim's freedom. It is from his own lack of freedom as it is manifest in Jim's enslavement, and in race–slavery generally, that Huck flees. The chains that he helps to forge for his friend are painful reminders of his own. As I have observed more than once, Huck is remarkably pliant in adapting to the demands and constraints of life at the widow's. Civilization cramps his style at times, but it beats loneliness. What Huck cannot abide is the guilt that issues from his involvement in that civilization as it bears on the lives of black people. He runs, in short, because he cannot free himself from guilty complicity in the way of life that enslaves Jim.

Thus we leave Huck, just where we found him at the outset, in recoil from civilization. In the course of the story, the precise terms and the dynamics of his bad faith have drawn into much sharper focus; but the essentials of his condition do not change. The good-hearted, resourceful boy continues to move blindly forward in the repeating cycle that self, circumstance, and culture have cast for him. For a while he will find relief in solitude. Before long, however, the solitude will become more haunted than ever, and the brief consolation of solitary detachment from the human sources of woe will give way to the brief comfort of being with people again. And so it will go, until Huck learns to live with his ghosts, or shapes himself more fully to a civilized identity, or surrenders completely to death itself, the complete oblivion that so occupies his troubled mind.

IX

Bad faith as I have defined it is a frequently benign cultural phenomenon involving the acquiescence in manifest departures from law or custom. Bad faith features the deception of self and other in the denial that such departures have occurred, and bears the clear implication that humans will sometimes permit what they cannot approve so long as their complicity is submerged in a larger, tacit consensus. Thanks to potent prohibitions against their acknowledgment, the operations of bad faith are most often unconscious and unobserved; the act of denial is itself denied. In its benign and even beneficial phase, bad faith enables a society to transcend the strict boundaries of its laws and conventions and the unanticipated limitations of its actors and circumstances. It may work in the service of flexibility and forgiveness, advance the spirit of healthy free play conducive to change, smooth the way toward the resolution of difference, and enhance equity. Bad faith has the potential to liberate the spirit of society from the strict letter of its codes.

The analysis of bad faith in *Tom Sawyer* is copiously illustrative of its positive uses. At the same time, however, Mark Twain's failure to recognize in himself and in Tom what he angrily condemns as hypocrisy in the citizens of St. Petersburg is evidence of his entanglement in the dimension of bad faith that he deplores. His outraged awareness of bad faith, and the evidence of his immersion in it, would continue to grow in the work that followed *Tom Sawyer*. But so—for a while at least—would his understanding of the benefits of the deception of self and other. Perhaps his most balanced assessment of what he recognized as an ineluctable fact of human social experience appears in his essay "On the Decay of the Art of Lying," which he presented for discussion at the Historical and Antiquarian Club of Hartford in 1882. Though his tone is frequently inclined to archness, there is little evident irony in the axiom that forms his point of departure. "No fact is more firmly established," he declares, "than that lying is a necessity of our circumstances." He is more playful in his insistence that lying is "a Virtue," in suggesting that the art of lying deserves "careful and diligent cultivation," and in the declaration that "an awkward, unscientific lie is often as ineffectual as the truth." It would be impossible, he goes on, to

> *live* with an habitual truth-teller; but, thank goodness, none of us has to. An habitual truth-teller is simply an impossible creature; he does not exist; he has never existed. Of course there are people who *think* they never lie, but it is not so—and this ignorance is one of the very things that shame our so-called civilization. Everybody lies—every day; every hour; awake; asleep; in his dreams; in his joy; in his mourning; if he keeps his tongue still, his hands, his feet, his attitude, will convey deception—and purposely.

Persuaded of the inevitability of deception, Mark Twain proceeds to weigh its uses and abuses. Lies are to be valued or condemned according to the pleasure or pain they produce. Thus on one side, "courteous lying is a sweet and loving art, and should be cultivated"; on the other, "an injurious truth has no merit over an injurious lie. Neither should ever be uttered" (xx, 361–64).

Such indulgent, gently playful distinctions form a brief prologue to the more circumstantial, more deliberate discussion of what Mark Twain calls "the *silent* lie—the deception which one conveys by simply keeping still and concealing the truth." This brand of deceit is a variety of bad faith. A silent lie is the mute refusal to acknowledge an awkward reality. Because it is silent, such deception betrays both an impulse to deny, and an impulse to deny that a denial has occurred. Such double denials go unobserved by deceiver and deceived because the silent lie conforms to and even reinforces an acceptable construction of reality. Most significant perhaps, "simply keeping still and concealing the truth" was evidently on Mark Twain's mind in 1882, and it was a topic that he could approach in a mood of good-humored acquiescence. Although his example is graphically exemplary of the perils of lying silently, the essayist is nonetheless quite positive in his address to a world in which "lying is universal—we *all* do it; we all *must* do it" (xx, 364–67).

This playful, precariously balanced point of view is rarely in evidence during the years that followed the publication of *Huckleberry Finn*. As his career wore on, and as experience and reflection combined to darken his perspective on the world, Mark Twain surrendered increasingly to feelings of contempt for "the damned human race." Thus his essay, "My First Lie, and How I Got Out of It," which appeared in 1899, is parallel in much of its substance, but hardly in its tone, to the earlier "On the Decay of the Art of Lying." Once again, Mark Twain proceeds from the assumption "that all people are liars from the cradle onward, without exception." People begin "to lie as soon as they wake in the morning, and keep it up, without rest or refreshment, until they go to sleep at night." Deceitfulness is the very essence of human nature, and it is so by virtue of an "eternal law." Since man "didn't invent the law," he is not responsible for its effects; "it is merely his business to obey it and keep still." This act of concealment, he goes on, is "the lie of silent assertion; we can tell it without saying a word, and we all do it" (XXIII, 146–47).

The lie of silent assertion is the silent lie all over again, but with some important new features. While a silent lie is any mute refusal to acknowledge the truth, the lie of silent assertion is the concealment of the knowledge that humans are by nature incapable of truthfulness. All people lie all the time, but they lie first in denying this law of their nature. It is also clearly implied that the vast majority fails to recognize that deceitfulness is the inexorable law of human nature. So comprehensive is their self-deception that they actually imagine themselves honest.

The parallels with bad faith are of course quite striking. Both schemes assume abundant departures from what is regarded as true or right, the denial that such departures have occurred, and the failure to acknowledge that anything has been denied. Mark Twain's further elaborations on the lie of silent assertion—or what we may be tempted to call the lie of truth—lend substantial confirmation to this parallel. He goes on to highlight the intimate connection between the lie of silent assertion and civilization. "In the magnitude of its territorial spread, it is one of the most majestic lies that the civilizations make it their sacred and anxious care to guard and watch and propagate." He dwells at length and quite bitterly on the way in which the lie of silent assertion at once generates and confers legitimacy on a world of lesser frauds and deceits. For one who comprehends the situation, it is an effort to try "to make it appear that abstention from lying is a virtue . . . Why should we help the nation lie the whole day long and then object to telling one little individual private lie in our own interest to go to bed on?" Most significantly of all, however, and at the dead center of Mark Twain's reflections on civilization and "the nation," is the clear and emphatic association of the lie of silent assertion with the crime of slavery. Thus in his primary illustration of the "majestic lies" of civilization he declares:

> For instance: it would not be possible for a humane and intelligent person to invent a rational excuse for slavery; yet you will remember that in the early days of the emancipation agitation in the North, the agitators got but small help or countenance from any one. Argue and plead and pray as they might, they could not break the universal stillness that reigned, from pulpit and press all the way down to the bottom of society—the clammy stillness created and maintained by the lie of silent assertion—the silent assertion that there wasn't anything going on in which humane and intelligent people were interested.   (XXIII, 147–49)

The lie of silent assertion explains what is otherwise inexplicable, how civilized people committed to freedom and justice and human equality and Christian love are able, either as active or passive participants, Southerners or Northerners, to witness the inhuman spectacle of race–slavery in their midst without registering any apparent concern or discomposure. Mark Twain assumes, as I do, that racism and slavery have always been an intolerable cultural contradiction in America, and that the pervasive lie of silent assertion—or the cognate version of what I have called bad faith—is oblique but unmistakable testimony to an abiding, profound uneasiness with these realities of our history and common life. This impossible acquiescence in the delusion that there isn't "anything going on in which humane and intelligent people" are interested is just as surely an enduring American phenomenon as it is an enduring crux in our understanding of *Huckleberry Finn.* The novel continues to speak to our condition because it makes us mindful of the legacies of race–slavery in our midst; but it is a great favorite with us, an American "classic," in good part because it seems to invite the dismissal or disavowal of as much of its darkness as we cannot bear to own. *Huckleberry Finn* draws us close to a harsh center of our reality, and we follow willingly, unthreatened by more discomposure than we can comfortably manage because the narrative enables the relatively effortless reader recapitulation of its lie of silent assertion.

This is a lie whose cultural authority is broad, continuing, and multilayered. Its breadth and continuity are clearly exemplified in the phenomenal popularity of *Huckleberry Finn,* and representative levels of its influence and expression are manifest in the text itself. The lie has been most visible in the behavior of Tom Sawyer. As Laurence B. Holland observes, the concealment of Jim's emancipation is a lie of silent assertion which enables Tom "to stage the rescue of Jim which is so cruel and intended to be so entertaining."[44] The same lie is accountable for the evident pleasure that the audience assembled at the Phelps plantation derives from Tom's "evasion." Their amusement is invulnerable to intrusions of conscious uneasiness over the plight of poor Jim, and the knack for enabling them to take unruffled pleasure from their cruelty is the final evidence of Tom's cultural authority. Neil Schmitz insists that the novel's conclusion "is an affront . . . because the humanity of its prime character [Jim] is patently, systematically ignored. Everything is drawn into the structure Tom creates." "Everything" here embraces the entire audience within the novel, including Huck, whose "tenuous sympathy for Jim's difficult position" is briefly audible, but ineffectual, and soon gives way to silence.[45] Schmitz goes on to argue that the novel's bad faith in matters of race and slavery is painfully manifest in its concluding portrait of Jim. That Jim should offer "to sacrifice his life (and the family he professes to love) for Tom's sake," he insists, is absurd. He is equally incredulous when "Jim's native goodness negates the crushing burden of his past" and "transcends the pain that has been inflicted on him." In denying Jim "the privilege of wrath, even resentment," the novel, and the culture it manifests, shrink from a conscious reckoning with the gravity of their crime and, more specifically, with the prospect of a fearsome retribution. "It is because Jim ought to come out of his shed with a knife (the brass candlestick Tom gives him, sharply honed) that he emerges with a dulcet grin, ready to sacrifice himself."[46]

As the title of his essay—"Twain, *Huckleberry Finn,* and the Reconstruction"—clearly suggests, Schmitz is centrally concerned to "place"

Mark Twain's novel in the period of its publication. "Jim's situation at the end of *Huckleberry Finn*," Schmitz asserts, "reflects that of the Negro in the Reconstruction, free at last and thoroughly impotent, the object of devious schemes and a hapless victim of constant brutality." Mark Twain conceived his novel in the fullest awareness of this "implacable reality," and yet recoiled as a witness into a lie of silent assertion, a bad-faith refusal to confront the harsh facts before him. The result is a portrayal of "Jim shorn of his subjective reality, no longer actively engaged in the process of living . . . trapped in the prison of the white man's mind."[47]

Though Schmitz breaks important new ground in situating *Huckleberry Finn* in a specific post-bellum frame of reference, he is hardly alone in the detection of evasiveness in Mark Twain's treatment of Jim. As I have noted, Henry Nash Smith also imagines the novelist retreating guiltily from the resurgent tragic thrust of his material.[48] In a similar vein, Laurence B. Holland argues that Mark Twain's "silent guilt" about his novel's evasion of a full moral reckoning was "all the stronger for remaining tacit, repressed or compressed within the lie of silence" that pervades the narrative.[49] The novelist's incomplete success at containing and submerging the discord emergent from his story is perhaps most evident in the failure of Tom's evasion to deceive completely. It may be glimpsed, too, in Mark Twain's rather stridently jocular disavowal of a "motive" or a "moral" in his tale (10), and in the tone of irritable fatigue with which Huck draws the narrative to a close. Moreover, the novel's almost obsessive preoccupation with fiction-making is at once a comment on the pervasive bad faith of the social reality it represents, and on what Holland describes as "the moral hazards entailed in the enterprise of fiction"[50]—especially, I would emphasize, in a fiction about the attempt by two boys to liberate an already freed runaway slave, set in 1840, narrated retrospectively by the most morally tortured of the participants, written by Mark Twain, humorist, son of a slave-holding Whig from Missouri, deserter from the Confederate militia, later a Lincoln Republican living in a posh suburb of Hartford, and published, after nearly a decade of intermittent, halting toil, in 1885. Indeed, if we demand of our novels that they dramatize the movement toward the resolution of significant human problems, then *Huckleberry Finn* is a failure. Jim is not really free at all, Tom and his admiring friends are blind to the travesty of freedom they have performed, and the novelist and his vernacular hero recoil from painful glimpses of their own complicity in the spectacle of injustice. Yet the novel continues to enjoy a vast readership. This is so, as I have said more than once, because it enables its American readers to approach the most profoundly troubling issue in their history without risk of being overcome with the fear and guilt that attach to the subject. We return to the novel not because of what it resolves, but because it seduces us with a comedic image of resolution that we cannot quite accept, but that we permit, by a lie of silent assertion, to stand in place of much darker revelations. We reread *Huckleberry Finn* because of what it spares us; but precisely because we never really finish it, we are obliged to repeat it. Thus we read our premier literary classic by choice and, paradoxically, because we are compelled to.

It is one key to the cultural authority of *Huckleberry Finn* that at a number of levels it enables the retreat to an illusion of resolution where none has occurred. For Mark Twain and Huck and many readers, the frustration and the guilt that attach to Jim's example and continuing predicament are variously submerged in Tom's "evasion." One way or another, we are all complicit with the egregious young romantic, and our uneasiness on that score registers in a certain discomfort with the novel's conclusion, and in an impulse to try the story just one more time. I have argued that such layered recapitulations of bad faith are profoundly significant indices of what, in cultural terms, we are. Mark Twain never came close to repeating this powerful, complex imaginative enactment of this twisted strand of his culture's bad faith. In his numerous subsequent treatments of racism and slavery he either seemingly stumbled on to the topic at the very end of literary fragments, or he attempted, never with much success, to withdraw to a safely detached perspective on his material. The subject either surfaced suddenly and quite unmanageably from the midst of promising projects, or it defied his attempts to frame it in a coherent philosophical perspective. In either case, the inevitable result was an incapacity to finish what he had started, and, further, an incapacity to conceal that failure in evasive illusions of resolution.

Perhaps the most telling example of the first of these characteristic failures is "Which Was It?" a long fragment of a novel recounting the nightmare of disaster dreamt by George Harrison, a rich, respected family man. The narrative does not reach the point at which the dreamer awakens to relief; rather, it terminates just as Jasper, an ex-slave, turns the tables on the degraded Harrison and begins to settle his people's "long bill" of revenge "agin de low-down ornery white race."[51] Having reached this nadir in the dream section of his tale,

Mark Twain stopped, leaving the white sleeper forever face to face with the nightmare of retribution poised on the dark side of his waking reality. In trying to account for this oddly suggestive ending, it may not be altogether fanciful to suppose that the line of Mark Twain's narrative drew him all unawares—as his narratives were wont to—into a confrontation with one of his own, and his culture's, deepest fears. So compellingly real was that horrific, unlooked-for prospect that it entirely eclipsed the original comic plot and declared itself de facto the proper, if not the consciously intended, end of the story. Viewed in this way, "Which Was It?" is a record of the failure of the lie of silent assertion to restore consciousness to its waking reality—in fact, its dream—of respectable affluence. It is also an oblique acknowledgment of the unbearable human terms of that all-white dream, and a warning, aptly embodied in the strangely complete incomplete story, against straying from the shelter of bad faith into the glare of too much truth.

"Which Was It?" bears the suggestion that Mark Twain was increasingly prone, as the years wore on, to gravitate toward a perspective on American history and culture that featured racism and slavery in bold if very somber relief. This is quite clearly the drift of *Huckleberry Finn,* though in that novel, as in nothing else Mark Twain wrote, the ostensible conclusion is merely the last of many evasions of a proper resolution. "Which Was It?" amounts to a version of the same thing, a single turn on the same repeating cycle, except that it actually achieves the resolution that *Huckleberry Finn* seems bound for, but at the same time cancels the dark, deeply sought, more deeply obstructed conclusion by presenting itself as incomplete. If the lie of silent assertion in *Huckleberry Finn* is the permanent deferral of an irresistible ending, then "Which Was It?" tells the same lie by lodging that ending in an unfinished replica of the original bad faith plot of human liberation. Neither text tells a complete story; in both the fact of incompleteness is the formal symptom of a pervasive lie of silent assertion; and the texts taken in tandem arrive at the resolution that bad faith obstructs in each taken separately.

Such partial renderings of a persistent train of personal and historical reflection figure prominently among the fragmented literary remains of Mark Twain's later years. And let me emphasize that it was an incomplete story, one cut short again and again in bad faith, that Mark Twain had to tell. His message, both as an individual and as a definitive culture-bearer, is the deferral of a reckoning with the full, painful implications of race–slavery. Incomplete literary works that "end" in truncated disclosures of this cultural pathology gather toward the full revelation of what is secretly known, only to resubmerge it in their formal literary status as negligible fragments. This telling incapacity to completely tell is manifest in "The Stupendous Procession," an unfinished allegory of civilized prospects at the opening of the twentieth century. Modern imperialist powers, bearing emblems of their territorial conquests, appear one after the other, until the spotlight falls, where it remains until the piece breaks off, on America. Indeed, it is clear that the sins of the European countries are of secondary interest to Mark Twain; his primary object is to review in vivid symbolic detail the errors of his own nation. The emphasis is everywhere on the cynical declension from founding ideals, and toward the end the focus comes more and more to rest on American racism as it descends on the citizens of our imperial acquisitions. A contemporary version of ante-bellum slavery is the sad lot of those peoples unfortunate enough to fall within the orbit of the Christian civilization of the United States. Having reached this general perspective on American corruption at home and American racist imperialism abroad, the unfinished manuscript closes with an angry summary of the moral state of the nation. Banners are imagined

> scattered at intervals down the long procession, and glinting distantly in the sunlight; some of them bearing inscriptions of this sort:
> "ALL WHITE MEN ARE BORN FREE AND EQUAL." *Declaration of Independence.*
> "ALL WHITE MEN ARE AND OF RIGHT OUGHT TO BE FREE AND INDEPENDENT." *Ibid.*
> 14th Amendment: "WHITE SLAVERY SHALL NO LONGER EXIST WHERE THE AMERICAN FLAG FLOATS."
>
> > "Christ died to make men holy,
> > *He* died to make white men free."
>
> (Battle Hymn of the Republic. "He" is Abraham Lincoln.)
> "GOVERNMENTS DERIVE THEIR JUST POWERS FROM THE CONSENT OF THE GOVERNED WHITE MEN." *Declaration of Independence.*

Finally, the Statue of Liberty appears with its "torch extinguished and reversed," Old Glory passes, "furled, and draped with crêpe," and over all looms the "SHADE OF LINCOLN, towering vast and dim toward the sky, brooding with pained aspect over the far-reaching pageant."[52] The thrust of this concluding indictment could not be more clear: American imperialism in the new century merely repeats, on an international stage, the tragic domestic drama of the century just passed. Nothing has been learned; there has been no moral progress; the present and future are bound to recapitulate the intolerable contradiction of race–slavery in the land of freedom and equality.

Mark Twain effectively silenced his public voice by leaving "The Stupendous Procession" unfinished and unpublished. The same censor enforced the suppression of publicly unspeakable declarations on the same subject in the long, but also unfinished "The Refuge of the Derelicts." Reflecting on one such pronouncement, Isabel V. Lyon, Mark Twain's secretary, records in her journal for March 21, 1905:

> Tonight Mr. Clemens read a very interesting unpublishable sketch. Unpublishable because it is what an old darkey says of the universal brotherhood of man—& how it couldn't ever be, not even in heaven—for there are only white angels there & in the old darkey's vision the niggers were all sent around to the back door. It's a wonderful little sketch but it wouldn't do for the clergy. They couldn't stand it. It's too true.[53]

The manuscripts of *The Mysterious Stranger,* closely related variations on the theme of human enslavement to history, the will of God, evolution, and the Moral Sense, came to a similar end. The "Schoolhouse Hill" fragment, by far the shortest, breaks off quite abruptly, almost in midstride. According to William M. Gibson, the editor of *The Mysterious Stranger* manuscripts, this sudden standstill is itself something of a mystery. "Why Mark Twain let this story lapse after a moderately promising beginning when he had dozens of ideas for continuing it is problematical" (9), Gibson concedes. We may begin to account for this otherwise puzzling circumstance by observing that "Schoolhouse Hill" is the only version of the story set in the ante-bellum South, and thus the only version to include American slavery among its examples of the manifold constraints on human liberty. Indeed, the narrative ends just as the slaves, uncle Jeff and aunt Rachel, begin to grow familiar with No. 44, the angelic witness to mortal degradation. It seems likely that the Hannibal installment on his somber theme, once it began to surface in its full range of personal and social implication, was more than Mark Twain could bear to pursue. Confronted once again with the sharp cutting edge of the tale he was bound, as if by blind compulsion, to tell, he withdrew abruptly to his own lie of silent assertion.

Let me turn finally to "The Secret History of Eddypus, The World-Empire," yet another of the significantly incomplete writings that Mark Twain produced during the last years of his life. "The Secret His-

tory" offers itself as an attempt made in 2901 A.D. to develop an account of the rise and fall of civilization that occurred one thousand years
earlier. This attempted historical reconstruction rests heavily on "Old
Comrades," a book by Mark Twain, the ancient Bishop of New Jersey,
and the only fully reliable written record to have survived the destruction of libraries that inaugurated the long interval of barbarism. As
John S. Tuckey suggests, the Eddypus fragment sets forth a cyclical
conception of history in which mankind struggles to draw itself "out
of ignorance and slavery to gain freedom and knowledge, only to be led
by its own cowardice and greed into fooling away its chances and being
returned to its chains." Tuckey goes on to develop the parallels between
"The Secret History" and *What Is Man?*, which was published in a
limited, anonymous edition, and the *Autobiography,* which was written
for posthumous publication. Among other things, Tuckey observes,
these are all "suppressed" works, not-so-confident gospels in which
Mark Twain spoke his mind only to disguise or conceal what he had to
say.[54] Like *Huckleberry Finn,* "The Secret History" thematizes suppression; it records a struggle to recover a usable past from beneath a mil-
lenial lie of silent assertion. Moreover, in the late fragment, as in the
novel, the act of telling recapitulates the denial of precisely the truth
that the tale reveals. Huck cannot say what the narrative shows: that
Jim is not really free. "The Secret History" draws the same general
conclusion from the unfolding narrative of the rise and fall of modern
civilization. Despite the great hope engendered by the Enlightenment
and the political revolutions at the end of the eighteenth century, the
liberation of "the mind and soul" that ensued was a faint flicker in a sea
of darkness. The sole illustration of this sweeping overview with which
the fragment terminates is the prophesy, ventured by "wise men" in the
young Republic, of "the early extinction of slavery in America." This
bright prospect came to naught because of the cotton bonanza that
followed in the wake of advances in agricultural technology. Slavery
became extremely profitable, with the result that it "was gratefully recognized by press, pulpit and people, all over the land, as God's best
gift to man."[55] Thus "The Secret History" fragment draws to a close
with an image of America withdrawing into a national lie of silent
assertion about its peculiar institution. The bad faith, Mark Twain insists, is American ("all over the land"), not Southern; and he is equally
clear, as early sections of the manuscript demonstrate, that race–slavery
is the primary cultural ingredient in the subsequent imperialist adventures that bring this brief dream of freedom to its final, nightmarish

conclusion. Civilization, he reflects, "was a sham at home and only laid off its disguise when abroad."[56]

The Eddypus fragment contains a coherent argument about the relationship between the bad-faith cultural pathology of race–slavery and the course of American empire. At the same time, however, it participates in the leading symptom of the disease it professes to deplore by failing to speak out against race–slavery in a forcefully complete, public manner. Rather, it retreats to the lie of silent assertion in making its last words indefinite, not definitive. "The Secret History" is in bad faith in the additional sense that it tends to submerge its moral outrage in a coolly detached perspective on its subject matter. More specifically, Mark Twain sets his portraits of slavery and civilization in a deterministic framework that makes no room for human design in the unfolding pattern of history. "Individuals do not project events," he argues; "individuals do not make events; it is massed *circumstances* that make them. Men cannot order circumstances, men cannot foresee the form their accumulation will take nor forecast its magnitude and force." Thus while he emphasizes that slavery is a cruel contradiction in America, he characterizes the failure of its prompt and timely abolition as a leading example of "the fell way in which the plans and foreordainings of men go down before the change-making orderly march of the serried battalions of blind Circumstance."[57] Where Circumstance rules, the argument implies, there is no human responsibility, and therefore no occasion for guilt or the laying of blame.

"The Secret History" is quite evidently one of the many later works in which, as Bernard DeVoto long ago observed, the image of man "enslaved and dominated by inexorable circumstance" is the humorist's desperate response to what he "is inwardly afraid he is being held to answer for . . . No one," DeVoto goes on, "can read this wearisomely repeated argument without feeling the force of an inner cry: Do not blame me, for it was not my fault."[58] As we have observed, the topic of slavery had for years stirred guilty agitation in Mark Twain; but its capacity to provoke answering retreats into the philosophy of determinism became manifest only after the publication of *Huckleberry Finn,* in the years of nagging domestic and international turmoil at century's end. The argument from necessity formed a shield against the arrows of his moral indignation, which he let fly in anger at the resurgence of the dread disease, but which invariably threatened to return on his own head. His dabblings in philosophy thus illustrate the second of his characteristic strategies with the topic of race–slavery, the withdrawal to postures of safe-seeming detachment. Determinism serves Mark Twain in "The Secret History" as "the Territory" serves Huck Finn, as a refuge from what he knows, and wants to forget, about his own complicity in the crime against black people. It is a lie of silent assertion which works well enough to permit the engagement with the consuming topic, but not well enough to sustain closure, or to conceal the fact that engagement without closure is precisely what the strategy is designed to produce. The determinist argument fills many pages, and it appears to be the primary thrust of the unfinished treatise, but it does not soften Mark Twain's perception of slavery as cruel and contradictory, nor does it cool the angry irony that flows through his concluding characterization of slavery as "God's gift to man." In fact, the moral outrage has not really subsided at all. But it appears in a frame of discourse so apparently incomplete as to invite critical neglect, and otherwise so philosophically detached as to seem untroubled by guilt.

Mark Twain did not settle naturally or comfortably into detached philosophical points of view on anything. He was constitutionally ambivalent, passionate, and much too independent and willful to repose for long in systematic perspectives, let alone narrow determinisms. A little philosophy served him well enough in his evasions of fear and guilt, but he was at least now and then capable of recognizing his rational excursions for what they were. A moment of such penetration occurs toward the end of "My First Lie, and How I Got Out of It," when he lapses into the exact species of bad faith that his essay has exposed and vigorously denounced. From the beginning of "My First Lie," it will be recalled, Mark Twain includes himself in an enlightened minority of perspicacious witnesses to the operations of bad faith. A member of this group is distinguished not only because he is aware that it is "the eternal law" of human nature to lie constantly, but also because that knowledge does nothing to inhibit his natural inclination, even when he deceives "his fellow-conspirators into imagining that he doesn't know that the law exists. It is what we all do—we that know. I am speaking of the lie of silent assertion; we can tell it without saying a word, and we all do it—we that know" (XXIII, 147). Membership in this elite devolves upon those who understand the dynamics and the awesome dominion of unacknowledged—and, for the vast majority of people, unrecognized—deception in human experience. What such insiders perceive, beyond the law of their nature, is the bleak, pathological dimension of the culture of bad faith—a civilization blinded by the lie of silent assertion to its profound deviation from its proudest human values. Mark Twain goes on to identify American slavery and the contemporary outbreak of imperial oppression as the premier expressions of the lie of silent assertion, and to inveigh against them. But then, having developed this commendable position, he concludes with what must seem a striking reversal:

> To sum up, on the whole I am satisfied with things the way they are. There is a prejudice against the spoken lie, but none against any other, and by examination and mathematical computation I find that the proportion of the spoken lie to the other varieties is as 1 to 22,894. Therefore the spoken lie is of no consequence, and it is not worth while to go around fussing about it and trying to make believe that it is an important matter. The silent colossal National Lie that is the support and confederate of all the tyrannies and shams and inequalities and unfairnesses that afflict the peoples—that is the one to throw bricks and sermons at. But let us be judicious and let somebody else begin.
> And then—But I have wandered from my text. How did I get out of my second lie? I think I got out with honor, but I cannot be sure, for it was a long time ago and some of the details have faded out of my memory. I recollect that I was reversed and stretched across some one's knee, and that something happened, but I cannot now remember what it was. I think there was music; but it is all dim now and blurred by the lapse of time, and this may be only a senile fancy.   (XXIII, 156).

To be sure, this is mimicry of bad faith, a self-conscious burlesque of the lie of silent assertion in action. But we take the humor seriously because it works, quite conspicuously by design, to displace the timely, morally urgent discussion that precedes it. His self-conscious mimicry notwithstanding, Mark Twain is in earnest in moving to empty consciousness of what it knows about human deceitfulness. His impulse to conceal this knowledge thus extends in its application not merely to his co-conspirators, but to himself as well; in effect, the member of the select "we that know" betrays a longing to join ranks with those that don't. And for good reason. As "My First Lie" clearly shows, the knowledge that it is "the eternal law" of human nature to lie does nothing to relieve the knower from guilt about his lying. To the contrary, that knowledge is the source of suffering, for it brings its possessor face to face with what he is powerless to respect or change in his own makeup. "We that know" are unwilling witnesses to what they quite perversely regard as their own degraded complicity in widespread human suffering. The vast majority of people, those who don't know about the lie of silent assertion, are all liars with dirty hands, but they live in blissful ignorance of what is, by the terms of "My First Lie," their natural condition. Indeed, it is the fullest expression of their compliance with the natural that they are totally and irreversibly self-deceived on the score of their constitutional deceitfulness. They believe that lying is wrong, and in this they are profoundly misguided; but they are saved from themselves by the unshakable conviction that they are essentially honest. "We that know" are equally persuaded of the moral obligation to tell the truth, but they frame that assumption in the consciousness that it is definitively characteristic of their species to lie. In the upshot, since the knowledge of their natural condition and the pressure of their unnatural morality are utterly incompatible with each other, it follows that peace of mind can result only from the severance of the conscious link between the two. Thus it is that Mark Twain beats a retreat from his painful awareness of his true nature to a righteous illusion of self that conforms to his eccentric moral prepossessions. Having penetrated to the core of their own and their culture's lie of silent assertion, it is the natural impulse of "we that know" to retell that lie, to their peers and to themselves, almost as soon as its existence and implications are recognized.

The long concluding passage from "My First Lie" is striking in a number of related ways. On one side, of course, it clearly anticipates young Satan's contemptuous treatment of the Moral Sense in *The Mysterious Stranger*. We are reminded, too, that the American jeremiad in the hands of a Colonel Sherburn, or of the Mark Twain who presides *in propria persona* over "My First Lie" and "The United States of Lyncherdom," may serve as the instrument of an unacknowledged disposition to be "satisfied with things the way they are." Less obviously perhaps, Mark Twain's bad-faith decision to "be judicious and let somebody else begin" to face the truth echoes the consensus among the villagers in *Tom Sawyer,* who

> had a strong desire to tar-and-feather Injun Joe and ride him on a rail, for body-snatching, but so formidable was his character that nobody could be found who was willing to take the lead in the matter, so it was dropped. He had been careful to begin both of his inquest-statements with the fight, without confessing the grave-robbery that preceded it; therefore it was deemed wisest not to try the case in the courts at present. (108)

In a variety of guises, and viewed from a variety of points of view, the lie of silent assertion was from the very beginning a staple of Mark

Twain's perspective on the world. It is evident here not only in the "judicious" retreat from morally responsible behavior, but also in the familiar suggestion that the main line of argument has been lost ("I have wandered from my text"). Alleged failures of memory and appeals to old age serve in the same way to draw attention away from the central, morally compelling business at hand. Philosophical determinism or dream, judicious temporizing or bad-faith affirmations of a degraded status quo, and the fading and blurring of vision caused by removes in space or time—all of these apparently very different states of mind involve detached points of view, equally detached, even resigned, tones of voice, and betray in the aggregate a pronounced inclination to back away from experience, to obscure or submerge or totally strike from the mind what cannot be tolerated at close range. They are the furtive mental postures, in short, of the lie of silent assertion, and they appear with increasing frequency in Mark Twain's writing toward the end of his career.

As the complex thematics of evasion in *Huckleberry Finn* clearly suggest, such retreats from the glare of consciousness tend to occur when the topics of race and slavery press to the foreground, and they generally achieve less than the full measure of oblivion they strive for. It is the painful dilemma of "we that know" to be fatally betwixt and between, compelled to witness what they are equally driven to forget, fitfully aware of their complicity in what they condemn, heedless of an indulgent necessity, uncertain as to which was the dream, and prone to light out when their reality gets too close or clear for comfort. Because too much of Cereno's answer is unbearable, "we that know" recoil in endless earnest to the lie of silent assertion in Delano's query, "You are saved: what has cast such a shadow upon you?" It is, of course, a dialogue of one. Just so, the voice of "My First Lie" at once cynically burlesques and innocently retells the lie of silent assertion. The result, in Melville's tale, as in so much of Mark Twain, is a perilous equipose of radical, incompatible opposites. Delano does not recognize the obvious because he cannot bear to; Cereno's is killing knowledge. So is Hank Morgan's. Hank is by nature inclined to enjoy bending other people to his imperious will, but he is also driven by a conception of himself as liberator of the numberless slaves of tyranny. This absolute split fosters an array of contradictions that reach their inevitable, shattering culmination in his righteous detonation of Arthurian Britain and final surrender to oblivion. *A Connecticut Yankee* does not end, it explodes in furious, blind confirmation of its narrator's bad-faith incapacity to free anything, himself included.

Hank Morgan succumbs because his unique circumstances work to draw out the contradictions in the cultural baggage that he brings with him from the nineteenth century. He endures the lonely, angry, nervously defensive self-righteousness that Tom Sawyer would experience were he suddenly transported to the center of an equally alien setting— or, on the other hand, that David Wilson does *not* experience under what appear to be similarly unfamiliar conditions. In fact, Dawson's Landing is cut from the same cultural cloth as the rest of Mark Twain's America, but it is far enough from upstate New York to afford the young advocate the marginality that he seems secretly to crave. He is culturally no stranger to the southern town. He knows it well enough to plumb its deepest mystery, and to recognize that his interests are best served if he operates from a position along the margin. For Wilson sees that the sleepy slaveholding community is in fact explosive with suppressed racial fear and hatred. I am suggesting, of course, that Wilson's earliest reported act in Dawson's Landing, his remark about what he would do with half of a barking dog, is no mistake; rather, it is the vehicle to the marginal position that he readily accepts and occupies without complaint. Wilson is a stranger by design. He is drawn, as Mark Twain was drawn again and again, back to the site of a formative encounter with his culture's pathological bad faith. But Wilson makes the trip, as Mark Twain never could, as an automaton, an utterly dispassionate isolato, as coolly detached in his relationship to the tormented Mississippi village as a technician to a machine. Mark Twain aimed to achieve something like the same distance from his materials; indeed, by his own account he set out to write a brief farce about Italian Siamese twins, but was overtaken all unawares by the much graver ironic doublings spawned by race–slavery in the tragedy whose title we are rather telling inclined to shorten to *Pudd'nhead Wilson*. It is a novel whose ironies emerge from an apparently placid narrative surface, and jar us, not altogether agreeably, from the detached critical response that the general tone of the story seems to invite. The novel opens to a serene panorama of "snug little" houses with "whitewashed exteriors" situated in the immemorial river village of better times gone by. These "pretty homes . . . fenced with white palings" are "opulently stocked" with all varieties of "old-fashioned flowers." So settled and conventionally appealing is the scene that we may not pause over the geraniums that spread "like an explosion of flame"[59] across the housefronts. We may not notice that the sleeping village of our mythic past appears, by no great stretch of the imagination, to be on fire. Or that the gown Roxy wears when she switches the babies is "a conflagration of gaudy colors" which, when set off with some "rather lurid ribbon," "a spray of atrocious artificial flowers," and a shawl "of blazing red complexion," makes her appear a "volcanic eruption of infernal splendors."[60] Such details, along with the narrator's occasional ironic intrusions into the flow of the narrative, are reminders of Mark Twain's complex, imperfectly controlled relationship to his story. In David Wilson's case, however, were it not for his Calendar, we might suppose that the deliberate, dispassionate outsider is oblivious to the violence thrusting upward from beneath the superficial calm of Mark Twain's troubled, deeply troubling novel.

Pudd'nhead Wilson's barbed aphorisms reveal that the enigmatic stranger is in fact one of the "we that know," an especially subtle, resourceful, perhaps desperate conspirator in the lie of silent assertion. He lies first by keeping so still that his fellow-conspirators nearly fail to recognize him for what he is. And, second, he lies in the silent assertion that the race—slavery in Dawson's Landing isn't something in which humane and intelligent people are interested. These are the same lies told by the strangers who appear in Camelot, Hadleyburg, Eseldorf, and other fictional evocations of Hannibal in Mark Twain's later works. As outsiders, and by virtue of their seeming indifference to the spectacle of human folly, these aloof, superior witnesses served Mark Twain as imaginative stays against the confusion of too much of his own reality. They are the vehicles of a virtual compulsion to examine and reexamine the human condition, but to do so at a comfortable remove from the thrust of implication. The *locus classicus* in this vein is, of course, *The Mysterious Stranger,* a collection of fragments in which a consummate stranger, an angel, the innocent young nephew of Satan, offers an assessment of man's estate. The leading feature of his commentary is determinism, the notion that humans are without choice in the formation of their behavior, and thus without responsibility for what they do. It follows, young Satan argues, that men and women are fools if they blame themselves for what they regard as their sins. In a degraded but totally determined world, guilt is the pinnacle of folly, and prayer for early release into the oblivion of insanity or death is the highest mortal wisdom.

The argument from necessity is a measure of the chasm that separates young Satan from his human companions, and it helps to account for his serene indifference to the spectacle that he surveys. He is unthreatened by any suggestion of a personal kinship with humanity, and he is apparently confident in the view that the mortal predicament, though replete with foolishness and pain, is blameless and inevitable. Looking through the angelic stranger to his maker, we recognize Satan's detachment and resignation as manifestations of Mark Twain's longing. The angel's serene indifference is the expression of his author's enduring wish to arrive at a settled philosophical remove from his own deep sympathy and guilt over human suffering. Since we are all slaves to necessity, his argument clearly implies, our anguish is misplaced and should be set aside.

Were Mark Twain and his angelic visitor the thoroughgoing determinists that they at times appear to be, *The Mysterious Stranger* would be a complete, rather mechanical text. But they are not. Neither the angel nor the humorist is comfortable for long with a conception of human nature that excludes some measure of freedom to choose; neither, in other words, successfully restrains the impulse to blame the human species for its trouble. Thus the notion that man is enslaved to necessity alternates with the notion that he is enslaved to his nature as it expresses itself in the operations of bad faith. "Satan was accustomed to say that our race lived a life of continuous and uninterrupted self-deception," recalls Theodor Fischer. "It duped itself from cradle to grave with shams and delusions which it mistook for realities, and this made its entire life a sham" (164). Satan's principal illustration of this general point is the Moral Sense, the foolishly proud human capacity to distinguish right from wrong. The Moral Sense, he observes with contempt, almost invariably leads to the rationalization of wickedness. Humans imagine that they are superior to the brutes in their possession of this rational power. In fact, and paradoxically, the Moral Sense brutalizes men and women by opening an array of moral distinctions to the play of their bad faith, and thus permitting them to suppose, by endless lies of silent assertion, that their most perfidious inhumanities are species of virtue. This penchant for "continuous and uninterrupted self-deception" in matters of right and wrong is the mother of a host of mortal woes, all of them entailing enslavement of some sort, most cruelly of humans to one another, and most painfully of the sinner to his conscience.

Mark Twain knew all of this from long personal experience, and there can be no doubt that he was more comfortably within himself launching barbs of contempt than in groping for philosophical repose. But he was no more able to sustain coherent discourse on the Moral Sense than he was on determinism, for neither approach to the dark, irrepressible theme of slavery seemed to yield a permanently satisfying resting place. Determinism relieves guilt at the price of obliterating choice. The freedom to choose, on the other hand, may in principle imply the potential for moral progress; but for Mark Twain such prospects invariably succumb in practice to the perverse play of man's fallen nature, and thus to the shackles of conscience and bad faith. Because he recoiled from the implications of both perspectives on human enslavement, Mark Twain could neither finish his story nor set it aside. Instead, his attitude swings, with Satan's, between intervals of detached indifference and periodic eruptions of angry condemnation. In such latter phases, of course, the futility of retreat to angelic detachment becomes manifest, and the implied philosophical solution to the moral—and esthetic—dilemma collapses into the problem. Were Satan's indifference to the mortal predicament a plausible solution, then he would maintain it. But he cannot. Nor, on the other hand, is he content to stand for long in wrathful judgment of a species whose fallen nature Mark Twain knew best from a long lifetime's self-scrutiny. The problem, we perceive, is the fundamental incompatibility between the writer's assumptions about human nature and the kind of freedom—from nature, history, conscience, others, and by implication, perhaps, from the God that young Satan's uncle disobeyed—that he attempts to confer on his angelic hero. The longing for such freedom is manifest in the conception of the extraordinary stranger; but its frustration is equally clear in the failure to embody that conception in a complete, coherent story.

It may be that in Satan we catch a glimpse of Mark Twain's groping rebellion against culture itself, against the compulsion to abide by the rules of what is, "we that know" recognize, a fiction, a fabrication. The denial of culture's constructedness is the grand progenitor of all subsequent bad faith denials, and the first and heaviest link in an endless chain of lesser, often benign, sometimes unbearable, but obligatory lies of silent assertion. Rather more narrowly, Satan is a manifestation of the urge D. H. Lawrence detected at the center of American culture, to be masterless, totally free of restraints. Most demonstrably, however, Mark Twain's obsession with an elusive, ungraspable conception of freedom expresses the frustration endemic to a culture committed to the principle that humans are created free, equal, and deserving of dignity, but which is burdened at the same time with a history that records the continuous, widespread, violent, and unabating disregard of those ostensibly sacred ideals. The shortest of *The Mysterious Stranger* fragments, "Schoolhouse Hill," clearly illustrates this most proximate of the cultural frameworks for Mark Twain's somber reflex on the score of freedom. Significantly, this version of the story is the most contemporary in setting, the most direct in its approach to race–slavery, and by far the shortest. It ends just as Satan begins to grow familiar with the slaves. Earlier on, it features the fabulous stranger's effortless overthrow of the school bully, and of his vengeful father, the local slave-trader, whose wrist gives way like a twig under the pressure of Satan's grip. "Apparently," ventures William M. Gibson, "Schoolhouse Hill" was designed as "an essay in the correction of ideas and a comedy set in the world of Tom Sawyer and Huckleberry Finn, whose boy-hero would like to reform and save it" (8). Such sanguine plans notwithstanding, however, there is no reasonable prospect for change, and scant occasion for humor, in the Hannibal of "Schoolhouse Hill." Satan crushes the slave-trader's bones not in order to edify him and to enforce a change of heart, but out of an angry impulse to punish. Evidently enough, he assumes that it is pointless to identify the man's contemptible trait and to argue against it. Thus he draws no moral from his bone-crushing exploit. Nor do the boys looking on. They are accustomed to sudden, irrational violence; they regard it as a form of amusement; they are "fascinated with the show and glad to be there and see it" (189).

James M. Cox anticipates my own argument by highlighting the incompatibility of the Moral Sense with "the deterministic thesis." The first of these, he observes, places the responsibility for human enslavement on man, while the second assigns it to God. "He is never able to integrate the two concepts," Cox insists, adding that "This central problem could well have been what drove Mark Twain to his repeated efforts to finish the manuscript." The way out of this dilemma, Cox ventures, was the dream ending which Mark Twain "confidently left for Paine to find." The dissolution of all contradictions in a solipsistic dream "was like a goal which" Mark Twain "could see but could not reach." Cox goes on to concede that "the inevitability" of the dream ending

> does not keep it from being a way out rather than a way through the dilemma which caused it. For little Satan's attack [on God] is what it reveals itself to be—an outburst of the pent-up indignation which the structure and style of the book could not discharge. More important, Satan's solipsism constitutes a decisive weakening of the criticism produced by his ironic innocence. Finally, the ending gives the lie to the

identity of the book, for Satan in his act of departing actually acquires the Moral Sense he has been remarkably and effectively free of in the successful moments of the narrative. The truth is that Satan must forego the emotion of indignation if he is to be free of the Moral Sense.[61]

Cox's analysis is characteristically penetrating, and I bring it forward here in order to build upon it in a small way, and to align it as fully as possible with my own developing thesis. I agree emphatically that slavery is Mark Twain's consuming topic in *The Mysterious Stranger,* and that contradictions in the framing of that issue figured decisively in the failure to complete any of several versions of the story. I am impressed, as Cox is, that Mark Twain wrote the dream ending but neglected to tie it to any of the fragments he left behind. He wrote the dream ending "as a goal to be reached," Cox reiterates. "Though he could end the story, he could not finish it. Instead, it finished him as a writer."[62]

The trajectory of my own argument inclines me to view Satan's inconsistencies as expressions of Mark Twain's wavering attempt to achieve a settled perspective on the question of slavery, and not as problems of characterization per se. The young angel is the vehicle of his maker's groping. Moreover, I am not persuaded that such inconsistencies are primarily to be found in the fragmentary dream ending. To the contrary, I find that the attack on God is everywhere implicit in the deterministic thesis, that Satan's advocacy of solipsism is hardly the first of his lapses from innocence, and, most vitally, that all such lapses into the Moral Sense give "the lie to the identity of the book" as Cox defines it. In effect, I want to locate the book's "identity" not in an immanent unity pointing toward an "inevitable" ending, but rather in its conspicuous, pervasive, significant failure to achieve coherence. Satan's inconsistency and the accumulation of incoherent fragments is testimony to an obsession with slavery as enduring as Mark Twain's incapacity to arrive at a permanently satisfying perspective on that topic. His failure to integrate the Moral Sense with his deterministic thesis hardly exhausts the evidence on this general score. Theodore imagines that travel will restore him to serenity, only to find, as Mark Twain found on his world lecture tour in the mid-1890s, that slavery is universally the law of "civilized" human experience. Insanity is held out as the answer for minds subjected to an unbearable reality, but Satan then adds that only the very few among the deranged who are able to "imagine themselves kings or gods" arrive at happiness. "The rest," he concludes, "are no happier than the sane" (164). Laughter is also advanced as a solution to the human predicament, but Satan's characterization of humor as a "weapon" of destruction rather than an aid to clarification and relief is ominous, especially in a thoroughly humorless, misanthropic performance by America's quondam clown prince. Against the "colossal humbug" of civilized life, Satan argues, most human resources are virtually powerless. "Only Laughter can blow it to rags and atoms at a blast. Against the assault of Laughter nothing can stand" (166). Humor does not expose abuses that they may be reformed; it flattens everything in its path. Laughter is volatile and violent, and its pleasures are those of explosive rage fully indulged. The advocacy of humor, in short, only barely conceals an overpowering impulse to obliterate.

The manuscripts of *The Mysterious Stranger* may thus be described as a succession of approaches to the question of human enslavement that are no sooner tried than they are found to be unworkable. Satan takes a deterministic line only to imply that humans have the freedom to choose; he counsels indifference and promptly gets angry; restful travel heightens distress; the serene promise of insanity is withdrawn; laughter is not really funny at all. At no point, however, does the miscarriage of any such approach result in a descent to permanent disenchantment. Rather, each failure to achieve resolution is followed by yet another optimistic assault on the problem. It is thus the alternating rhythm of collapse and recoil that emerges as the dominant pattern in *The Mysterious Stranger,* and not a movement toward resolution of any kind. This is as true of Satan's apparently conclusive solipsism as it is of any of the other approaches. With determinism and laughter and the rest, the dream ending presents itself as a perfectly plausible conclusion to Mark Twain's restless fable—so plausible, in fact, that generations of readers and critics have been inclined to view it as the humorist's last, settled view of the human condition. But the dream ending is simply another false start, a promising approach that is finally just as vulnerable to collapse as all the other promising approaches in *The Mysterious Stranger.* All versions of the story emphasize the remoteness in time and place of the setting, and the two longest fragments, "The Chronicle of Young Satan" and "No. 44, The Mysterious Stranger," open to virtually identical images of drowsing detachment from the trials of ordinary life.

> It was 1702—May. Austria was far away from the world, and asleep; it was still the Middle Ages in Austria, and promised to remain so forever. Some even set it away back centuries upon centuries and said that by the mental and spiritual clock it was still the Age of Faith in Austria. But they meant it as a compliment, not a slur, and it was so

taken, and we were all proud of it. I remember it well, although I was only a boy; and I remember, too, the pleasure it gave me.

Yes, Austria was far from the world, and asleep, and our village was in the middle of that sleep, being in the middle of Austria. It drowsed in peace in the deep privacy of a hilly and woodsy solitude where news from the world hardly ever came to disturb its dreams, and was infinitely content.   (35)[63]

This is a familiar scene, of course, an installment on "the matter of Hannibal" in which remoteness in time and space from the implicitly troublesome present is the literal correlative of sleep, and brings profound peace of mind. A number of observations follow. Most significantly, the passage reveals that *The Mysterious Stranger* begins where it ends, in a dream state that promises serenity, but which cannot be sustained. It is as though Theodor commences, or recommences, to tell his story with Satan's concluding advice—"Dream other dreams, and better!"—firmly in mind. He is initially inclined to offer his narrative as a sort of dream, and he seems determined to fabricate the happiest conceivable version of the materials that pass through his mind. Almost from the beginning, however, there are obstacles to the fruition of his design on serenity. I refer, of course, to the irony that cuts sharply through his placid tone, a flash of self-conscious uneasiness from beneath the mantle of innocence, and a reminder that consciousness, even as it drifts toward sleep, has a border on discord. As the pages that follow make clear, the dream of contentment, like all prospects of resolution and repose, is vulnerable to the sudden emergence of harsh perspectives on the omnipresent theme of human slavery.

In numbering dreams among the promising approaches to experience in *The Mysterious Stranger,* we are properly reminded of Mark Twain's tendency, especially in his later years, to approach the calamities in his life as passing nightmares.[64] Sleep was not always a threshold on serenity, he well knew, and at times, as in "Which Was It?" it is a gateway to horrors far worse than those of waking consciousness. The same may be said for memory, an obvious analogue to dreaming in Theodor's opening description of his childhood in Austria, and the mental frame in which most of Mark Twain's major narratives are set. Memory has the potential to filter and soften, as sleep does, and its nostalgic evocations of boyhood are quite evidently cognate with Theodor's dream. *Tom Sawyer,* I have argued, is a product of just such a selective and softening mental process. So is "Old Times on the Mississippi," though its continuation in *Life on the Mississippi* gives the lie to the preceding nostalgia, and demonstrates that memory is as liable to lapses from repose as any other state of mind in *The Mysterious Stranger.* The chasm that separates *Tom Sawyer* and *Huckleberry Finn,* both recollections of the same place and time, serves to illustrate the same phenomenon, and presents us, in Jim, with a point of departure for an understanding of that characteristic liability.

Frequent alternations between the positive and the negative poles of a wide variety of conditions and mental states, it must be clear, are a staple of Mark Twain's art.[65] In elaborating this point as it applies to *The Mysterious Stranger* and to other works, however, it is noteworthy that descents from the positive to the negative, from success to failure, from contentment to unrest, quite often hold out gratifications to those enduring the apparent breakdown. Hank Morgan's failure to free the enslaved masses cannot be separated from his egotistical showman's addiction to center stage, which flourishes in a culture of aristocrats and slaves, and which influences his emergent persuasion that the species is constitutionally incapable of freedom. We see a version of the same phenomenon in "The United States of Lyncherdom," where outrage and dismay imperfectly conceal an inclination to cultivate the horrific spectacle of violent racial injustice. Just so, the Satan who descends from serene philosophical indifference to righteous, bone-crushing violence takes a contradictory plunge into the contemptible Moral Sense. But this apparently unthinking failure of consistency repays Satan with an opportunity to show off in front of the admiring boys. Like Hank, Satan is willing to sacrifice consistency and the high ethical line to cheap heroics, especially when such self-indulgence is virtually proof against detection, even his own.

As the examples of Hank Morgan and young Satan suggest, the ostensible agents of truth and justice may be moved by a deep, concealed interest in the preservation of the degraded status quo. Colonel Sherburn's seemingly reluctant surrender to the necessity of gun-play—"I'll endure it till one o'clock" (184), he says of Boggs's drunken abuse— and his apparently close brush with the lynch mob are in fact carefully orchestrated episodes in a drama that culminates in the decisive reconfirmation of his local preeminence. Sherburn cultivates adversity as a stage for his jeremiad, a triumph of imperious, bloody-minded showmanship whose violent moral indignation cannot fully disguise the Jeremiah's stake in the conditions which he professes to deplore. In seeming to suffer the town's contempt, Sherburn at once exploits and preserves the shameful status quo. The same may be said for Pudd'nhead Wilson. The retiring stranger advances scientific evidence of the twisted social implications of race–slavery, but his disclosures are decisive contributions to the restoration of the conditions of extreme injustice with which, in his machine-like detachment, he has made his peace. From the outset, it seems likely, Pudd'nhead views the pathological bad faith in Dawson's Landing not as a moral wrong to be exposed and corrected, but as a circumstance ideally adjusted to his craving for remote, passionless control—a circumstance, therefore, to be preserved and exploited. Thus he deliberately cultivates the misunderstanding that lands him permanently on the margin of the godforsaken little community, a stranger, serenely dead to a world that he has known, we surmise, too well for comfort.

Complex intentionality of a similar stripe prompts young Satan's declaration that the world's "colossal humbug" is powerless to resist the leveling "assault of Laughter." When we reflect that the angelic outsider is also persuaded that the world's humbug is ineradicable, we recognize that the universal sham of reality is the first essential to his continued pleasure as a cosmic humorist. His drift in all this is evidently complex. On one side, he wants to reform the world; on the other, he aims to exploit its folly as fodder for broadsides of annihilating Laughter. Satan's simultaneous, apparently incompatible impulses to reform and obliterate humanity are evidently part and parcel with his inclination, on occasion, to adopt the Moral Sense as his perspective on the mortal condition. His vacillation between serene indifference and angry moral disapproval, I have argued, reflects Mark Twain's uncertain grappling with the contradiction of race–slavery and racist imperialism in the land of human freedom and equality. Satan's indifference is the emotional corollary to a deterministic explanation for the glaring contradiction, while his anger follows upon the assumption that humans are morally responsible. This deep division in the angel's thinking opens on yet another. For while Satan's anger implies the assumption of an ideal of behavior accessible to human emulation, it also releases in him precisely the selfish, destructive, exploitative tendencies that he condemns in the Moral Sense. Thus his descent from indifference to passionate involvement, though prompted perhaps by a glimmering of hope for reform, is also thinly disguised self-indulgence in violent humor, intimidation, and showmanship. The indignant idealist in Satan thus competes with a violent, compulsive showman—a Colonel Sherburn—who cultivates and exploits human degradation for his own selfish ends.

This collapse of optimism into varieties of crude subjection serves, in turn, to confirm the foregoing analysis of the Moral Sense, and to reinforce the inclination to retreat to the serene indifference of the deterministic thesis. It is evidence as well that the apparent incoherence of *The Mysterious Stranger* finds its order in a revolving cycle of incompatible opposites engendering and canceling each other. The story has no ending because it is precisely the nature of this circular pattern to continue to rotate, to forever fail to achieve the resolution it forever seems to promise. Such perpetual motion has its source in a consciousness that is itself deeply divided. Espousal of determinism suddenly gives way to notions of free will, indifference to advocacy; the approach to the ideal collapses in unprincipled self-indulgence; and so on. But the division is not merely between the stages of consciousness; it is within them as well. The appeal to laughter bends simultaneously to prospects of reform and license; the right-minded punishment of the slave-trader is also cynical showing off. In due course, the guilt caused by the regular betrayal of shameful ulterior motives leads, in the name of stern philosophical truth, to the detection of necessity at work within the persistent oppositional structure. This step manifestly recapitulates the pattern it ostensibly seeks to break, and thus propels the cycle forward. But it is an especially decisive step because it illustrates that the consciousness at work in *The Mysterious Stranger* reacts to the revelation of its capacity for self-deception—to a glimpse of the selfish ends served by its high-minded intentions—by retreating to the illusion that such hapless duplicity is necessary, inevitable, and thus outside the range of its control or responsibility. The result is a pattern of consummate bad faith, in which the simultaneous push and pull of righteous and selfish motives propels consciousness through constant repetitions of the withdrawal to determinism and temporary repose, all the while deflecting attention away from the endlessly deferred reckoning with the theme of human freedom. Ironically, the revolving lies of silent assertion in the foreground obliquely dramatize the more comprehensive, pathological bad-faith evasion that they serve primarily to obscure. *The Mysterious Stranger* thus enacts and reenacts the fragments of a story that Mark Twain could not put aside, but that he could not bear to tell in full. As a way out where there was no way through, he contrived to retreat in symptomatic bad faith to the illusion of a perpetual cycle of necessary, irreducible indeterminacy.

X

Huck Finn ends his narrative only to take it up again. "The End. Yours Truly, Huck Finn." I take this to be a complex, very telling moment. Huck wants out of this story he has felt obliged to tell and to share, but that he has come to find such a "trouble" in the telling that he vows never to "make" another book. He is quite emphatic about "The End." But his emphasis betrays the lingering suspicion that in ending his narrative he has merely stopped it, not really finished it. He has not resolved the vexing question of race—slavery that his story has circled back to, time and again. He is not comfortable with what he glimpses of the "evasion" of Jim's freedom, or with his own ready complicity in that travesty. But to fully resolve his uncertainty and uneasiness, he senses, he must address hard realities about himself and his culture. In the outcome, and without knowing quite how or why, Huck tries to stop what he cannot finish by running away. "The End."

"Yours Truly, Huck Finn" protests too much in a similarly ironic way. Most obviously, the words that follow "The End" betray the fact that just saying so is not, in this case, enough. "The End" is clearly not the end. What *has* concluded, Huck may be heard to say, is a story, a fiction, a mere book. The Huck Finn on the outside of the book, he implies, is more "Truly" real, more himself, than the fictional character on the inside. His opening gestures of esteem for "true" books notwithstanding, Huck concludes his maiden effort in the literary line by implying that his own narrative is not to be trusted. I am not what this fiction makes me seem to be, he hints; I am something better, freer, less civilized. Quite ironically, Huck falls back on the immemorial literary convention of the ending as a way of separating the truth from what is merely conventional. Just so, he uses language to draw the line between what his story says and what he more "Truly" is. That line is as manifestly fictional, of course, as the one that separates "The End" from what follows.

We are strongly inclined to forgive Huck his bad faith. This is so in good part because by forgiving Huck we forgive ourselves. We blink our own bad faith in blinking his. But we are also guided by the sense that Huck is not really conscious of what his actions add up to, and therefore not morally accountable. Perhaps. But perhaps we are blinking here too. After all, Huck is morally self-conscious enough to throw away the snake-skins, and adept enough at self-deception to forget what he has done. And he must recognize how deeply divided he is in his feelings toward Jim; he must see that he is as likely to betray his black friend as to protect him. What Huck cannot have perceived is that his responses to Jim are all geared, in one way or another, to the civilization he runs from. To be sure, Huck is marginal to the dominant culture; but his marginality works primarily to distort the culture's operations in him, not to obstruct them. Thus while most culture-bearers dress and eat and pray without straining at the rigid conventions that inform their behavior, Huck is sufficiently remote from the cultural center to be aware, at intervals, of the gap separating the conventional from what seems natural. This gap is most painful for him in matters of race and slavery. For the fully acculturated people around him, the utter contradiction of their leading institution is deeply submerged under a blanket of bad-faith denial. By multiple lies of silent assertion that some cruelty is not cruel, that some injustice is not unjust, that some humans are not fully human, they have contrived to live in relative equanimity with a staggering contradiction. For his own part, and because of his marginality, Huck is imperfectly sheltered against an awareness of the unbearable significance of race–slavery. He is sufficiently the outsider to feel love and respect for Jim, and to experience guilt when he violates the trust of his friend. But he is sufficiently the insider to have internalized the prohibitions against any behavior even remotely suggesting abolitionism, and thus to question his own positive impulses toward his companion on the raft. Unlike Tom and his admirers, who are blind to the enormity in their midst, Huck is on one side able to glimpse the crime, and on the other properly in awe of the consequences of its acknowledgment. He retreats to bad faith out of the fear of fully expressing, even to himself, what it is that he has seen. As the result, he is as helpless to acquiesce in his culture's bad faith as he is to draw himself out of it; thus he wavers between contrary, incompatible states of mind.

Perhaps we forgive Huck, then, not because he is morally unself-aware, but because his marginality leaves him powerless to control or transcend this swing back and forth between contradictory states of mind. He does what he does, we may feel, out of the necessity of his nature and circumstances. But if this is so, then we have effectively denied Huck moral choice, and thus either relinquished him as a hero, or else inadvertently betrayed that it is his moral helplessness which we feel drawn to. Huck would of course reject such notions out of hand.

True, as he approaches his decision to go to hell for Jim's sake, he tries "to kinder soften it up somehow for myself, by saying I was brung up wicked, and so I warn't so much to blame" (269). But he knows better, and ends by accepting the responsibility for his decision. It is ironic, of course, that having made up his mind, Huck almost immediately recoils into the identity and bad-faith scheming of Tom Sawyer. The role of liberator in a world of resolute slaveholders is too much for him, and he collapses under the enormous weight of his decision. But never again does he toy with the notion of necessity; to the end, even as he lights out, Huck imagines himself a free moral agent.

I am suggesting, of course, that the impulse to exempt Huck from responsibility for his choices may spring from a need to exonerate ourselves. If we argue that Huck's marginality renders him a witness to the constructedness and cruelty of his culture, but also incapacitates him to change anything, then he is qualified for membership in the elite "we that know." Members of that group, it will be recalled, recognize that it is their nature to silently deny the truth, acknowledge that the denial of slavery is the leading illustration of that law, and then, still in obedience to the rule of their natures, promptly deny the law, and the cruelty of slavery along with it. The net result in psychological terms is a state of mind forever divided and alternating between contempt for the world it fabricates and acquiescence in the world it receives. Mark Twain is quite clear in "My First Lie" that the awareness of the laws of human nature does nothing to exempt humans from their sway. Indeed, he concludes his discussion of necessity by bending to its influence. What he does not suggest, however, is that the ready agreement by the "we that know" that such inexorable laws apply to human behavior is itself their most significant lie of silent assertion, for it acknowledges and validates the universal sway of mute deceit. Bad faith rules, by necessity, in all human affairs. In other hands, this conclusion might seem a reluctant surrender to stern reality. In Mark Twain's hands, however, it is a subtle part of bad faith to make voluntary moral decisions seem obligatory, especially when those decisions bear directly—as they do in "My First Lie" and *The Mysterious Stranger*—on race–slavery. The "we that know" do not surrender to necessity, they retreat in guilt-stricken bad faith from too much of their own reality.

Huck is tempted briefly by this logical line of retreat to the doctrine of moral necessity, a line that he has no doubt heard often enough in St. Petersburg. But he resists valiantly, if with imperfect success. Mark Twain was similarly tempted, and similarly disposed to resist his own impulse, as his failures to make a coherent virtue of necessity demonstrate. And we, the readers and critics of Mark Twain, respond to a milder version of the same impulse, which presents itself in the name of such imperatives as freedom, boyhood, innocence, and nature, to release Huck from any responsibility for the profound moral evasion that he recounts at the end of his narrative. We may do this in a direct way, by declaring that he must "light out" in order to preserve his innocence and freedom from civilized contamination. Or we may take an indirect approach and dismiss the long conclusion, the evasion, as Tom's story, or as a grave lapse in Mark Twain's literary judgment. However we act upon it, our impulse to exempt Huck is a symptomatic bad-faith recapitulation of our hero's willful self-deception. But of course we fail to win anything approaching complete release from the heavy moral claims that the narrative at once imposes on consciousness and invites consciousness to set aside. We are no more able to finish this story than Huck or Mark Twain are. Rather, we end it, as the hero and the humorist did; and though we are as thoroughly unsettled as they are by our passage through the narrative, we return to it, again and again, as we might to the memory of an unresolved childhood trauma.

Something is not right in *Huckleberry Finn,* and we know it. But the same bad faith that gives rise to our uneasiness works to obscure its source, leaving us, with Huck and his maker, rather nervously inclined to run away. But only, as I have said, to come back all over again. So long as we continue to come back to *Huckleberry Finn,* to puzzle over it and quarrel about it and vow yet once more in vain to put it behind us, for that long we can be sure that we have not given way to the potent cultural impulse to conceal, ignore, forget, permanently light out from, or consign to necessity our failures to redeem fully the promise of our grandest ideals.

Notes

Introduction

1. C. Vann Woodward, *The Burden of Southern History* (New York: Vintage, 1961), p. 189.

2. Louis Hartz, *The Liberal Tradition in America* (New York: Harcourt, Brace and World, 1955), p. 7.

3. Peter L. Berger and Thomas Luckmann, *The Social Construction of Reality* (Garden City, N.Y.: Doubleday, 1966), pp. 5–6.

4. Ibid., pp. 103, 187.

5. In his very useful overview, *"The Social Construction of Reality:* Implications for Future Directions in American Studies," *Prospects,* 8 (1983), 49–58, R. Gordon Kelly observes: "Although Berger and Luckmann nowhere say it so baldly, their argument appears to lead ineluctably to this conclusion: If reality is socially constructed, men can *restructure* it—on the basis of an understanding of the processes in and through which the reality of everyday life is maintained" (53).

6. Carolyn Porter, *Seeing and Being* (Middletown, Conn.: Wesleyan University Press, 1981), p. xviii.

7. Ibid., p. xix.

8. Ibid., p. 47.

9. Ibid., p. 49.

10. Ibid., pp. 234–35.

11. Ibid., p. xi.

12. Gregory S. Jay, "America the Scrivener: Economy and Literary History," *Diacritics,* 14 (Spring 1984), 39–40.

13. Berger and Luckmann, *The Social Construction of Reality,* p. 90.

14. Pierre Macherey, *A Theory of Literary Production,* trans. Geoffrey Wall (London: Routledge and Kegan Paul, 1978), p. 238.

15. In Louis Althusser, *Lenin and Philosophy,* trans. Ben Brewster (London: New Left Books, 1971), p. 164.

16. Stephen Greenblatt, "Invisible Bullets: Renaissance Authority and Its Subversion," *Glyph 8* (1981), p. 41.

17. Ibid., p. 53.

18. D. A. Miller, "The Novel and the Police," *Glyph 8* (1981), p. 140. Miller's assertion that "the novel shows disciplinary power to inhere in the

very resistance to it" finds ample confirmation in what I have observed of Mark Twain's major works. "At the macroscopic level," Miller goes on, "the demonstration is carried in the attempt of the protagonist to break away from the social control which thereby reclaims him" (pp. 143–44). This would seem to apply, in somewhat different ways, to both Huck and Jim.

19. Edmund S. Morgan, *The Challenge of the American Revolution* (New York: Norton, 1976), p. 141.

20. Ibid., p. 142.

21. Frederick Douglass, *Narrative of the Life of Frederick Douglass* (New York: Signet, 1968), pp. 35–37.

22. John Langston Gwaltney, *Drylongso: A Self-Portrait of Black America* (New York: Vintage, 1981), pp. 100, 103–04, 105–06, 128. See also pp. 4, 19, 21, 98–101, and *passim*.

23. Lawrence W. Levine's *Black Culture and Black Consciousness* (New York: Oxford University Press, 1977) enhances our understanding of the slaves' perspective on bad faith, both within the society of the white oppressors, and within the black community itself. See especially Chapter 2, "The Meaning of Slave Tales."

24. David Brion Davis, *The Problem of Slavery in Western Culture* (Ithaca, N.Y.: Cornell University Press, 1966), p. 62.

25. Ibid., p. 261.

26. Charles Dickens, *Martin Chuzzlewit* (London: Oxford University Press, 1951), p. 341. Eric J. Sundquist's "Slavery, Revolution, and the American Renaissance," in *The American Renaissance Reconsidered: Selected Papers from the English Institute, 1982–83,* ed. Walter Benn Michaels and Donald E. Pease (Baltimore: The Johns Hopkins University Press, 1985), pp. 1–33, offers useful insights into this process of denial.

27. Woodward, *The Burden of Southern History,* pp. 178–79. Paul M. Gaston's *The New South Creed* (New York: Alfred A. Knopf, 1970) is very useful on relevant Southern mythologies in the decades after the Civil War.

28. Winthrop D. Jordan, *White Over Black* (Chapel Hill, N.C.: University of North Carolina Press, 1968), pp. 178, 384, 373, 197, 489, 429.

29. Eugene Genovese, *Roll, Jordan, Roll: The World the Slaves Made* (New York: Vintage, 1976), p. 5.

30. As quoted by Genovese in *Roll, Jordan, Roll,* p. 426.

31. Ibid., pp. 595, 597. Orlando Patterson's recent, very forceful comparative study, *Slavery and Social Death* (Cambridge, Mass.: Harvard University Press, 1982), challenges accepted scholarly views in a number of vital areas and should give rise to valuable debate. Patterson's concluding chapter on "Slavery as Human Parasitism," with its acute observations on the varieties of reality inversion and ideological self-deception endemic to slaveholding societies, is especially relevant to my work.

32. James M. Cox, *Mark Twain: The Fate of Humor* (Princeton, N.J.: Princeton University Press, 1966), p. 175.

33. Ibid., p. 176.

Part I

1. *The Adventures of Tom Sawyer,* ed. John C. Gerber, Paul Baender, and Terry Firkins, in *The Works of Mark Twain* (Berkeley: University of California Press, 1980), p. 33. Hereafter references to this edition will be cited parenthetically in the text.

2. Bernard DeVoto, *Mark Twain's America* (Cambridge, Mass.: Houghton Mifflin, 1932), p. 304.

3. Ibid., pp. 304, 306–07.

4. Walter Blair, *Mark Twain & Huck Finn* (Berkeley: University of California Press, 1960), p. 75.

5. Henry Nash Smith, *Mark Twain: The Development of a Writer* (Cambridge, Mass.: Harvard University Press, 1962), p. 91.

6. James N. Cox, *Mark Twain: The Fate of Humor,* (Princeton, N.J.: Princeton University Press, 1966), pp. 131, 146.

7. Ibid., pp. 147–48.

8. Ibid., p. 141.

9. Ibid., p. 147.

10. Early on in his chapter on *Tom Sawyer,* Cox acknowledges that the children imitate the adults of St. Petersburg: "Tom Sawyer and his gang . . . are children at play—their world is a play world in which adult rituals of love, death, war, and justice are reenacted in essentially harmless patterns" (131). He goes on to acknowledge that Tom "has no sustained desire to escape" the constraints of village life, "and no program of rebellion." In the same voice, however, Cox insists on a clear distinction between Tom's "pleasure" and the adults' "dull play" (140–41). My general position on Tom's relationship to the community, and some of its details, are clearly anticipated in Judith Fetterley's fine essay, "The Sanctioned Rebel," *Studies in the Novel,* 3 (1971), 293–304. Though she follows Cox in settling on a dramatic model for the analysis of Tom's role in St. Petersburg, Fetterley stresses the similarities between the attitudes and behavior of adults and children (300–301), and argues that the townspeople endure Tom's egotism and aggressiveness because he amuses them and affirms their values. "For indeed the focus of *The Adventures of Tom Sawyer* is on the harmony between Tom and his community and on the satisfactions of the symbiotic relationship between them" (303).

11. Cox seems to have something like this in mind when he asserts that "in Mark Twain's world of boyhood, the imagination represents the capacity

for mimicry, impersonation, make-believe, and play"; *Mark Twain: The Fate of Humor,* p. 148.

12. Ibid., p. 141.

13. The parallels between my characterization of Tom Sawyer and historian John Dizikes' more general portrait of the American gamesman are numerous enough to suggest that Mark Twain's young hero was patterned after a familiar Jacksonian type. Like Tom Sawyer, the gamesman "acknowledged the rules in order to circumvent them when it suited him. Getting around, bending, or undermining the rules, without clearly breaking them, was, for the gamesman, a fundamental part of the game." Dizikes goes on to note the gamesman's skill at calculation, his tendency to work by indirection, his gravitation to "situations of ambiguity and uncertainty," and his absolute commitment to victory. Finally, all successful gamesmen expressed their "nerveless self-control" and asserted their mastery of all situations by putting on a poker face. "The poker face," Dizikes argues, "was a game face in a land where all life was treated as a game, and it was never abandoned because the game never ended" (*Sportsmen and Gamesmen,* [Boston: Houghton Mifflin, 1981], pp. 38–42, 287).

14. James Joyce, *A Portrait of the Artist as a Young Man* (New York: The Modern Library, 1944), p. 252.

15. Mark Twain, "How To Tell a Story," in *The $30,000 Bequest* (New York: F. P. Collier and Son, 1917), pp. 263–64. Mark Twain is strongly inclined to think of his story-telling as a trick on the reader, or even as a military strategy designed to outwit and defeat an enemy.

16. *Adventures of Huckleberry Finn,* (Berkeley: University of California Press, 1985), p. 165. Hereafter references to this edition will be cited parenthetically in the text. For a much fuller discussion of Huck's involvement in bad faith, especially as it influences his friendship with Jim, see my essay, "The Silences in *Huckleberry Finn,*" *Nineteenth-Century Fiction,* 37 (1982), 50–74.

17. Again, see "The Silences in *Huckleberry Finn.*"

18. Smith, *Mark Twain: The Development of a Writer,* p. 82: "The rivalry of Tom and Sid serves merely to introduce such boyish crimes as Tom's swimming without permission."

19. Ibid., p. 82: "Nothing comes of the hint that Sid picks up about the murder of Dr. Robinson from Tom's talk in his sleep."

20. For a much more detailed discussion of Mark Twain's complex feelings about Henry, see my essay, "Why I Killed My Brother: An Essay on Mark Twain," *Literature and Psychology,* 30 (1980), 168–81.

21. Hamlin Hill, "The Composition and the Structure of *Tom Sawyer,*" *American Literature,* 32 (1961), 379. Blair's essay, "On the Structure of *Tom Sawyer,*" appeared in *Modern Philology,* 37 (1939), 75–88.

22. Fetterley, "The Sanctioned Rebel," p. 300.

23. "The Turning-point of My Life," *Great Short Works of Mark Twain,* ed. Justin Kaplan (New York: Harper and Row, 1967), pp. 224–25.

24. *The Autobiography of Mark Twain,* ed. Charles Neider (New York: Harper and Brothers, 1959), pp. 77–78. In the margin of the holograph manuscript of the novel appears Mark Twain's reminder to himself that "Becky has measles" (as noted on p. 9 of the Introduction to the Gerber et al. edition of *Tom Sawyer*). It might have been appropriate for Becky to come down with measles either before or after Tom takes her punishment for ripping the page in the teacher's anatomy book. At both points she is the possessor of a painfully compromising secret. But Mark Twain seems to have sensed that the illness was more properly the self-induced affliction of a boy with trouble in mind. His personal experience undoubtedly influenced his final judgment in the matter. The measles episode seems to have figured rather prominently in Mark Twain's memory. In a June 6, 1900 letter to Will Bowen's widow, Clemens opens by responding to what appears to have been Mrs. Bowen's inquiry: "Yes, I really wanted to catch the measles, & I succeeded" (*Mark Twain's Letters to Will Bowen,* ed. Theodore Hornberger [Austin: University of Texas Press, 1941], p. 27).

25. I take it to be a leading element in bad faith's potency, durability, and resistance to change that it bears with it the "history" of its own evolution and developmental necessity. Or, to put the case another way, a culture's specific bad faith—its ways of lying to itself—persists relatively unchanged over time because it persuades its practitioners that marked deviations from its path are either impossible or the surest steps toward disaster. Thus I do not mean to suggest that the cycle of fear and guilt in Tom's experience, or the implied development of bad faith as a social arrangement from some remote, primal terror are in any sense objective. Rather, they are integral to the structure of bad faith, and such objectivity as they seem to possess is symptomatic of the good health of the subtle social arrangement that they at once express and reinforce.

26. This is not the place for prolonged discussion of Tom's (and Huck's) materialism. It seems clear enough, however, that the lust for money functions in a variety of interesting ways in the novel. It can be argued, for example, that the reflex desire for material wealth is one cultural acquisition that Huck shares, up to a point, with his friend. It is noteworthy, too, that while money intermittently blinds the boys to danger, the quest for gold also leads them into evil's lair. Finally, the novel fully supports the conclusion that riches are the just reward of success in a culture of bad faith.

27. Victor Turner, *The Forest of Symbols* (Ithaca, N.Y.: Cornell University Press, 1967), pp. 104, 106, 99, and *passim*.

28. I address this issue in my essay, "The Silences in *Huckleberry Finn*."

29. *Paradise Lost* concludes (XII, 646–49): "The world was all before them, where to choose / Their place of rest, and Providence their guide: /

They hand in hand, with wand'ring steps and slow, / Through Eden took their solitary way."

30. From p. 552 of the original manuscript, held at Georgetown University, as quoted by John C. Gerber et al. in their "Introduction" to *Tom Sawyer,* pp. 17–18.

31. Ibid., p. 17.

32. Becky's reaction to the radical social deprivation of the cave is reminiscent of what Berger and Luckmann, in *The Social Construction of Reality,* pp. 101–02, call "anomic terror." In an adequate "symbolic universe," the individual finds a place to "locate" and integrate the anticipation of his or her death, and is thus "constantly protected against terror." "To be anomic . . . means to be deprived of this shield and to be exposed, alone, to the onslaught of nightmare." The complementary social and psychological dimensions of Becky's condition are also present in this analysis of anomie. "While the horror of aloneness is probably already given in the constitutional sociality of man, it manifests itself on the level of meaning in man's incapacity to sustain a meaningful existence in isolation from the nomic construction of society."

33. The major phases of Mark Twain's lifelong journey home are aptly described as "the Matter of Hannibal" in Henry Nash Smith's essay, "Mark Twain's Images of Hannibal: From St. Petersburg to Eseldorf," *Texas Studies in English,* 37 (1958), 3–23. Readers of the middle and later chapters of *Life on the Mississippi,* and of the brief "Villagers of 1840–3," will be aware of the horrors that were poised in memory at the threshold of Mark Twain's consciousness. James M. Cox describes these dark intervals in *Life on the Mississippi* as "guilt fantasies cast in the form of nostalgic recollections and boyhood adventures." Cox goes on to observe, quite acutely I believe, that "although there is an element of play in Mark Twain even at his most nostalgic, there is a strong presence of the sensitive author recounting the guilt, injury, and fear of his bygone youth as he tells of burning the jail house and killing the prisoner, of diving into the river and touching the hand of his drowned companion, and of lying in terror while the thunder storms raged in the night" (*Mark Twain: The Fate of Humor,* p. 164). I discuss Mark Twain's difficulty with these memories in "Why I Killed My Brother."

34. My use of "myth" overlaps in significant ways with Richard Slotkin's definition of the term in the first chapter of *Regeneration Through Violence: The Mythology of the American Frontier, 1600–1860* (Middletown, Conn.: Wesleyan University Press, 1973). I share the persuasion that "True myths are generated on a sub-literary level by the historical experience of a people and thus constitute part of that inner reality which the work of the artist draws on, illuminates, and explains" (4). No doubt in good part because of the fact that he is dealing with our national literature in its earliest, founding phases, Slotkin is strongly inclined to focus on "ultimate questions" and to frame his analysis in religious terms. My own commentary reflects the strongly "socio-

logical" cast of the literary materials I have elected to study, but it is none-theless rooted in the notion, as articulated by Slotkin, that "Myth is essen-tially conservative, depending for its power on its ability to play on conscious and unconscious memory, to invoke and relate all the narratives (historical and personal) that we have inherited, and to reach back to the primal levels of individual and collective psychology" (14).

Part II

1. As quoted in Arthur Lawrence Vogelback, "The Publication and Re-ception of *Huckleberry Finn* in America," *American Literature,* 11 (1939), 269–70. Victor Fischer's "Huck Finn Reviewed: The Reception of *Huckleberry Finn* in the United States, 1885–1897," *American Literary Realism,* 16 (1983), 1–57, very substantially supplements Vogelback's work.

2. The standard account of the composition of the novel appears in Wal-ter Blair's "When Was *Huckleberry Finn* Written?" *American Literature,* 30 (1958), 1–25.

3. Henry Nash Smith, *Mark Twain: The Development of a Writer,* (Cam-bridge, Mass.: Harvard University Press, 1962), p. 174.

4. *Pudd'nhead Wilson* (New York: W. W. Norton, 1980), p. 9.

5. Ibid., p. 19.

6. Mark Twain's familiar, extremely telling account of his general ap-proach to composition, along with a somewhat arch but nonetheless revealing discussion of the genesis of *Pudd'nhead Wilson,* appears in "The Author's Note to 'Those Extraordinary Twins'."

7. Judith Fetterley, "Disenchantment: Tom Sawyer in *Huckleberry Finn,*" *PMLA,* 87 (1972), 69–73.

8. Ibid., p. 71.

9. Ibid.

10. Ibid., p. 72.

11. I am guided here by Sacvan Bercovitch's brilliant *The American Jere-miad* (Madison, Wisconsin: University of Wisconsin Press, 1978).

12. *Adventures of Huckleberry Finn,* ed. Leo Marx (New York: Bobbs-Merrill, 1967), p. 174.

13. *Great Short Works of Mark Twain,* ed. Justin Kaplan (New York: Har-per and Row, 1967), pp. 195–97.

14. As quoted in Hamlin Hill, *Mark Twain: God's Fool* (New York: Harper and Row, 1973), p. 25.

15. Ibid., p. 19.

16. Letter from Mark Twain to Rudolf Lindau, 14 April 1901, as quoted in Hill, *Mark Twain: God's Fool,* p. 29.

17. *Great Short Works of Mark Twain,* pp. 199–200.

18. Ibid., p. 200.

19. Justin Kaplan, *Mr. Clemens and Mark Twain* (New York: Simon and Schuster, 1966), p. 297.

20. *A Connecticut Yankee in King Arthur's Court* (Berkeley: University of California Press, 1979), p. 162. Hereafter references to this edition will be cited parenthetically in the text.

21. Smith, *Mark Twain: The Development of a Writer*, p. 124.

22. Ibid., pp. 129–30.

23. *The Autobiography of Mark Twain*, ed. Charles Neider (New York: Harper and Brothers, 1959), p. 7.

24. *Great Short Works of Mark Twain*, p. 155.

25. Smith, *Mark Twain: The Development of a Writer*, pp. 131–33.

26. *The Autobiography of Mark Twain*, p. 14.

27. In *The Writings of Mark Twain*, Author's National Edition, 25 vols. (New York: Harper and Brothers, 1907–18), XIX, 283. Subsequent references to works in this edition will be cited parenthetically in the text with appropriate volume and page numbers.

28. In *Which Was the Dream?* ed. John S. Tuckey (Berkeley: University of California Press, 1968), pp. 82–83. See also *Following the Equator* (VI, 96), *Joan of Arc* (XVII, 51, 257; XVIII, 51, 56), and *Tom Sawyer Abroad* (XX, 32–33, 36).

29. See also the "mournfulness of death" that confronts Hank when he returns to England (410).

30. *The Mysterious Stranger*, ed. William M. Gibson (Berkeley: University of California Press, 1970), p. 324. Hereafter references to this edition will be cited parenthetically in the text.

31. *Great Short Works of Mark Twain*, pp. 199–200.

32. Daniel G. Hoffman, *Form and Fable in American Fiction* (New York: Oxford University Press, 1961), p. 331.

33. Ray W. Frantz, "The Role of Folklore in *Huckleberry Finn*," *American Literature*, 27 (1956), 315.

34. Richard P. Adams, "The Unity and Coherence of *Huckleberry Finn*," *Tulane Studies in English*, 6 (1956), 91.

35. James M. Cox, "Remarks on the Sad Initiation of Huckleberry Finn," *Sewanee Review*, 62 (1954), 395.

36. George C. Carrington, Jr., *The Dramatic Unity of Huckleberry Finn* (Columbus, Ohio: Ohio State University Press, 1976), pp. 8–11.

37. *Great Short Works of Mark Twain*, p. 158.

38. *The Autobiography of Mark Twain*, pp. 98–102.

39. See my article, "Why I Killed My Brother: An Essay on Mark Twain," in *Literature and Psychology*, 30 (1980), 168–81.

40. Carrington, *The Dramatic Unity of Huckleberry Finn*, p. 133. Carrington goes on to note that "Huck's gratuitously evil act . . . dooms both Jim and himself to a pattern of betrayal and failure in their actions, their relations

with other men, and their relations with nature. This is Huck's 'original sin,' and he never escapes it, as Jim predicts." Though we develop this point in rather different ways, certain features of Carrington's line of interpretation anticipate the argument advanced here.

41. James M. Cox points out that "in turning over to Tom Sawyer the entire unpleasant business of freeing Jim, Huck is surely not acting out of but remarkably *in* character." He goes on to add that it is Huck's "successful evasion which we as readers cannot finally face" (*Mark Twain: The Fate of Humor*, pp. 173, 179).

42. Quoted by Justin Kaplan in *Mr. Clemens and Mark Twain*, p. 313.

43. Spencer Brown, in "*Huckleberry Finn* for our Time," *The Michigan Quarterly Review*, 6 (1967), 45, argues that there is a selfish element in Jim's decision not to identify the corpse in "the house of death." "Huck is really free (free of his father, and thus no longer in danger, he can go back home, or wherever he pleases); but Jim needs Huck for his flight to freedom."

44. Laurence B. Holland, "A 'Raft of Trouble': Word and Deed in *Huckleberry Finn, Glyph* 5 (1979), 82. In this penetrating, indispensable essay, Holland makes brief but apt use of Mark Twain's essays on lying. He does much more; and his commentary, though at times frustratingly compressed and elliptical, is deeply insightful and always stimulating. Much of what Holland has to say bears on issues that I address here, and at times his arguments and suggestions concisely anticipate my own much more fully developed lines of thought. We do not always agree. For example, I would insist that Tom's lie of silent assertion involves more than the suppression of the truth about Jim's freedom. The deeper, ultimately more damaging lie is the denial that he has denied anything "in which humane and intelligent people were interested."

45. Neil Schmitz, "Twain, *Huckleberry Finn*, and the Reconstruction," *American Studies*, 12 (1971), 61. James M. Cox also gives emphasis to Huck's evasiveness when it comes to freeing Jim (*Mark Twain: The Fate of Humor*, pp. 173, 179–80). Laurence B. Holland argues that Huck actually misleads the reader when he creates the impression that he does not know of Jim's legal freedom at the time of his narration of the decision to "go to hell" to rescue his friend. "When he looks back and remembers the incident on the raft when he tore up the letter to Miss Watson," Huck "knows that Jim has already been freed. But to reenact the drama which constitutes his heroism, to recreate it in its vividness and moral urgency, Huck must in memory keep to the lie of silence." Holland properly emphasizes that Huck's behavior in Chapter 31 "burgeons with a pressure of moral urgency and commitment . . . which exceeds anything actually true of Huck's behavior before or since," and goes on to locate the source of Huck's unwonted feelings in Mark Twain. Still, to suggest, as Holland does, that Huck consciously misrepresents himself in Chapter 31 is to strain to the point of contradiction the conception of the boy's character that emerges from the rest of the novel. Huck is a racist, not

an abolitionist, and he is everywhere careful to conceal his shameful regard for his black friend. Except where Jim is concerned, however, he is not at all prone to conceal his moral lapses, or to inflate his movements of goodness. Given this much, and in spite of Huck's penchant for deceit and self-deception when it comes to Jim, I am inclined to view his seeming "lie of silence" as an epiphenomenon of the retrospective first-person narrative form.

46. Ibid., pp. 64–66.

47. Ibid., p. 60.

48. Smith, *Mark Twain: The Development of a Writer,* pp. 129–33.

49. Holland, "A 'Raft of Trouble'," p. 84.

50. Ibid., p. 81. J. Hillis Miller, in "Three Problems of Fictional Form: First-Person Narration in *David Copperfield* and *Huckleberry Finn,*" published in *Experience in the Novel: Selected Papers from the English Institute,* ed. Roy Harvey Pearce (New York: Columbia University Press, 1968), p. 44, describes *Huckleberry Finn* as "a fiction by which Twain attempted to approach his childhood and therefore to reach his own inmost reality." He goes on to review the copious array of fictions that dominate the lives of the people within the story, and concludes that "these fictions within fictions keep before the reader a picture of interpersonal relations as a complex system of deceit within deceit in which each man lies to his neighbor."

51. *Which Was the Dream?,* p. 415.

52. *Mark Twain's Fables of Man,* ed. John S. Tuckey (Berkeley: University of California Press, 1972), pp. 418–19.

53. As quoted by Tuckey in his Introduction to *Mark Twain's Fables of Man,* p. 9.

54. Ibid., pp. 18, 20–24.

55. Ibid., pp. 380–82.

56. Ibid., p. 327.

57. Ibid., pp. 379–80.

58. Bernard DeVoto, *Mark Twain at Work* (Cambridge, Mass.: Harvard University Press, 1942), p. 116.

59. *Pudd'nhead Wilson,* p. 3.

60. Ibid., p. 13.

61. Cox, *Mark Twain: The Fate of Humor,* pp. 280–83.

62. Ibid., pp. 283–84.

63. See the virtually identical opening to "No. 44, The Mysterious Stranger," on p. 221.

64. See William M. Gibson's useful background discussion in his "Introduction" to *The Mysterious Stranger,* pp. 28–33.

65. I develop this general point in "Seeing the Elephant: Some Perspectives on Mark Twain's *Roughing It,*" *American Studies,* 21 (1980), 43–64, and in "Patterns of Consciousness in *The Innocents Abroad,*" forthcoming in *American Literature.*

Index